Writing for the Street, Writing in the Garret

MELVILLE, DICKINSON, AND PRIVATE PUBLICATION

Michael Kearns

THE OHIO STATE UNIVERSITY PRESS • COLUMBUS

Library of Congress Cataloging-in-Publication Data
Kearns, Michael S., 1947–
 Writing for the street, writing in the garret : Melville, Dickinson, and private publication
/ Michael Kearns.
     p. cm.
 Includes bibliographical references and index.
 ISBN-13: 978-0-8142-1140-3 (cloth : alk. paper)
 ISBN-10: 0-8142-1140-2 (cloth : alk. paper)
 ISBN-13: 978-0-8142-9239-6 (cd-rom)
 1. American literature—19th century—History and criticism. 2. Authorship—History—
19th century. 3. Authorship—Sociological aspects. 4. Melville, Herman, 1819–1891—
Political and social views. 5. Dickinson, Emily, 1830–1886—Political and social views. I.
Title.
 PS201.K43 2010
 810.9'003—dc22

                                        2010018578

This book is available in the following editions:

Cloth (ISBN 978-0-8142-1140-3)
CD-ROM (ISBN 978-0-8142-9239-6)

Cover design by James A. Baumann
Type set in ITC Galliard
Printed by Thomson-Shore, Inc.

9   8   7   6   5   4   3   2   1

Contents

Chapter 5

Not "Convenient to Carry in the Hand":

Illustrations

Preface and Acknowledgments

Around a decade ago, my teaching of America's nineteenth-century "cultures of letters" (the phrase is the title of a superb book by Richard Brodhead) led me to notice some similarities in the writerly lives of Herman Melville and Emily Dickinson. For instance, each writer refused a mentor's request for a photograph, each writer grew up in a family that had suffered significant financial reversals, each spent a major part of her or his creative life in western Massachusetts, and each suffered with eye ailments. These apparently superficial similarities took on more significance when I began to consider how conflicted was each writer's relationship to those cultures (and in fact to recognize that there were indeed cultures, that there was not a single "scene of writing"—Brodhead's phrase—within which they worked) and how dramatically distant the two seemed from each other in scholarly studies. In fact, any serious work that included one of these writers seemed to ignore the existence of the other, almost as if they occupied distinct but parallel universes.

To a cursory glance, of course, they did: female versus male, private writer versus public author, unmarried versus married, stay-at-home versus world traveler, writing as an avocation versus writing as a profession, poet versus novelist, and so forth. But as I continued to think about and explore the similarities, I began to realize that the differences separating the two writers might be to an extent a vestige of earlier approaches to American literary history, in which male authors were studied as public voices, and in which scholars whose work went beyond concentrating on a single writer would emphasize either one genre (Chase's *The American Novel and Its*

Tradition, The Continuity of American Poetry by Pearce) or one theme (Levin's *The Power of Blackness*, Feidelson's *Symbolism and American Literature*). Even the groundbreaking work that began to incorporate what had been considered the "low" or "popular" culture of nineteenth-century America (such as *Cultures of Letters*, Reynolds's *Beneath the American Renaissance*, Walker's *The Nightingale's Burden*, Petrino's *Emily Dickinson and Her Contemporaries*) typically would not cross more than one of those universe boundaries. For these reasons, the dramatic differences between Melville and Dickinson made the similarities all the more interesting to me.

As Brodhead shows, the economics of writing, the labor of writing, the relationships between writers and readers, and the stratification by genre all became well established during the decades immediately after the Civil War. I began to realize that the picture was even more complicated in the case of writers whose interest lay outside of print publication. To tease out these contradictions, I turned to the work of the French sociologist of literature Pierre Bourdieu and of his chief American exponent John Guillory, applying their analyses to the noncommercial markets that interested Melville and Dickinson, markets within which circulated such genres as portfolio poetry, the commonplace book, the scrap book, the personal letter, and the self-published limited-print-run book. During this period all of these genres, and others, operated within markets that created and circulated symbolic capital but had almost nothing to do with the production of economic capital (aside from the production of the paper, copy books, and empty scrap books that constituted the raw physical material of the genres). Yet these extra-economic markets were significantly influenced by the dominant economic markets: "The conjunction of mass literacy and fully reproducible text made print the most advanced medium of marketed and marketable culture and thus made literature a leading early instance of an autonomous aesthetic field whose construction was both opposed to and facilitated by that impersonal and heteronomous cultural market" (Paulson 403).

Decades ago William Charvat noted that to create literature in the middle of the nineteenth century was to seek to establish one's authority both in conjunction with and in opposition to a market driven by the economics of large-scale production and consumption. According to Charvat, the writers of this era were always struggling with two opposing pressures, "creative and social," with the latter understood to include the economic aspects of copyright, printing, and distribution (297). In fact *Writing for the Street, Writing in the Garret* can be understood as an application and elaboration of Charvat's key point that such economics is "ancillary—and subordinate to—the historical study of . . . cultural dynamics" (297). I would only disagree with Charvat that "literary economics" lacks relevance for the study of "non-professional writers like Thoreau, Whitman, and Emily Dickinson." As Bourdieu has shown with his extensive statistical analyses of the business of French culture—and perhaps as Charvat understood but was too cautious to assert—these dynamics are grounded in various types of capital. Bourdieu explains that understanding how a writer responds to the available fields and markets requires describing "the space of available possibilities (in particular, the economic and symbolic hierarchy of the genres, schools, styles, manners, subjects, etc.), the social value attached to each of them, and also the meaning and value they received for the different agents or classes of agents in terms of the socially constituted categories of perception and appreciation they applied to them" (*Field* 89–90). The value of a work of art is produced not or not only by the artist but also by "the field of production as a universe of belief" that includes "belief in the creative power of the artist" (Bourdieu, *Rules of Art* 229).

Writing for the Street, Writing in the Garret lays out these spaces for two of American's major nineteenth-century authors, demonstrating that each can be understood as negotiating between the romantic notion of the individual genius composing in solitude with no concern for an audience (writing in the garret) and the writer whose only interest is to earn money by pleasing a mass audience (writing for the street). Melville himself voiced this opposition in a quatrain titled "In a Garret" from his late volume *Timoleon:* "Gems and jewels let them heap—/ Wax sumptuous as the Sophi: / For me, to grapple from Art's deep / One dripping trophy!" (*Collected Poems* 228). I adopt the metaphors "street" and "garret" as one way to avoid "the dubiously dichotomizing terms 'elite' (serious) and 'mass' (popular) culture" (Davidson 17) while still acknowledging the salience of those concepts for the writers themselves and for their actual audiences. Much can be learned by looking at both Melville and Dickinson as seeking a middle way between street and garret: aiming overtly (or, in the case of Melville, desiring to aim) for actual albeit extremely small audiences (perhaps only a single reader) in order to earn symbolic capital (prestige) which could then enhance the author's authority as a cultural spokesperson and critic.

I also emphasize that the two must be thought of specifically as writers. The garret was not just a metaphor for evoking a romanticized notion of the suffering artist unappreciated by her or his generation; it also metonymically invoked the physiological wear and tear caused by the physical work of putting pen to paper. Writing is not roofing or bricklaying, but it has always carried a set of occupational hazards that manifest themselves in headaches, eye strain, and back and leg pains (especially sciatica), not to mention a general weariness that can result from sitting at a table in an icy room eight hours a day (as Melville did during much of the composition of *Moby-Dick*). A writer's choices regarding implement and paper, chair and desk, lighting, time of day, length of time spent writing, use of a scribe or reader, use of other books—all of these influence the writer's goals and successes.

WRITING IS easier now, physically, than it was for Melville and Dickinson. I don't have to strain to write by whale-oil lamp or kerosene lantern; central heating and an electric blanket compensate for my poor circulation; I don't have to pay someone to transcribe my handwriting into a legible text for an editor to consider. Moreover, while I have done much of the writing in garret-like isolation, I have benefited from an NEH Summer Stipend, a Faculty Creative Work and Research Award from the University of Southern Indiana, the encouragement of colleagues in the Emily Dickinson International Society (Ellen Louise Hart, Paul Crumbley, Barbara Kelley, Cindy Mackenzie, and Ellie Heginbotham, especially), and the intellectual stimulation provided by one of the best students from which a teacher could ever learn, Craig T. Fehrman.

When a book is ten years in the making, it would be impossible to recognize all the individuals who have contributed. The following people, however, have been extremely helpful as I have collected images for the final draft: Jaclyn Penny of the American Antiquarian Society, Sean Casey and Kim Reynolds of the Boston Public Library's Rare Books and Manuscripts Department, Betsy Sherman of the Berkshire Historical Society, Heather Cole of the Houghton Library, and Kathleen Reilly of the Berkshire Athenaeum.

To my wife, Amy, however, I owe the largest debt of gratitude. In the early stages of the work, she insisted on believing in what I was doing even when I lost faith. Even more important, she refused to let me rely on scholarly jargon but kept pushing me truly to understand and express in my own words what I was trying to say. She was, and remains, my Hawthorne and my Sue.

1

Marketing by Mug

Writing to Evert Duyckinck on 12 February 1851, Melville offered this extensive comment on the state of America's literary economy:

> As for the Daguerreotype (I spell the word right from your sheet) that's what I can not send you, because I have none. And if I had, I would not send it for such a purpose, even to you.—Pshaw! you cry—& so cry I.— "This is intensified vanity, not true modesty or anything of that sort!"— Again, I say so too. But if it be so, how can I help it. The fact is, almost everybody is having his "mug" engraved nowadays; so that this test of distinction is getting to be reversed; and therefore, to see one's "mug" in a magazine, is presumptive evidence that he's a nobody. So being as vain a man as ever lived; & beleiving [*sic*] that my illustrious name is famous throughout the world—I respectfully decline being *oblivionated* by a Daguerretype (what a devel [*sic*] of an unspellable word!). (*Correspondence* 180)

The "purpose" to which Melville refers is the Duyckinck brothers' plan for "a series of articles on contemporary authors, with portraits," to be published in *Holden's Dollar Magazine*, presumably with less "puffery" and more emphasis on quality than had characterized that magazine under its previous editors (Horth 178–79). By highlighting his use of the word "mug," Melville may have intended to evoke not only the common meaning of "face" but also the association with what was deemed low, common, ugly, foolish, and incompetent. (These associations were present in

English in the middle of the nineteenth century, according to the *Oxford English Dictionary;* the phrase "mug shot" to refer to a photo in a police record apparently entered the language somewhat later.) Melville fictionalized the same situation in his novel *Pierre; or, The Ambiguities;* Pierre reflects that "instead of, as in old times, immortalizing a genius, a portrait now only *dayalized* a dunce. Besides, when every body has his portrait published, true distinction lies in not having yours published at all. For if you are published along with Tom, Dick, and Harry, and wear a coat of their cut, how then are you distinct from Tom, Dick, and Harry?" (254).

Duyckinck apparently had requested not only the daguerreotype but a contribution to *Holden's Dollar Magazine,* to which Melville in the same letter replied:

> I can not write the thing you want. I am in the humor to lend a hand to a friend, if I can;—but I am not in the humor to write the kind of thing you need—and I am not in the humor to write for Holden's Magazine. If I were to go on to give you all my reasons—you would pronounce me a bore, so I will not do that. You must be content to beleive [*sic*] that I *have* reasons, or else I would not refuse so small a thing.—(*Correspondence* 180; emphasis in original)

Melville's disinclination to write for *Holden's* almost certainly had to do with his sense that this particular publication was simply not worthy of his effort; it was intended by the Duyckinck brothers to cater to what George Duyckinck referred to as "the million"—literature for the masses, indeed (Yannella 65–66). Melville had referred to this mass audience in his 1850 review of Hawthorne's *Mosses from an Old Manse* as "superficial skimmers of pages" ("Hawthorne and His Mosses" 251). At this time in his writing career, he was aiming for "true distinction," and he held the belief, typical for his time, that recognition as an artist entailed, paradoxically, not being recognized—that is, not being recognized by a mass audience. Soon after writing to Duyckinck, in fact, he satirized the brothers in the "Young America" portions of *Pierre* (Books XVII and XVIII) and sympathetically portrayed the romantic hero of that book as a "poor be-inked galley-slave" catering to "Mediocrity" (Yannella 70–71, quoting from *Pierre* 261). As early as the publication of *Mardi* he had written to his father-in-law that attacks by critics "are matters of course, and are essential to the building up of any permanent reputation" (letter of 23 April 1849 to Lemuel Shaw, *Correspondence* 130).

Thomas Wentworth Higginson made a similar request of Emily Dickinson; her reply in July of 1862 was more congenial than Melville's but similar in how the writer distances herself from what she terms a dishonorable activity:

> Could you believe me—without? I had no portrait, now, but am small, like the Wren, and my Hair is bold, like the Chestnut Bur—and my eyes, like the Sherry in the Glass, that the Guest leaves—Would this do just as well?
>
> It often alarms Father—He says Death might occur, and he has Molds of all the rest—but has no Mold of me, but I noticed the Quick wore off those things, in a few days, and forestall the dishonor—You will think no caprice of me—(*Letters* L268)[1]

Only one photographic image of Dickinson is known to exist, the daguerreotype taken by William C. North in Amherst in late 1846 or early 1847 (Kromer Bernhard 595–96). According to Kromer Bernhard, Dickinson's brother and sister "were vehemently opposed to publication of the daguerreotype" after her death, feeling that this image failed to capture "the play of light and shade in Emily's face" (Kromer Bernhard quoting Millicent Todd Bingham 598). Perhaps, as Kromer Bernhard says, "the Dickinson family did not value North's daguerreotype of Dickinson" (598); perhaps Dickinson herself did not value it. It would seem most unlikely for a mature writer seeking possibly a magazine audience and at least the opinion of one of the era's leading persons of letters—if not a wider audience—to send an image taken when an adolescent. Possibly, also, Dickinson's experience with the medium in general was not of the sort that would have led her to trust it; Mary Loeffelholz, for instance, comments insightfully on how Dickinson seems to have imagined and represented "the nexus of physiognomy and the rhetoric of temporality" (464). Juxtaposed against Melville's letter to Duyckinck, however, several of this letter's details stand out: her desire to "forestall the dishonor" ("to see one's 'mug' in a magazine, is presumptive evidence that he's a nobody") and her desire not to seem capricious ("Pshaw! you cry—& so cry I"). Such similar comments from two individuals so different merit closer study in the context of the marketing of and markets for literature.

PHOTOGRAPHY, CAPITAL, AND CLASS

The requests from Duyckinck and Higginson together with the replies of Melville and Dickinson invite some broad questions. What did it mean, socially, culturally, and economically, to have a photographic image made?

To send or receive one? What did it mean to have one's image published in a magazine or in some other form allowing for mass circulation? These questions can be answered in part with a review of the cultural work performed by the daguerreotype and subsequent photographic technologies, work that contributed to the creation of economic and symbolic capital.

The daguerreotype was introduced into America in 1840 (just a few months after Daguerre announced the process), reached its zenith early in the 1850s, but remained widespread throughout the decade, the practitioners numbering 938 in 1850 and 3,154 in 1860, according to United States census data, with an estimated three million daguerreotypes produced in 1853 (Taft 60–61, 63). Although "by 1857 [daguerreotyping] was a minor branch of the photographic trade," into the 1860s it had a market among "*first-class* people" (Taft 101, 122, 136, quoting an unnamed writer from 1862). Other forms of photographic imaging became popular during the 1850s, but the census continued to list only the occupation of "daguerreotypist," suggesting that the term was still widely used in 1862, functioning perhaps the way "Xerox" or "Kleenex" does today—as a generic label. Lacking Higginson's letter, we don't know whether he specified a type of image. He might, for instance, have asked her for a *carte de visite,* which exploded on the scene in 1860, so much so that it sparked the immediate development of the family-album industry (Taft 140–41). Melanie Hubbard argues that this is exactly what was requested ("'Turn it'" 118). However, the *carte de visite* was much smaller than a standard daguerreotype, and the image was not of the same quality—much less suitable for reproduction, were that in Higginson's mind. In any case, Dickinson could certainly have known that during this period the process for mass-producing an image (by reproducing the image photographically on wood and then if needed on a more durable medium) improved dramatically, meaning that any image could easily become a commodity (Taft 422–23). On the other hand, if Higginson requested an actual daguerreotype, he could have intended his request to imply an association with cultivation and privilege—an association with the likely readers of the *Atlantic,* for instance. The historical details reveal that the phenomenon of the photographic image was involved, but in a complex way, in the era's discourse about social and economic class. An image could be destined for "the street," implying mass production and an appeal to a range of audiences from low-brow to high-brow, or it could be shown to and circulated in its singular form among select individuals and thus preserve (in the case of an image of an author) an association with the elite and the romantic—"the garret." The language used by Melville and Dickinson in their replies strongly evokes the social-class aspect of this street/

garret distinction; they cared deeply about preserving their reputation in the eyes of an (unnamed) elite. The mark of "true distinction," after all, was to have no image published.

Dickinson's attitude toward photographic images probably was also influenced by what Betsy Erkkila describes as her privileged "class position" as "the daughter of a conservative Whig squire" (*Wicked Sisters* 45). Erkkila notes that Dickinson, in contrast to "many of the women writers of her age" such as Stowe and Fuller, "returned to a pre-Revolutionary and aristocratic language of rank, titles, and divine right to assert the sovereignty of her self as absolute monarch" (51). Erkkila links Dickinson's "poetic revolution" with the "elitist, antidemocratic values" of her household. These values would scorn sitting for a daguerreotype, which could have a leveling effect because it could serve as the basis for a mass-produced and distributed image. Dickinson's class and economic position probably helped prevent her from feeling pressured by Higginson's request (as well as by those from people wanting to publish her work).

The photographic image was also central to another related discourse, that of the American "national character," which exhibits elements of both garret and street. Whether Higginson intended to appeal to the vanity of his barely known correspondent, his and Duyckinck's requests could have been understood by their interlocutors within this national context. Duyckinck wanted to include Melville's image in a proposed "series of articles on contemporary authors, with portraits," to include such notables as Hawthorne and Prescott. This was a strikingly new possibility in publishing. Richard Rudisill writes that "[b]y 1850 . . . the medium of engraving made national distribution of pictures possible" (13–14). The daguerreotype itself could not be reproduced, but it could serve as the basis for a wood engraving or an electroplate from which thousands of reproductions could be made. According to Rudisill, this technology served the national need to create definitive images of icons central to the national identity, for example George Washington, and to make these images available for personal possession (31–32). The literary ventures of figures like Duyckinck were probably intended to contribute to this national search for a visible identity and an "American" character type. Rudisill makes the claim that photographic images in America at this time functioned as "[t]he ultimate determiner of a type of national iconography of character" by "condition[ing] the process of visual perception along particular lines of development so that people came to conceive of certain kinds of visual images as being true, or permanent, or typical" (225). This conditioning could take place because, first of all, images were available for possession by individuals on a scale not seen before: even the lower-class household could pay homage to George Washington, Benjamin Franklin, Ralph Waldo Emerson, and others by displaying images either purchased individually or taken from magazines. Second, the images were understood to be accurate representations—exactly what the owner of the image would have seen had he or she been standing where the camera had stood. Third, the images defined as true and accurate a particular style: a frontal view emphasizing the torso and head, with relatively less reliance on elaborate backdrops and props than was common in European images.

This solidification and marketing of the American character by means of the photographic image was the enterprise in which Duyckinck explicitly invited Herman Melville to participate and in which Higginson may have been inviting Emily Dickinson (or in which she could have felt invited) to participate. But there were two dark sides to the enterprise. Most obviously, an artist could feel owned by a mass public without necessarily profiting from the sale, while the publishers who succeeded in creating the most desirable, representative images stood to profit enormously from getting these images into "households and public places in every part of the nation" (Rudisill 225). These publishers would garner economic capital; they would also define a standard by which a household's patriotism and Americanness could be assessed.

In addition to this economic aspect, from which artists with a romantic sense of their role might want to remain aloof, the lifelikeness of photographic images caused many people to feel that evil or at least mysterious forces could be at work: the phenomenon of photography was like animal magnetism or mesmerism in its cultural function. Alan Trachtenberg, who has done the best recent work on the daguerreotype as a cultural phenomenon, writes that by 1851 it was a "common experience" to notice that whether the viewer sees a "shadow or image, or indeed *one's own visage* flashed back from the mirrored surface, depends on how one holds the palm-sized cased image, at what angle and in what light" ("Seeing and Believing" 461–62; emphasis added). That is, not only can the image either seem to be present or absent, as is the case with any image under glass, but the surface may also replace the subject's image with that of the viewer, an outcome that surely would have appalled Emily Dickinson. Equally appalling would have been the sensationalistic literature in which daguerreotyping played a major role: young men falling in love with a daguerreotype and stalking the sitter, daguerreotypes falling in love with each other, a daguerreotypist capturing the soul of someone by taking that person's portrait. These and similar plot elements reflect the symbolic weight carried by daguerreotyping in America at this time (Trachtenberg, "Mirror" 62–71).

This symbolic weight stemmed in part from the American desires to transcend time and to represent national characteristics, desires dramatically embodied in Emerson's emphasis on sight as a means to insight, especially the famous "transparent eyeball" passage in *Nature* (Rudisill 17–19, 27, 31). As the link to Emerson suggests, the daguerreotype "both reflected and activated national faith in spiritual insight and truth obtained from perceiving the works of God in nature" (Rudisill 5). Some of these significances were embodied by Hawthorne in his character Holgrave, from *The House of the Seven Gables,* who saw the camera "as a sort of insight machine by which limited human capacity is enabled to receive the truth which nature provides out of herself. It becomes a means of intensifying human perception to the point that man can produce pictorial records of the essence underlying nature and within man himself" (Rudisill 233). The camera could do this because it used light, which was regarded as nature's painter.

Dickinson read *The House of the Seven Gables* at a time in her life—her early twenties—when she was prone to "cut out the vivid bits [of her reading] and paste them into her unfolding life" (Habegger 246). She could have come to understand the daguerreotype as Hawthorne did, a cultural practice doing cultural work, according to Trachtenberg: "By questioning popular assumptions about the medium, by casting a skeptical eye on the claims of a photographic power independent of self-reflective structures of meaning, Hawthorne represents photography as a new political mode of seeing with unforeseen consequences" ("Seeing and Believing" 479). Thus she could have regarded photography as a "political mode of seeing" with consequences for gender relations. As the sensationalistic literature dramatized, for a woman those consequences were profoundly troubling. Likewise, "Melville was uneasy with the nascent cult of personality that he saw emerging with the growth of photography. . . . A fairly private man, Melville balked at the new demands the image-hungry public was starting to make" (Hayes 482). Yet Melville might have benefited from having his image made public: "He was, after all, quite handsome, and those who knew him tended to project the romantic experiences he related in *Typee* onto him. Recording her first impressions of Melville, Sophia Hawthorne commented, 'Mr Typee is interesting in his aspect—quite. I see Fayaway in his face'" (Hayes 482). I will return shortly to this possibility.

Clearly, if photography is regarded as an "insight machine," the images embodying those insights can become not only descriptive but prescriptive. Both photography and language led Dickinson to ask basic questions about capturing reality: "[D]oes technology reveal or create the soul? Does the material world simply express something interior but already present, or does it somehow create that interior? And what does it mean that our representations, upon which we depend for our consciousness, can kill, fix, replace, and misrepresent the world?" (Hubbard, "'Turn It'" 126). These same questions intrigued Melville; throughout his writing career he thematized the relationship between a surface and whatever might be beneath that surface and thematized as well the human drive to read deep significations into surfaces. He surely noticed that various banks had appropriated for the paper currency they issued the well-known whaling painting by Ambroise Louis Garneray which he mentions in chapter 56 of *Moby-Dick* (Kelly 346–49). Given his symbolic imagination, he probably remarked on how those bank notes not only asserted the economic significance of whaling but also, by reproducing the likeness mechanically, eliminated the individuality of each whaleman. He could even have concluded that this appropriation ultimately reduced the whalemen to pieces of currency that passed from hand to hand, in the same way that a printed book or image turned an author into a commodity.

The responses of Melville and Dickinson to their mentors' requests evoke considerations of class having to do both with economy and with the social and cultural position of the artist. Both writers associated the reproduced image with commonness, Melville insisting that the publication of one's "mug" marks one as common, Dickinson going so far as to intimate that there's a "dishonor" in even having such an image made. The language used by Melville and Dickinson reflects the struggle in mid-nineteenth-century America over "literary legitimacy," that is, determining "who are authorized to call themselves writers" (Bourdieu, *Field* 78). Are the legitimate authors those whose images are widely distributed or those who scorn such distribution? As Bourdieu explains, the question is complicated: "one of the most significant properties of the field of cultural production . . . is the extreme permeability of its frontiers," a property that explains "the conflicts between rival principles of legitimacy" (79). These conflicts are significantly influenced by economic and social class, education, and institutional and personal connections, with the major dichotomy being between economic and symbolic capital. A third important type, cultural capital, functions in part as a cultural space in which economic and symbolic capital can be converted one to another: "*Symbolic capital* refers to degree of accumulated prestige, celebrity, consecration or honour. . . . *Cultural capital* concerns forms of cultural knowledge, competences or dispositions" (Randal Johnson 7). Symbolic capital is accrued by the producers of art; in its most basic form, it equates to prestige. Cultural capital is accrued by "social agents" and allows these agents fully to participate in a culture's artistic activities.

As models by which authors might construct their own sense of legitimacy and might be understood within literary marketplaces, writing for the street and writing in the garret functioned as mutually exclusive methods of achieving legitimacy in mid-nineteenth-century America. Symbolic capital is like social class; it is valuable to the extent that it is not available to every "Tom, Dick, and Harry," and in particular it is associated with genius and inspiration because of the still widespread belief that art is produced by especially talented individuals rather than by a system in which the artist is only one component. While almost any household could lay claim to a bit of cultural capital simply by putting magazine photos of Washington, Franklin, Prescott, and Emerson on their walls, accruing symbolic capital required not just knowledge but artistic activity—or at least the impression of artistic activity—specifically, artistic activity carried out in the garret. The artist should display no interest in what everyday people on the street might think of (or be willing to pay for) her or his products.[2]

For symbolic capital to be accrued, art must be marketed, a process that requires what Bourdieu terms a field of restricted production, which he contrasts to a field of large-scale production. These two fields, which are essential for understanding Melville's and Dickinson's relationships to their audiences and sense of themselves as authors, can be sketched as follows:

Field of restricted production:

- Works within this field tend to be "destined for a public of producers of cultural goods" (Bourdieu, *Field* 115).

- The field has its "own [autonomous] criteria for the evaluation of its products" (115).

- Works tend to be *pure, abstract,* and *esoteric* (123).

- Works are "consecrated" by such "agents" as salons, literary and critical circles, journals, publishers (121).

- Works are understood to "create their public" (127).

Field of large-scale production:

- Works are intended for "the public at large" (115), hence evaluative criteria are heteronomous.

- The producer "submits to the laws of competition for the conquest of the largest possible market" (115).

- "[C]onsecration" is irrelevant, market share being the only criterion for success (115).

- Works are understood to be "created by their public" (127).

All forms of capital can circulate within these two types of field, but the natural home of symbolic capital is the former, and that of economic capital is the latter. Symbolic capital is autonomously evaluated within a field of restricted production, whereas a field of large-scale production exists to serve the needs and expectations of an entire public and thus circulates economic capital through the entire society. Evaluative criteria within a restricted field will emphasize style over function and will tend to support class distinctions, because these criteria appeal to a more educated and affluent public that has been trained to and can afford to mingle with the "agents of consecration"—those individuals and institutions that create a work's symbolic value (117–23).

Neither type of field should be seen as monolithic, although at first glance the two types appear identical to "high" and "low" culture as that bifurcation began to develop in America in the nineteenth century. The most restricted field would be the single-member audience, or an audience consisting of single individuals each of whom receives a unique copy of the work. Metaphorically—and sometimes literally—this work is understood to be produced in a garret, that is, with an eye toward the most autonomous criteria, "internal norms of perfection." To say that a work is "understood to be produced" in a particular way is to describe how the work will be received: as if it was produced solely for the sake of art, not even for the appreciation of those with the power to consecrate, because to appear to court consecration is already to move away from the ideal of art for the sake of art.

Nineteenth-century American literary culture assumed that a work produced in a garret could succeed in the street (in a field of large-scale production) as Fanny Fern dramatizes in *Ruth Hall*. (I discuss this in chapter 2.) But such a possible outcome has little influence on the producer of the work if that producer is an artist in a garret. This is because a good produced within a field of restricted production is "a two-faced reality, a commodity and a symbolic object" whose symbolic and commercial values "remain relatively independent, although the economic sanction may come to reinforce their cultural consecration" (Bourdieu, *Field* 113). One of Bourdieu's most important points is that consecration cannot be accomplished by the artist, in spite of "the ideology of creation" held by most artists since the beginnings of romanticism and ostensibly held as well by the creators of symbolic capital. Instead, this value is created first by the "cultural businessman" who markets the work and ultimately by the field of production as a whole, "understood as the system of objective relations between these agents or institutions and as the site of the struggles for the monopoly of the power to consecrate, in which the value of works of art and belief in that value are continuously generated" (78).

Bourdieu also insists that a work's symbolic capital, created within the field of restricted production, "always in the long run guarantees 'economic profit'" (*Field* 75). This "guarantee" is in part a matter of definition: "'Symbolic capital' is to be understood as economic or political capital that is disavowed, misrecognized and thereby recognized, hence legitimate" (75). But the guarantee is also a function of how the culture industry operates: "For the author, the critic, the art dealer, the publisher or the theatre manager, the only legitimate accumulation consists in making a name for oneself . . . a capital of consecration implying a power to consecrate objects (with a trademark or signature) or persons (through publication, exhibition, etc.) and therefore to give value, and to appropriate the profits from this operation" (75). Bourdieu emphasizes that the "disavowal" of economic reality "is neither a simple ideological mask nor a complete repudiation of economic interest," but rather involves the realistic acceptance and "practical mastery of the laws of the functioning of the field in which cultural goods are produced and circulate" (76). Or, as Melville wrote in a letter to James Billson in December 1885, near the end of his writing life, literary "fame" is nothing more than a reputation that is manufactured by publishing houses (*Correspondence* 493), a letter in which he also, interestingly, refers cheerfully to sending Billson a photograph.

The long-term guarantee of economic profit manifests itself in the Melville and Dickinson "industries" that arose in the twentieth century, as I will demonstrate in chapter 5, and as Melville himself seems to have understood early on: "All ambitious authors should have ghosts capable of revisiting the world, to snuff up the steam of adulation, which begins to rise straightaway as the Sexton throws his last shovelful on him.—Down goes his body & up flies his name," he wrote to Evert Duyckinck on 5 April 1849 (*Correspondence* 128). But the material, biographical, and textual evidence also shows that both writers were well aware of the "two-faced reality" of works produced for careful reading and that this awareness influenced their opposition to the commercial endeavor. According to Bourdieu, the "commercial value" of a work of art is commensurate with "the cost of production," which is "the product of a vast operation of *social alchemy* jointly conducted, with equal conviction and very unequal profits, by all the agents involved in the field of production"—not just those agents involved in the production of any single object but those involved in the production of all objects that have symbolic value (*Field* 81). Because they adhered to the romantic "ideology of creation" but were critical of this "vast operation of social alchemy," Dickinson never, and Melville only at the beginning of his career, unthinkingly embraced wide-scale publication. In fact, Melville shows in stories such as "Bartleby" and "The Tartarus of Maids," not to mention in much of the economic subtext of *Moby-Dick* and the experiences of Pierre in New York City, that a manufacturing economy troubled him greatly not only because laborers shared little if at all in the profits but because the process tended to erase both the laborers and their labor. His sense of irony would have led him to approve of Bourdieu's phrase "social alchemy."

For the individual artist, the laws and principles described by Bourdieu operate through what he terms "habitus," a "practical mastery" that allows the artist to feel "'what needs to be done,' where to do it, how and with whom. . . . Choosing the right place of publication, the right publisher, journal, gallery or magazine is vitally important because for each author, each form of production and product, there is a corresponding *natural site* in the field of production, and producers or products that are not in their right place are more or less bound to fail" because they will not find a "receptive audience and sympathetic critics" (*Field* 95; emphasis in original). Habitus and social origin especially influence the development of a new artistic position: "As a rule those richest in economic, cultural and social capital are the first to move into the new positions" (68). As I explain in chapter 2, Dickinson and Melville understood—although the latter refused for years to accept—that their "natural sites" were those associated with the garret rather than with the street. It is a truism in Dickinson studies, but an important one, that she could afford not to publish; Melville of course, as he wrote in the famous "dollars damn me" letter to Hawthorne, tried to "get a living by [writing] the Truth," but this turned out to be for him the shortest path to "the Soup Societies" (*Correspondence* 191, letter of 1 [?] June 1851).

Melville's and Dickinson's reaction to the enterprise of photography provides a helpful although partial view of their habitus. To participate in this enterprise, they apparently believed, was to allow evaluation to be based on the public's perception of something extraneous to the work— the artist's "mug." Unlike the work itself, which should be able to make its own way with respect to an audience, a photograph would soon lose its vitality, its "quick." In fact the image would limit the writer's identity to a preestablished shape, as Dickinson was possibly emphasizing with her repeated reference to the image as a "mold." Their reactions to their mentors' requests are consistent with Bourdieu's description of a writer seeking to amass symbolic capital within a field of restricted production. This writer is not concerned with popularity or financial success, does need to be taken seriously, will be unwilling to produce ephemera, and—most important—must work within a system of production that also controls the criteria for evaluation, criteria that are explicitly not based on market share.

It is an oversimplification to state that a writer who desires to accrue symbolic capital must embrace a "poetics of failure," as André Kaenel describes Melville's reaction to Duyckinck (35). Certainly, Melville expressed the belief that commercial success would make metaphysical greatness impossible. However, when Melville was writing to Duyckinck he probably was still hoping for economic success, as shown by his negotiations for the publication of *The Whale* in both England and the United States. "All the evidence shows that Melville, when he entered the literary life, thought of himself not as an artist but as the kind of practical writer who can be called, without prejudice, a journalist . . . [intending] to communicate, in familiar language and literary forms, materials which readers could absorb and understand without special antecedent knowledge and without any great concentration or effort" (Charvat 208). By the time of writing what was to become *Moby-Dick*, Melville was experiencing a tension between his desire to make a living by reaching a mass market and his recognition that to contribute something important to his culture could mean limiting his audience to the "thought-divers" he had earlier identified as the most valuable readers (*Correspondence* 121)—that is, he definitely had identified another audience who would require different strategies and yield different rewards from those he experienced when writing and seeking a publisher for *Typee*. When responding to Duyckinck's request, Melville probably still believed that he could command both economic and symbolic capital. Perhaps he even believed what he wrote to Duyckinck, that his fame could only be "oblivionated," not enhanced, by a published daguerreotype.

Given the dramatic decline in his economic capital, perhaps Melville should have listened to his mother, who advised that if he did not do the same thing that Hawthorne, the historians George Bancroft and W. H. Prescott, and others were doing and allow a daguerreotyped image to be widely distributed, he would "appear very strangely stiff" (Horth 785). Apparently she understood that the way toward gaining either influential friends or a reading public would be smoothed by an impression of conviviality and conventionality and that this new technology was one means to that end. Melville's image had already been established verbally, in the public's eye, by his first two novels; as he disparagingly and no doubt out of frustration noted in his famous June 1851 letter to Hawthorne, he was known as the man who had "lived among the cannibals" (*Correspondence* 193). Had he allowed his "mug" to be seen in the daguerreotyped company of such literary notables as Bancroft and Hawthorne, that public identity might have been altered or even replaced, given the power of a visual image. The 1847 oil portrait done by Asa Twitchell shows a soulful-looking young man with large, gentle eyes, a full head of well-combed

Figure 1. Oil portrait of Herman Melville, 1847, by Asa Twitchell. Used by permission of the Berkshire Athenaeum, Pittsfield, Massachusetts.

hair, and a modest beard—not at all primitive or cannibalistic. (See figure 1.) Similarly, the 1861 *carte de visite* image taken by R. H. Dewey shows Melville as serious and respectable—certainly no longer the romantic-looking person painted by Twitchell, but obviously a mature and worthy member of society. (See figure 2.) The Twitchell image or a similar one could have helped prepare even a fairly large audience for the writer's turn toward what reviewers disparaged in *Mardi* and *Moby-Dick* as "metaphysics"; the Dewey image could likewise have helped Melville reshape himself in the public eye as a poet.

Dickinson may have had a more nuanced understanding than did Melville of the influence of visual images on the acquisition of symbolic and cultural power. Her description of herself in the letter to Higginson seems calculated to evoke a sense of romantic mystery: her hair is both "bold" and like the "Chestnut Bur" (did she really mean spiky, like the hard covering around the chestnut?), and her eyes are "like the Sherry in the Glass"

Figure 2. *Carte de visite* image of Herman Melville, taken by R. H. Dewey, 1861. Used by permission of the Berkshire Athenaeum, Pittsfield, Massachusetts.

(visual image of color and probably sparkle) "that the Guest leaves" (mystery). Offering him a verbal portrait also enhanced the sense of intimate, imaginative connection necessary for accruing symbolic capital within the fields of portfolio poetry and personal letter. This description, she says, is her living self ("the Quick"), not a lifeless replica ("Mold"). While the mainstream literary economy was increasingly identifying an author's work with the author's photographic image, Dickinson presented a self in terms that were self-consciously not economic.[3]

Although Dickinson's situation and personality set her against the new technologies of photographic reproduction, those technologies were not intrinsically inimical to symbolic capital, especially because the production of symbolic capital was ideologically linked to America's developing identity.

The daguerreotype contributed to this identity by providing "symbolic representations of objects" in the context of which Americans could identify themselves (Rudisill 31). Both Melville and Dickinson could have done what Poe and Whitman did, embracing the opportunity offered by the new medium actually to enhance their literary stock. The photographic images of Poe—most dramatically the virtual disappearance of the philtrum (the vertical indentation above the center of the upper lip)—show that he "learned how to shape his personal image for the camera" just as he shaped the verbal images in various biographical sketches (Hayes 486). In a sense he was turning himself into a visual icon. Whitman did the same several decades later. Beginning in 1876, each edition of *Leaves of Grass* "opened with a frontispiece portrait, never the same, all showing him as he looked contemporary with the book" (Trachtenberg, *Reading* 67). This technique paralleled what Whitman had done verbally, anointing his persona "Walt" and insisting that *Leaves of Grass* was physically identical with its maker.

Both Poe and Whitman were attempting to craft their photographic images to conform to the culture's notion of a poet. Poe modeled himself according to the romantic tradition, emphasizing his slender build and large forehead. Poe's marketing acumen allowed him to recognize this vacuum in the field of the visual icon: America as yet recognized no poet as representing the nation on the world stage, so he may have felt he could establish his credentials by becoming a visual as well as a verbal presence and contributing his photographic image to the nation's developing sense of the American character. Whitman, perhaps even more than Poe, embraced the culture's desire to create a single commodity by fusing the poet with his work. Whitman benefited from Emerson's descriptions of the American poet, creating in the first edition of *Leaves of Grass* a complete package: visual image (the famous photo of him in casual attire, looking very much like "one of the roughs" rather than like one of the consecrated poets), a statement of purpose echoing and extending Emerson's description (the preface), and a body of poetry that could never be mistaken for anything that had been produced up to that time in America. The fact that Whitman's book in its many editions took half a century to begin to be influential may say less about its revolutionary quality, however, than about Whitman's attempt to bypass the producers of symbolic capital, as he handled the marketing of both book and self.

The daguerreotype was an important component of this process of production. The success of American daguerreotypes in world competitions reinforced the national sense that American technology was superior and reflected a particular knack for inventiveness and pragmatic problem-

solving that was believed to be part of the American character. Daguerreotyping was also tied to "photography's cultural work within a society
rapidly undergoing unsettling change toward market-centered urban capitalism" (Trachtenberg, "Seeing and Believing" 463). In *Reading American Photographs,* Trachtenberg notes that Oliver Wendell Holmes wittily
but also insightfully equated photographs with money: both were "intan-
gible tokens of exchange," but the former did not fluctuate in value (19).
Daguerreotyping began in America as the province of lower-class work-
ers but rapidly became professionalized, with two main groups of practitioners, "the rural and small-town itinerant" and "the city entrepreneur
with an established gallery" (21–22). "By the early 1850s, professional
daguerreotypists were insisting publicly, through their newly founded
journals and in advertisements, that amiable and pleasing images required
the same craft and sensibility as painted miniatures"; these individuals
linked their "economic self-interest to the cultural and political interests
of their clientele," appealing to "the superior taste of superior people"
(25). Practitioners of the profession of photography felt themselves to be
on a mission to reflect and preserve images of the best characters, both of
public figures and of private persons (31–32)—or at least they paid lip service to this mission for economic gain. There emerged among the middle
class a "discourse on the daguerrean portrait, a discourse of instruction
and advice to both operators and sitters: how to arrange the body, where
to allow the light to fall, what background and furniture to provide, what
to do with sitters' hands and legs and eyes, with linen and wool and lace"
(26). This discourse contributed to the larger "obsession with 'character,'
how to achieve it, how to show it and preserve it, and most of all how to
recognize it in others" (27). Trachtenberg argues that "[t]he millions of
surviving daguerreotypes . . . show people learning a new way of seeing
themselves in the eyes of others, seeing oneself as image" (29).

Melville and Dickinson opposed that "new way" because it connoted
turning the individual into object that could become a commodity and
could even become fetishized in the sense described by Karl Marx. That is,
capitalism "produces objects of desire only insofar as it produces subjects,
since what makes the objects desirable is only the constitutive trace of subjectivity those objects bear" (Michaels 20)—or, capitalism produces both
the object and the subjects who desire it, and the value of that object is the
amount by which subjects desire it, an amount whose "trace" is carried by
the object. While commodities must have some usefulness, "their value as
exchangeable commodities is 'physically imperceptible'" (Michaels, quoting Marx, 20–21). When commodities come to be regarded neither as
things that have a use in themselves nor as the products of human labor

but as specific exchange values, they have become fetishized: "Commodities come to look neither like things as such nor like things that represent human labor but like things that are somehow human" (26). Dickinson and Melville would have found this kind of transformation appalling, but other, more practical considerations were also at play in their dislike of photographic images. For instance, Rudisill references Dickinson's letter to Higginson and comments that the "wooden image" embodied in the one known daguerreotype may have "conditioned her aversion to photographs and other likenesses" (212). He also notes that it was common to be dissatisfied with one's own image and to desire an image of loved ones in case of death, as Edward Dickinson did of his children (210–12, 217–20). Both writers also disliked fads and doubted that any human construction could "accurately" record a phenomenon. They probably also reacted against the mechanical nature of the various photographic media, in the same way that some visual artists denigrated images produced by so-called "drawing machines" and the camera obscura—these images were considered not works of art but the products of a relatively unskilled craft. For the majority of Americans "the mechanical nature of the process guaranteed its freedom from human fallibility"; "the medium was acceptable because it served human needs and because it was both utilitarian and reliable as to its truth" (Rudisill 230–31). But these characteristics would not have resonated positively with Dickinson and Melville.

FIELDS OF RESTRICTED PRODUCTION AND THE LEGITIMIZING OF ARTISTS

Bourdieu developed his theory as a way of describing and explaining what happened to culture in France during the nineteenth century, when producers of symbolic goods (artists, intellectuals, salon owners, publishers, and so forth) became increasingly free "from aristocratic and ecclesiastical tutelage as well as from its aesthetic and ethical demands" (*Field* 112). The potential market grew; even more important for the development of fields of restricted production was the diversification of society, which allowed a greater variety of producers to achieve a measure of economic independence (112). This independence was accompanied by the development of a "cultural industry" within which a work of art could not be reduced "to the status of a simple article of merchandise" (113–14). This combination of conditions did not exist in early nineteenth-century America, which had no extensive patronage system. More importantly, the market for culture during colonial and early federalist times was relatively small and the profit margin narrow, leading producers to pirate British goods rather than invest in homegrown authors. By the middle third of the century, however, while printing costs were declining, the American reading public was expanding rapidly both geographically (to the south and west) and among the educated, especially women (Charvat 304–5). These two developments gave American writers a better chance of achieving economic independence.

Toward the end of this period, a somewhat diverse set of fields developed within the market, but there was still no commercial field of restricted production that could accommodate works whose evaluation was independent of commercial considerations ("autonomous" evaluation in Bourdieu's terms). As late as 1859, in an Editor's Table column in *Harper's New Monthly Magazine*, the point is made that the phenomenal demand for "cheap literature," by which is meant "cheap, portable editions of books," is "nothing more than the wants of the public asserting themselves and calling for supply" ("Readers by the Millions" 838). Literature is termed "the most democratic thing in existence" as a result of the intellectual and spiritual "elevation" of society (838). Thus it is that America has become "a nation of readers" who are "just entering on the incipient stage of literary tastes" (839). The unnamed author concludes that "[a]uthors were never so sure of sympathy, appreciation, and substantial recompense as now. The real state of the case is, that the people consider literature as their property—a new estate superadded to trade, commerce, politics—and they intend to enjoy their sovereignty over it without 'let or hindrance'" (840). Stephen Railton aptly notes that authors reading this passage would feel a "conflict . . . between the imperatives of self-expression and the demands of performing for this American public" (20). "Readers by the Millions" implies that this large public audience constituted a field of restricted production that was emerging out of a field of large-scale production. This emergent field would support "our higher literature" economically. However, because this field was skewed toward the conservative end of the spectrum, where evaluation was governed by the same heteronomous criteria albeit somewhat refined, "self expression" had relatively little value. Moreover, this author is quite clear that any such "higher literature" produced will be owned by the public, a concept in keeping with the purpose of American copyright law, as I discuss in chapter 3, but inimical to autonomous evaluation. There did exist in America at that time, as there still does, a conflict between the leveling tendency of democracy and the desire to create a culture that preserved distinctions between social classes; as Robert Milder says, "The problem of establishing intellectual and aesthetic standards in an egalitarian society was and remains a difficult and politically volatile one in American society" (63–64).

Other conditions, too, inhibited until late in the nineteenth century the development of a field of restricted production like the one Bourdieu describes in France. Genres were demarcated by gender, with the novel being recognized, at least in antebellum America, as a "woman's form," enforcing Victorian ideals of duty and self-control" while avoiding "anarchistic, self-expressive tendencies" (Baym 21, 24). Reviewers also tended to oppose the development of new artistic positions; they recognized that geniuses often break rules but were likely also to regard rule-breaking as a result of simple unruliness or of the author engaging in egoistic self-expression and self-advertising (Baym 253). Similarly, the poetic models available in America, whether in the magazine verse or in the volumes by Bryant, Longfellow, Emerson or other widely read men, were of little help for a writer desiring to pursue new directions by transgressing conventions. In sum, because both cultural forces and market pressures privileged conservative novels and poetry, American writers searching for a field of restricted production within the publishing industry were less likely to succeed than were their continental counterparts. Insofar as such a field existed, it was dominated by the "higher literature," whose producers (not just writers, of course, but publishing houses, magazine editors, and reviewers) controlled the available symbolic capital. Only toward the end of the century did a field of restricted production develop in which producers could accrue both symbolic capital and at least a modicum of economic capital (resulting from traditional print publication) on the basis of criteria established within the field. However, as I will show in chapters 2 and 3, there were several such fields outside of the realm of commercial print publication, fields which Dickinson targeted throughout her writing life and that Melville committed himself to no later than his agreement in 1879 to allow the remaining copies of *Clarel* to be pulped.

In America, the literary marketplace had become, by the middle of the nineteenth century, a scene of significant economic profit, as Americans developed the talent and skills to produce not only books but the materials needed for books (paper, type, printing presses, and so forth), and as the number of readers increased dramatically. These conditions led to the significant development of the form of legitimacy Bourdieu associates with bourgeois taste. The art-for-art's-sake form of legitimacy was also beginning to develop but was taking a different shape from that described by Bourdieu in France: like bourgeois taste, it was located within the growing middle class and manifested itself in items produced by that class—keepsake books, commonplace books, poetry portfolios, and other forms of handwritten work.

The value of such forms had been established by Emerson. In pieces such as "Self-Reliance," "The American Scholar," "The Poet," and "Nature," Emerson emphasized that the American artist or intellectual should serve as a conduit for the spirit of the people but should also follow an inner light not subject to mass-market pressure. "The poet has a new thought," Emerson wrote in "The Poet"; "he has a whole new experience to unfold; he will tell us how it was with him, and all men will be the richer in his fortune. For, the experience of each new age requires a new confession, and the world seems always waiting for its poet" (200). He offered this anecdote: "I remember, when I was young, how much I was moved one morning by tidings that genius had appeared in a youth who sat near me at table. He had left his work, and gone rambling none knew whither, and had written hundreds of lines, but could not tell whether that which was in him was therein told: he could tell nothing but that all was changed,—man, beast, heaven, earth, and sea. How gladly we listened! how credulous!" (200). This anecdote expresses several tenets of romantic ideology specifically relevant to a field of restricted production and supporting the principle of autonomous evaluation: the myth of individual creation, the connection of the artist to nature more than to society (nature is thus available as a standard of evaluation separate from society), and the uniqueness of the artist's production. Emerson was also influential with the conduit metaphor, according to which truth flows, essentially unaltered, from nature through the poet to an audience—the youth knew only that "all was changed," and his audience listened "gladly" and credulously—and with the principle of self-reliance, which according to Donald Pease challenged both the national "Revolutionary mythos" and the dominance of "memory" in the formation of individual identity (35–36, 208), a challenge consistent with a view of art and the artist as autonomous at least with respect to the nation's ideology and mythos. The fields fulfilling these conditions were portfolio poetry and the letter—indeed, any work circulated only in manuscript. I will discuss these fields in chapter 2, but here I want to emphasize that within them evaluation is grounded in (a) the sense of personal, noncommodified relationship between writer and reader; (b) a realm of external, divine nature rather than domesticity or society; and (c) the uniqueness and inspiration of the work of art.

A second set of conditions allows for evaluation according to criteria (a) and (c) but is located within the domestic realm. These conditions received no single articulation but can be inferred from their artifacts: commonplace books, diaries, and so forth written privately, like portfolio poetry and letters, intended to be shared yet unlike those forms evaluated according to the criteria of sentiment and usefulness. Sharing these works was intended to create a sense of intimate community, yet the materials out of which these forms were made (blank copybooks, blank diaries, etc.) were part of a system of economic capital. I will say more about this category of forms in subsequent chapters.

BOTH DICKINSON and Melville esteemed "publication by manuscript"—that is, participation in an extremely limited field—not only because they felt authorized by the romantic ideology of creative inspiration and the American emphasis on self-reliance but also because publishing had become so commercialized in America. Perhaps they would have felt more at home under the old system of book production, which "resembled nothing more closely than the provincial book trade of England" and was "decentralized . . . unspecialized and undercapitalized" (Winship, *American Literary Publishing* 11–12). But the new system, with its mechanization of printing and binding and the "well-organized national book trade" based on advances in transportation, banking, and marketing, contradicted romantic ideology. This trade "included a number of specialized firms, many of considerable size, dedicated to a particular branch of book manufacture and distribution: papermaking, typefounding, stereotyping, printing, binding, jobbing, or retail bookselling" (Winship 11–12). Authors who desired to create art would also have been troubled by the expanded role of the publisher as "the entrepreneur of the book trade, the one who makes the decisions and takes the risks necessary to keep the whole enterprise in motion" (13). Within the nineteenth-century American book trade, publishing occupied the center; creation was only one branch, along with financing, manufacturing and supply, and distribution and reception (13–14). Furthermore, creation includes editors, illustrators, book designers, and anyone else who has a hand in preparing what is ultimately "published." Social and cultural contexts can influence any of these branches in obvious or subtle ways; for instance, "economic censorship may arise from a lack of financing for particular works," and audiences exert financial pressure (13–14).

Wholly rejecting commercial publishing, however, was not an easy, clear-cut choice, because many publishers themselves espoused an "artisan ideology" and believed (or at least found it expedient to assert) that "progress, liberal values, and the democratization of society and, by extension, the reading public were intertwined" (Zboray 182). Like the romantic ideology of artistic creation, the publisher's artisanal self-concept was out of step with social, political, and economic reality but could still influence how an author conceived of her or his relationship with a publisher. In reality, the publisher was a capitalistic entrepreneur rather than "an heir to the artisan tradition," books were not generally more accessible to the public (although newspapers were), and the "rationalized system of production" was transforming laborers from "men" (as in "journeyman") to "hands" and "girls" (182–85). Thus, in America as in France, the ideological celebration of artists and artisans conflicted with the reality that the true cultural entrepreneurs were not artists but, especially, publishers; they were the bestowers of legitimacy. To esteem publication by manuscript was explicitly to oppose economic institutions and, as I show in chapter 3, also to oppose the essential state legal institution of copyright law. These "positions"—of poet, pure writer, artist—were ideologically useful but otherwise scarcely connected to the realities either of the mass literary marketplace or of the slightly restricted marketplace implied in "Readers by the Millions."

Melville's and Dickinson's distaste for the marketing of art and artists, especially marketing by "mug," must be viewed not only within this cultural framework but also as a specific reaction to specific individuals and practices. Among the leading entrepreneurial publishers were George and Evert Duyckinck, the Harper brothers, and George Putnam, all of whom were involved either directly or indirectly in both magazine and book publishing, understood the importance of market share, and not only responded to readers' tastes but attempted to shape those tastes. George and Evert Duyckinck "knew how to turn a dollar, had a business instinct and talent to make money . . . [and] were attempting to cash in, and with some success, on the emerging mass market in publishing that appeared in the two decades before the Civil War" (Yannella 70). Similarly, *Harper's Monthly* was intended from its inception in 1850 to be a national publication; it was able to reach this goal because of its extensive piracy of British works, the publisher's early commitment to technology, and a surge in literary nationalism (Phegley 64). The magazine always had "one unifying mission: the initiation of common readers into the culturally informed middle class"; it carried out this mission by targeting married, middle-class women readers and by insisting on their responsibility to inculcate literary culture into their families (73–74). "*Harper's* defined itself as a magazine for the literate but under-educated masses, but not of them," intending to guide these masses toward the "best literature of the day" as determined by the magazine's editors (74). This mission was best fulfilled by aiming at the female audience, which was deemed more malleable: "If women readers could gain literary taste and an appropriate sense of national duty, they would transform the public realm by nurturing the literate and literary

Americans of the next generation" (75). The magazine attempted to control "American sentimental fiction" by serializing what it deemed the best models, such as Dickens's *Bleak House* (79–80); this attempt helps explain why Melville, who had been a major author in the Harper line, was not more strongly supported—for example, the magazine printed only one extract from *Moby-Dick* but serialized all of *Bleak House* (80–84).

By the time he turned to the writing of magazine fiction, Melville had become much more aware of the market complexities than he had been when he wrote to John Murray, offering him *Mardi* and "reiterate[ing] his confidence that his reputation has reached the status of 'guinea author,' deserving of publication in a more expensive format" (*Correspondence* 114). But even with *Mardi*, Melville was feeling conflicted about the value of his reputation and thus in the same letter desired that *Mardi* not be associated with his earlier work: "Unless you deem it *very* desirable do not put me down on the title page as 'the author of Typee & Omoo.' I wish to separate '*Mardi*' as much as possible from those books" (114–15). The publication of "Bartleby" in *Putnam's Monthly* within a month of the completion of the serializing of *Bleak House* constitutes Melville's critique of the values endorsed by the house of Harper and specifically of *Harper's* and that magazine's apparent unwillingness fully to support American authors who did not fit the sentimental realism rubric (Phegley 85). Another example of his market awareness is his rethinking of *Israel Potter*, after that work was rejected by *Harper's*, in order to "meet the editorial policies" of *Putnam's*, which began in 1853 "as a critical commentary on the times and as a direct contrast to the political conservatism" of the older magazine (Post-Lauria 118). The editors of *Putnam's* aimed for a critical and representational style, feeling that "the sentimental style of *Harper's* fiction severed the link between social problems and the teller's emotional response to them by highlighting abstracted sentiment rather than the actual subject" (123). On the other hand, *Putnam's* was also strongly pro-American, whereas *Harper's* was more oriented toward England, making the former perhaps a better vehicle for what Melville wanted to thematize in *Israel Potter* (129). "*Putnam's* editors hoped for precisely such independent and direct writing from their contributors. Melville's story of a rebellious hero whose life dramatized the contradictions inherent in commonly held ideologies of the Founding Fathers reflected magazine policies perfectly" (130).

The publishing of poetry was influenced by the same considerations as was the publishing of prose, but these considerations did not always play out in the same way. For instance, the house of Harper treated Melville's volume of Civil War poetry as if they expected or hoped that it would do well. Compared to Whitman's *Drum-Taps* and other single-authored volumes, *Battle-Pieces and Aspects of the War* "was a quality production: as attractively printed and bound as any of the single-author volumes, with clean, distinct typeface and more generous margins, by a leading house (Harper's) that promoted it vigorously. Harper's ran six poems in its monthly magazine (with one of the best, on Sherman's march to the sea, displayed in an unusual large-type two-page spread format); distributed a quarter of the volumes as review copies; and touted the book in a *Harper's Magazine* review" (Buell 127). These signs of legitimization, however, must be read in their immediate context. The favorable review occupied 8 lines of a densely printed 2-column 3½-page "Literary Notices," in which the lead item, *Personal Recollections of Distinguished Generals* by William Shanks, filled a full page. The review, the shortest in this article, reads, in its entirety, thus:

> Mr. Melville has broken a long silence in a manner hardly to have been expected of the author of "Typee" and "Mardi." Among these poems are some—among them "The March to the Sea" and that upon "Stonewall Jackson, ascribed to a Virginian"—which will stand as among the most stirring lyrics of the war. ("Literary Notices," *Harper's Monthly Magazine* 34, no. 200 [January 1867]: 265)

Likewise, the fact that the magazine ran six poems signifies less than it seems, because typically the only author identification was to be found in the table of contents. That said, Buell is correct that the "literary commodity" of the Civil War poem seems to have served Melville as a source of energy and focus (134), and the poems he produced were surely pushed by the house of Harper because his name carried symbolic capital even as the poems would (or were expected to) contribute to that capital. The reviewer's desire to invoke Melville's prestige may explain the unusual mention of *Mardi,* which was typically recognized (albeit not positively) as more metaphysical and poetical than Melville's other early works. In every other Melville notice I have located from the house of Harper, if only two titles are referred to they are *Typee* and *Omoo.*

If Melville's value as a "commodity" was not strictly economic, profit nevertheless was uppermost in the minds of the Harper brothers. Dickinson was certainly aware that profit could not be ignored in the publishing business and that it was in part based on the author's visage as a commodity. During her lifetime, the only poem of hers that appeared first in a magazine was "Some keep the sabbath," published as "My Sabbath" in the 12 March 1864 issue of the *Round Table,* which was founded in December 1863 by Charles Humphreys Sweetser and Henry Edward Sweetser (Scholnick 166–67). This was to be an independent, wide-ranging publication, but the Sweetsers realized that they would have to take in advertising in order to keep afloat (168). Dickinson's poem "Publication is the auction" may have addressed the practice of "paying off the reviewers and periodicals," a practice that the *Round Table* also condemned (171). Further, Dickinson's term "auction accurately describes a literary marketplace where authors were in fact bought and sold. For instance, in 1852 *Graham's* offered fifty dollars per poem to the two most popular American poets . . . [Longfellow and Bryant], but it insisted on dictating the length of the poems, their subject matter and treatment, and the frequency of composition" (171). Scholnick concludes: "In publishing in the *Round Table* Dickinson did not have to worry about being the victim of advertising; here was one periodical that did not print contributors' names. And in view of her close family connections to the Sweetsers, no doubt she did not have to worry about entering the literary marketplace and auctioning her work to the highest bidder" (180). (Scholnick mentions that they did append to their first volume the names of their regular contributors—170.) Given the Sweetsers' idealism, it is not surprising that they were critical of Longfellow, because they felt that popularity was inconsistent with "the real work of poetry" (179). Circumstantial evidence suggests that Dickinson may have authorized publication of this poem, but there is no material link to prove that she did so: when the poem first is known to have appeared in manuscript, in 1861 or 1862, Charles Sweetser was still a neighbor of Dickinson's and was "much interested in poetry" (Franklin, *Poems* 1:258–59).

These specific examples of *Israel Potter*, "Bartleby," *Battle-Pieces*, and "Some keep the sabbath" illustrate the complexity of the literary marketplace contemporaneous with Melville and Dickinson. Thoughtful and informed as these writers were, they knew that while writing itself is simple, to consider going before a public in a relationship mediated by a publisher involved advertising, pandering to the public's desire to know as much as possible about the author (and thus in a sense to possess the author's identity), the exploitation of laborers, a concentration on economic profit—in short, capitalistic entrepreneurism clothed in patriotic and romantic ideology. The artist's "mug" might be considered one focal point of all of these issues: it could be easily mass-produced and thus easily owned by thousands or even millions of anonymous individuals, and it catered to the cult of the author even while turning the author into just one element in the production stream. They also knew that other marketplaces existed that were not based on commercial publication. Within these noncommercial venues, work could earn symbolic capital without requiring the writer to make her- or himself a commodity—name, visage, and work blended by an entrepreneurial publisher into a single marketable package.

CLEARLY, DURING the two decades of daguerreotyping's market prominence, it produced economic capital. To a lesser extent, daguerreotyping and the other forms of photography that replaced it were also associated with the production of cultural capital: these methods could portray and thus help codify the American "character" and were recognized in Europe as an example of the emerging American excellence in mechanical matters.[4] In this context, Melville might have found himself regretting his decision to deny Duyckinck's request—who knows but that he might have ended up as part of some display of American types. But ten years later, the daguerreotype craze having swept the country, it is easy to imagine Dickinson appalled by the idea of participating, aware as she was of the "oblivionating" of the unique individual that Melville presciently noted in 1851. During the craze, individual portraits accounted for "over ninety-five percent of all daguerreotypes made in America" (Rudisill 198). Daguerreotypists, especially in cities, advertised their service by creating large galleries of their work, including both the famous and the ordinary persons who had sat for them; in fact "photographic portraiture" was at times described as fine art for the masses (213). Melville and Dickinson believed that there could be no such thing: in their eyes, the garret and the street were irreconcilable realms. The latter was the abode of "superficial skimmers," of the "admiring Bog" as Dickinson termed them in "I'm nobody" (Fr260), and to lower oneself to their level was to be at best "dayalized." For a writer with an eye toward immortality, Melville and Dickinson felt, photographs were a mark of failure.

2

"The Endless Riband of Foolscap" and Publishing by Manuscript

In November 1851, Melville wrote to Hawthorne, "I should have a paper-mill established at one end of the house, and so have an endless riband of foolscap rolling in upon my desk; and upon that endless riband I should write a thousand—a million—billion thoughts, all under the form of a letter to you" (*Correspondence* 213). He was probably expressing his deepest wish: that he could inscribe his best thoughts to the most carefully selected audience and that no limitation on these thoughts would be imposed by his medium. This form of publication would serve his desire to accrue symbolic capital while avoiding dingy commerce, saving him from the drudgery of writing as a job of work in which he was forced to exchange his intellectual and physical labor for always-insufficient advances and royalties. Dickinson was able actually to carry out such a plan throughout her writing life. By choosing not to strive for economic capital or even for a public readership, she preserved her ability to earn symbolic capital within the most restricted type of field of production: the individual recipient of a letter or poem. (However, because sharing letters was common practice, she could certainly expect that her words would reach a larger audience than their explicit addressees.) This field of production is exclusive; the evaluative criteria are autonomous (established by the artist who is also the person solely responsible for producing the work), and the maker creates the "public" simply by transmitting the good.

As with each writer's decision not to embrace the "street" by pursuing marketing by mug, the desire to participate in such an exclusive field of production to an extent resulted from distinctions of economic and social class. Bourdieu regards aesthetic distance as a class function: the expectations that art will reflect life and that an audience should be emotionally involved with a work of art are typical of the "popular" aesthetic; in contrast, the more restricted the field, the greater the aesthetic distance between audience and work, with culture and cultural capital arising from and being granted by a social aristocracy (*Distinction* 32–35). Cultural capital can result from education, wealth, or birth; the latter is strongly associated with "high culture." Dickinson definitely had this advantage; Melville had at least a taste of it. In mid-nineteenth-century America, however, as I will explain, this dichotomy between an aesthetic of popularity and an aesthetic of exclusion was complicated by the ideological celebration of labor as a source of value, a celebration characteristic of the American middle class. Similarly, the culture industry's dichotomy between rarity and vulgarity would be less compelling in America. It was certainly invoked by both Dickinson and Melville in the images and diction they attached to a large and indiscriminate public ("an admiring bog," "dayalized [as] a dunce"), but they also regarded their writing work as a valid type of labor, as deserving of respect as what craftspeople did.

The artist exerts the greatest power within a field of extremely limited production by including along with the work a description of the criteria by which it should be evaluated, a practice that conduces to the greatest possible autonomy. Melville probably came to understand this dynamic at least a year earlier than his endless-ribbon letter to Hawthorne. On 1 May 1850, he wrote to Richard Henry Dana Jr., "[D]id I not write these books of mine almost entirely for 'lucre'—by the job, as a woodsawyer saws wood—I almost think, I should hereafter—in the case of a sea book—get my M.S.S. neatly & legibly copied by a scrivener—send you that one copy—& deem such a procedure the best publication" (*Correspondence* 160). The chief evaluative criterion invoked by Melville is experience shared by author and reader—in this case, that of having lived as a common sailor. Melville does not say he would send Dana just any new creation but specifies "a sea book." This is not to say that a book's content would have to be limited to shared experience but rather that in sending a manuscript to a discerning reader Melville would pitch it in such a way as to invoke what he took to be the particular grounds shared by that reader. Thus, in offering to send Hawthorne a sample from *Moby-Dick*, he would not stress whaling but rather the book's metaphysical qualities and its association with hellish depths of thought.

He had invoked the same criterion in a letter to Dana seven months earlier (6 October 1849), when *White-Jacket* was about to be published.

Then he had written that were his novel to be "taken hold of in an unfair or ignorant way," he would be grateful for "a word to the purpose"—presumably, vouching for the accuracy of *White-Jacket*'s portrayal of life aboard a man-of-war. This earlier letter's somewhat stuttering manner suggests that he felt uncomfortable making the request: "[M]ay I hope that you will do so [say a word to the purpose], if you can spare the time, & are generous enough to bestow the trouble?—Your name would do a very great deal; but if you choose to keep that out of sight in the matter, well & good.—Be not alarmed,—I do not mean to bore you with a request to do any thing in this thing—only this: if you feel so inclined, do it, & God bless you. [new paragraph] Accept my best thanks for your kindness & believe me fraternally Yours—a sea-brother—" (*Correspondence* 140–41). If this letter truly reflects what Melville felt, he expected that "a sea-brother" would be the right reader for *White-Jacket*. Both letters attempt to establish with Dana a highly limited field for the production of prestige: by lending his name in support of or in validation of *White-Jacket,* Dana would enhance the prestige of its author. This loan would certainly have a positive economic impact as well, which may account for Melville's embarrassment in making the request; he wanted to preserve or enhance his ability to earn money with his writing, but he disliked having to go begging and surely worried that Dana would think less of him as an artist.

These three letters to Dana and Hawthorne also dramatize the conflict Melville felt between trying to preserve the potential for economic capital he had established when beginning his career with the publication of *Typee* and *Omoo,* and desiring to reach a more discriminating audience of "thought-divers." This story has often been told. The simple version portrays Melville as the romantic visionary unappreciated by most of his peers and unable to accommodate himself to the expectations of a mass audience. A more nuanced version, better grounded in an understanding of the literary culture of the time, portrays Melville as learning to appeal to a variety of audience types. In addition to the mass audience, to which Melville probably never aspired, there was a substantial middle-class readership divided roughly among (1) the readers referred to contemporaneously as "general," "common," or "popular," which included both sexes and "read largely for entertainment"; (2) those who "attempted to regulate literary production as well as the aesthetic tastes of general readers; such reviewers, literary critics, clergymen, particular authors, and other people of high social standing represented a separate audience usually referred to by their contemporaries (and themselves) as 'intellectual' or 'cultivated' readers"; (3) the group between these two, "literary" readers, who "blended the receptiveness of general readers to progressive ideological views with the particularly formulated aesthetic standards demanded by cultivated readers" (Post-Lauria, *Correspondent Colorings* 4–5). By the time he was writing *Redburn* and *White-Jacket,* Melville accepted his "social responsibility and civic duty" as an author and understood that "preservation as an author depended on loyalty to established practice rather than a deliberate literary isolation" (82–83); he had been affiliated with the New York City literary circles long enough to understand the expectations of the "cultivated" and "literary" types. He preserved this same orientation, according to Post-Lauria, as late as his magazine-fiction period, when he was sufficiently respected to be regarded as the "trademark" writer of *Putnam's,* a position he lost when the magazine's new editors began to try to appeal to "the general reader of sentimental fiction" (213, 228).

But in addition to these middle-class audiences, Melville was also aware of other, highly limited markets; throughout much of his writing career, as shown by the letters to Hawthorne and Dana, he recognized that private publication was the best way to reach those markets. His expressed desire for an "endless riband of foolscap" and for the economic freedom to send Dana a manuscript was not, or not only, a flight of fancy and an expression of frustration with mass-market publishing and the physical limitations of handwriting. He also understood that symbolic capital could be earned exactly as Dickinson did a few years later—"publish" by sending handwritten works to the shapers of taste (the producers of symbolic capital).

Dickinson can be read as if she benefited from Melville's experience, as if she learned from him to aim strictly for the noncommercial, nonprint fields of restricted production: mainly portfolio poetry, letters, and commonplace books. To present one's work within these fields is not intrinsically equivalent to publication, however. A writer might send a copy of a poem to a friend for many reasons. This becomes an act of publication when the writer selects individuals who have the power to consecrate and who will not perform that function for mass-circulated works. This means of earning symbolic capital requires the author to accept and be able to occupy a social class position at least somewhat elevated, in order to nurture relationships with the individual recipients of works produced in extremely limited quantities. Melville would not want to "bore" Dana, because to do so was a sign of low breeding, just as he did not want to "bore" Duyckinck by providing all of his reasons for rejecting the *Holden's* offer. Similarly, Dickinson's economic class enabled her to avoid what many other talented women of her generation had to do, write for money, and in conjunction with her family's high social standing it also helped her develop the habitus necessary to function well within those nonprint, middle- and upper-middle-class fields. A final requirement for such publication is that the physical object must reflect special preparation—a rough pencil draft doesn't count.

EARNING SYMBOLIC CAPITAL WITH THE LABOR OF WRITING

The young poet described by Emerson in his essay "The Poet" actually "had left his work, and gone rambling none knew whither, and had written hundreds of lines" (200); no labor is mentioned. But if this poet were a mature adult instead of a youth, he and his audience might feel that to leave whatever work he had been doing (the implication is schoolwork) and not to reflect any effort in the writing itself was a poor strategy for earning an audience's goodwill. How Melville and Dickinson understood themselves as engaging in the work of writing and in the work of literary authorship was influenced by how their society constructed the social, cultural, and economic functions of labor. In particular, their preference for producing their work by hand was validated by their culture's high estimation of manual labor: a manuscript tangibly embodies the manual labor required to produce it, unlike a printed, mass-produced book, which erases that labor. The ideology of antebellum America—the ideology that shaped Melville and Dickinson during their formative years and demonstrably influenced their attitudes toward the work of writing throughout their lives—deemed manual labor "more 'productive' of wealth than other kinds of labor," partly because its results were visible (Bromell 26–27). But such labor was also seldom represented in art, literary or otherwise, because the trades tended to guard their secrets, insisting that they be learned in an apprentice fashion rather than from books, and because values were generally expressed in abstract terms that were ill suited for the concrete nature of manual labor (32–33). A third cause, a Marxist would argue, is that "bourgeoisie culture . . . establishes itself on the concealment of manual labor," especially the "experiential qualities" of that labor (34). All of these factors contributed to the consistent distinction in the literature of antebellum America between work of the "mind" and work of the "hand" (34–35).

In this system, intellectual labor was most likely to accrue cultural capital; such labor typically was described in figures that made it seem manual and tangible, but the descriptions tended to ignore both the actual labor of writing (pushing a pencil or pen across paper, researching, thinking) and the actual tasks involved in authorship (reading proof, negotiating with publishers, and so forth). To earn cultural capital, a writer had to engage in art rather than craft but at the same time had to be advertised or understood as laboring no less than a carpenter or mason. The garret, of course, was an ideal site for such labor; any primitive or rustic locale was another.

Writers such as Melville, Thoreau, Stowe, and Douglass were aware of the contradictions inherent in the mind/hand distinction and "sought to broaden the reach of literature not by diffusing it through a transcendental order, but by focusing it through the prism of the human body" (Bromell 242–43). Both Melville and Thoreau of course had performed manual labor, so while both to some extent accepted the "ontological distinction between mind and body," both also questioned the utility of that distinction (39). For example, Melville's "Paradise/Tartarus" diptych shows him "at pains to indicate that the work of writing is in some way a party to this [social and class] division of labor. . . . [Writing] has become a privilege that requires the exploitation of others" (73–74). This statement is generally accurate if we replace "writing" with "authorship." The writer has no need of a copyist and can make do with the most coarse materials; the author, however, depends on others to produce the physical manifestations of her or his work. This manifestation can be a book or magazine; it may also be a professionally copied manuscript or a fair copy made by the author himself or herself using high-quality paper. In some visually obvious way the work must reflect significantly more and different labor than just placing words on paper.[1]

Ruth Hall, the autobiographical novel by Fanny Fern (Sara Payson Willis), provides a vivid dramatization of the labor involved in both the practice of writing and the profession of authorship while also invoking the romantic image of the writer by locating her labor in a garret. Describing the early days of Ruth's authorial career, Fern presents in great detail the physical demands of writing as well as the physical and emotional demands of embarking on this career:

> . . . often there was only a crust left at night, but, God be thanked, she should now *earn* that crust! It was a pity that oil was so dear, too, because most of her writing must be done at night, when Nettie's little prattling voice was hushed. . . . Yes, it was a pity that good oil was so dear, for the cheaper kind crusted so soon on the wick, and Ruth's eyes, from excessive weeping, had become quite tender, and very often painful. Then it would be so mortifying should a mistake occur in one of her articles. She must write very legibly, for type-setters were sometimes sad bunglers . . . but, poor things, *they* worked hard too—they had *their*

sorrows, thinking, long into the still night, as they scattered the types, more of their dependent wives and children, than of the orthography of a word, or the rhetoric of a sentence.

Scratch—scratch—scratch, went Ruth's pen. . . . One o-clock—two o'clock—three o'clock—the lamp burns low in the socket. Ruth lays down her pen, and pushing back the hair from her forehead, leans faint and exhausted against the window-sill. . . . (125–26)

This passage and others portray the "work of the hand" involved in writing as physically demanding in itself and also demanding because of the conditions under which it was carried out, conditions that can be summed up as "the garret life."[2] The garret (literally, a room in the top floor of a building or a room directly underneath the roof) began to be associated with poverty in the eighteenth century; by the nineteenth century, as many literary references show, the association had expanded to include artists, especially writers (*OED*). This association connects with the desire to create cultural or symbolic capital; material success, which affords an artist the ability to live in greater comfort and closer to street level, conventionally disqualifies the artist from garnering prestige or being able meaningfully to participate in important cultural dialogues. To succeed is to sell out; it is only by living as she does that Ruth can write truthfully, and because *Ruth Hall* trades on the conventions of sentimental fiction, Ruth is able to succeed financially. (I elaborate on this relationship in chapter 4.)

The romantic image of the writer's life could have appealed to Melville in part because it explained his family's decline and justified his own poor economic showing as a writer. Both of his grandfathers were "holdovers from the glorious past" of the American Revolution, whereas "his father lived in a fanciful future" (Delbanco 19). The latter tried to make a living as a retailer but "never became at ease in the increasingly impersonal system whereby European exports were sold in bulk to American auction houses, from which they were bought by wholesalers and distributed to the retail trade—a business in which good taste and personal charm counted for less than the ability to anticipate rising markets by buying low and falling prices by selling high" (20). In other words, the new market system was beyond Allan and seems never to have interested the son who would become famous. The garret life, however, connotes a different type of class distinction, based not on money but on the pursuit of truth and aesthetic perfection. Melville's most complete description of that life is to be found in *Pierre, or, the Ambiguities*. Pierre was not literally living in a garret when he moved to New York City to take up authorship in earnest, but his chamber at the so-called Church of the Apostles had all of the garret trappings: it was "meager even to meanness," a "beg-garly room"—a phrase Melville uses three times over two pages (270–71). Because his room lacked heat aside from that given off by a single chimney passing through it, he had to be wrapped in coat, cloak, and surtout in order to write, with hot bricks under his feet and also "under his inkstand, to prevent the ink from thickening" (301). He spent "eight hours and a half" in these conditions every day—no wonder that the narrator exclaims, "Civilization, Philosophy, Ideal Virtue! behold your victim!" (302–3). It is a small but important detail that Pierre was not drafting in pencil but was composing immediately in ink; little wonder, then, that his pub-lisher finally threatened legal action, although Melville's rendering of that moment seems intended to create sympathy for Pierre, the letter coming from "STEEL, FLINT, & ASBESTOS" (356).

The emphasis on Pierre's workday and the fact that he seems to work even on Thanksgiving, Christmas, and New Year's emphasizes his condi-tion as a manual laborer (303). Similarly, Melville's description of himself as no more than a manual laborer, in his second letter to Dana, calls atten-tion to the sheer physical effort involved in producing a literary good, not just the writer's effort but that of the "scrivener" who would actually produce the finished good. This hypothetical laborer might be his wife, who prepared some of his copies for printers during this period, or some-one actually paid to do the work. Melville knew that his handwriting was a poor medium for presenting a manuscript and that publication required the preparation of a fair (clean and legible) copy, one that bore no traces of the writer's struggles and uncertainties—the manuscript book would seem to have been produced as easily and spontaneously as were the lines of Emerson's young poet. Yet Melville's description also implies that in order for a good produced in this way to accrue symbolic capital, it needed to be a finished product—ready for distribution—and might already have involved the paid labor of someone other than the writer. Two samples of Melville's hand show why he would need a scrivener. Figure 3, a page from one of his journals, can with some effort be made out, as long as the reader is willing to make a couple of leaps. Figure 4 shows what would become the opening of chapter 14 of *The Confidence-Man*. Hayford and MacDougall offer a transcription of the uncanceled words of the second line, "may arise from the author's conception" (417), but a reader who lacked the final published version or any other intermediary might find the page as inscrutable as the brow of the white whale. There is no ques-tion that a typesetter would prefer a scrivener's script over Melville's. Dana need not know that the manuscript copy would probably be prepared by one of the women in Melville's household rather than by a professional

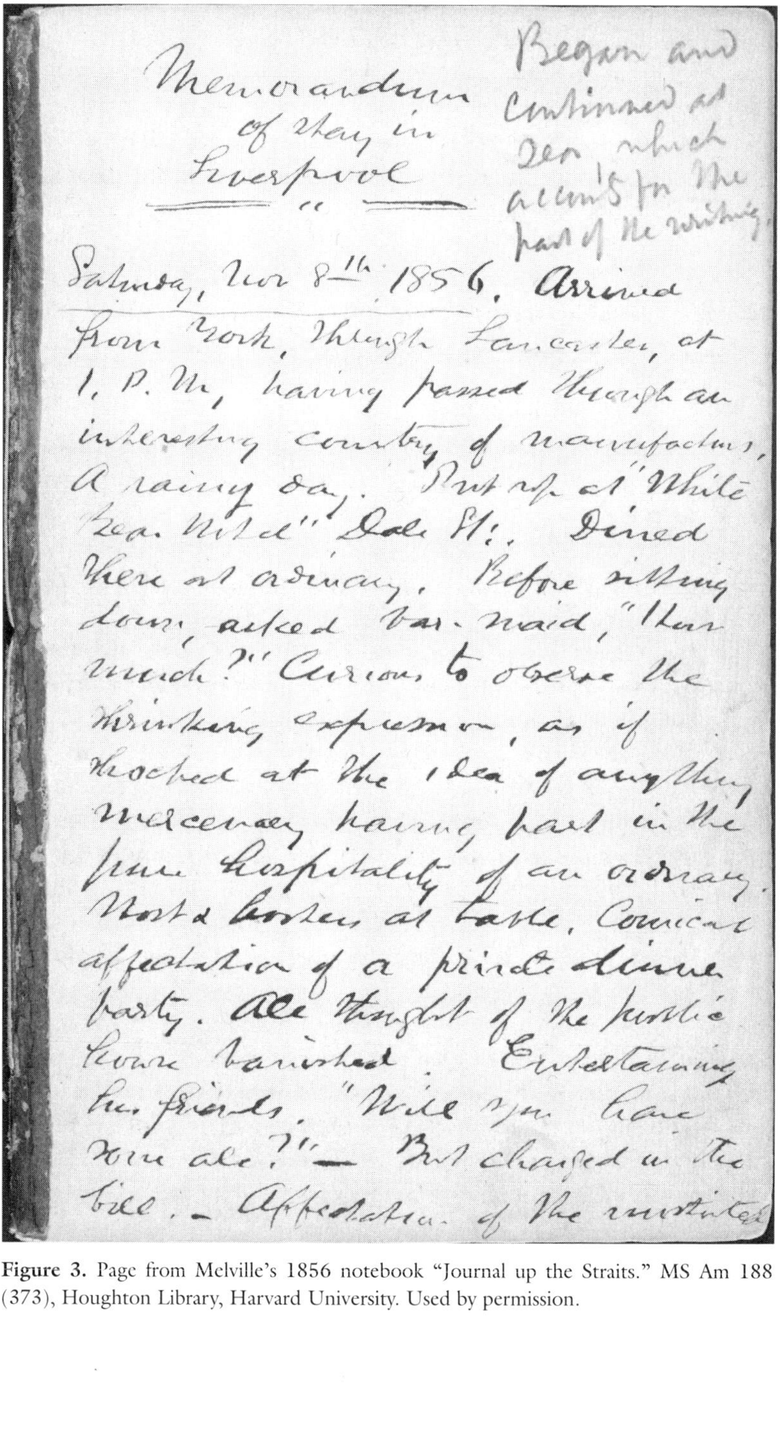

Figure 3. Page from Melville's 1856 notebook "Journal up the Straits." MS Am 188 (373), Houghton Library, Harvard University. Used by permission.

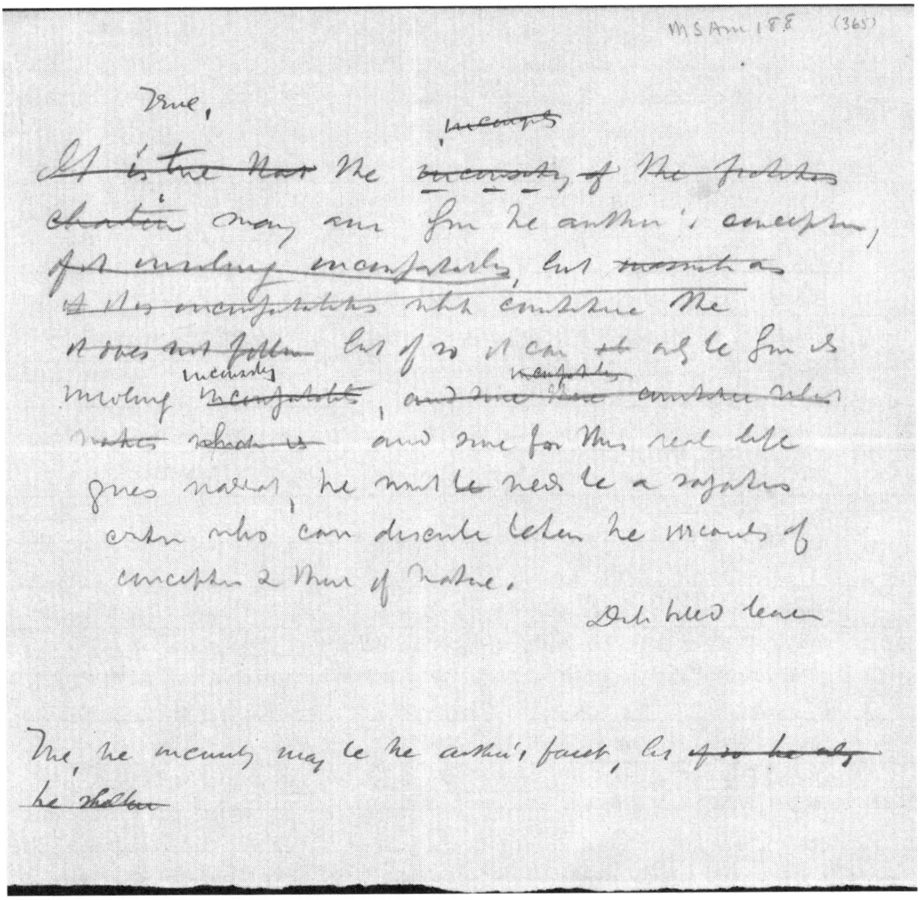

Figure 4. Manuscript fragment of chapter 14 of *The Confidence-Man*, in Melville's hand. MS Am 188 (365), Houghton Library, Harvard University. Used by permission.

paid to do the work, a fact of the Melville household's precarious economy that would have been unseemly to bring before polite society.

In his correspondence with Dana, Melville discriminated sharply between the mere wood-sawing labor of producing a book like *Redburn* and the (presumably pleasurable) crafting of a "sea-book" for a single discriminating reader. *Redburn* he characterized as labor for hire; he was producing a good that was sold in the mass market and over which he seems to have wanted no control, any more than a woman working in a paper mill could dictate who bought the paper or how it was used. The manuscript book embodies a romantic conception of labor (an expression of the whole individual, done for pleasure, valuable simply because of that genesis), whereas the marketed book is probably involved in the pragmatics of getting a living. The manuscript book can also be understood as the most pure expression of the work of writing, in contrast to the marketed book, which typically required the "writer" to turn "author," attending to an editor's demands, a public's tastes, the legal niceties of copyright and compensation, none of which has anything to do with the activity that often draws people to the work of writing—exercising creativity, imagination, originality, self-expression.

Melville's early reviewers did in fact emphasize that both "literary labor" and the laborer should be invisible, one reason for the critical blasting of *Mardi* (Weinstein 204). In this novel Melville attempted to redefine the production of literature as "meaningful and rewarding work" and refused to allow either his text or himself to "become part of an economy that requires an erasure of his labor" (208). He continued this reification of the labor of writing in *Moby-Dick,* attempting as well to involve actual readers in that process (209–10, 212). On the other hand, Melville's extensive and unattributed borrowing in his early books may count as erasing rather than foregrounding both accountability and writerly work. Fully to discuss this issue requires consideration of copyright and of nineteenth-century attitudes toward literary borrowing, topics which I take up in chapter 3. But it is clear that, in Weinstein's words,

> as [Melville's] career unfolded, his notion of economy shifted and expanded so as to force complex reconsiderations of the market economy and his literary labors in it. These reconsiderations, in turn, forced Melville to create within his fictions alternative economies with quite different mottoes ("I prefer not to" being the most memorable), which enabled him to avoid inflicting upon his characters and himself the psychic and bodily violations he had found to be the consequences of a market economy. (221)

Clearly, Melville regarded literary labor as distinct from the wood-sawing type involved in producing commodities for the mass market. Equally clearly, however, as Weinstein demonstrates, he insisted that literary labor was real work and, to be worthy of prestige, could not be the casual production of a dilettante. This attitude was probably influenced by his experience of the physical act of writing as involving drudgery and even pain, a topic I take up in chapter 4.

Melville certainly dramatizes in his fiction the labor of writing, but the labor within his household that was required to produce the fair copies of his work has been erased until very recently. This drudgery certainly weighed at times as much on the women of his household as did the labor of writing on their brother. According to Parker, in the winter of 1853–54, for instance, Augusta "had been in charge of servants while being Herman's sole copyist. . . . What with using daytime for copying and perhaps for necessary sewing, Augusta had no time for reading and for her essential correspondence unless she stayed up far into the night with her candle" (*Herman Melville* 2:207). Some of her copying "was done under great pressure of time, unlike three years before, when she had had the luxury of copying the whale book at her own pace, well behind Herman because he was writing slowly, by his standards" (2:208). However much Melville may have attempted to create fictional economies within which his characters could avoid becoming commodified or erased, the household component of his writerly economy enjoyed no such consideration; this remained the case throughout his writing life.

DICKINSON'S CHOSEN method of publication by handcrafting challenged the commodification of a writer's "mind"—indeed, the commodification of verbal art in general—as well as the division between mental and manual work. This method also both participated in and critiqued the division of labor into a male (business) and a female (domestic) realm. Her case demonstrates that for a woman, writing and the manual labor involved in homemaking could reinforce one another. Just as Thoreau's patch of beans served both economic and nutritive functions (not to mention symbolic), a loaf of bread could serve for Dickinson both socially and domestically, and writing about the loaf or the patch served spiritual, intellectual, and ultimately cultural ends. Furthermore, neither the actual items nor their verbal representations needed to be mediated through a capitalist market in order to be valuable: the actual goods could be bartered or given as gifts, while the verbal goods could enter the antimimetic market. In this way Dickinson could avoid becoming soiled by handling cash and would remain superior to "bourgeois shop culture," thus preserving her sense of aristocratic gentility (Stoneley 584, 589).

Some of the poems Dickinson sent with gifts as well as those she sent as gifts explicitly thematize writing as a physical crafting rather than "intellectual head work." Her poem "I send two sunsets" (Fr557) emphasizes that a verbal rendering of a sunset is in one way superior to the natural event—it is portable, as are the products of all handicrafts. The poet's offhand "as I / Was saying to a friend" calls attention to the ostensible ease with which the poet accomplished her creation; in the same amount of time that it took "Day" to create an "ampler" sunset, the poet "finished Two—and several Stars." Even when her theme seems to be the power of the poetic imagination to create a tangible reality, as in the brief poem "To make a prairie" (Fr1779), she tended to choose language that evokes a sense of handcrafting: the prairie is "made," not "created." The online *Emily Dickinson Lexicon* in fact shows seven uses of the verb "to create" in its various forms, compared to 202 uses of forms of "to make"; six of the occurrences of "create" connote divine creation, but so do a great many of the occurrences of "make," suggesting that Dickinson regarded even God as a crafter and laborer. ("Creation," always capitalized, occurs in eight poems.) Of the twenty-seven occurrences of "work" (including both noun and verb)—not a great number, but enough to suggest that this concept interested her—at least half denote physical labor. The theme of working/making fits well with Dickinson's use later in her writing life of pieces of paper having already served some function in the domestic realm (such as receipts and advertising fliers). It is quite possible, as scholars have recently suggested, that Dickinson saw little if any difference between handcrafting a strictly verbal article and embodying that article in scraps of paper gleaned from the domestic realm.

Of equal importance is the fact that Dickinson tended to avoid, use in a disparaging way, or emphasize the limitations of the language of finance and capitalistic commerce. "Merchant" and "invest" are deemed undesirable choices in "Publication is the auction"; personal "economy" seems a "scheme" or a "sham" like "estimates," "ultimates," and "arithmetic" in "The days that we can spare" (Fr1229). News about "The Stock's advance and Retrograde / And what the Markets say" is "as null as nothing" (Fr1049). The unnamed persons referred to as "they" in "I took one draught of life" (Fr396) seem to be shaped by that language. They tell the speaker that she has "paid . . . / The market price" for that "draught" (a word fascinatingly multivalent in this context, with the dominant meaning being "drink" as in "I took a drink" but a secondary suggestion of "bank draft" lurking just below the surface); she goes on to note that they "weighed" and "balanced" her and found her to be "worth / A single Dram of Heaven!" The concluding exclamation point is equally ambiguous, suggesting that this evaluation is either appropriately high or astonishingly low—cheap, we might say.

In "What would I give to see his face," she notes that she would give, among other things, "'shares' in Primrose 'Banks' / . . . spicy 'Stocks' / . . . Bags of Doubloons" (Fr266). The explicit association of these answers with Shakespeare's character Shylock, however, emphasizes that the foundational concepts of finance and commerce are wholly inadequate to obtain the end she desires. The concluding lines of this poem further ironize such an approach:

> Sign me the Bond!
> "I vow to pay
> To Her—who pledges *this*—
> *One hour*—of her Sovereign's face"!
> *Ecstatic* Contract!
> *Niggard* Grace!
> *My Kingdom's worth* of Bliss! (emphasis in original)

The poem strongly suggests that the speaker wholly misunderstands what is needed actually to gain sight of "his face." She begins by noting that to give herself would not suffice; only then does she begin to offer these additional purchase options. But like Antonio, who negotiates with Shylock in *The Merchant of Venice,* the poem's speaker seems to believe that the ultimate price ("my life") is not only inadequate but irrelevant compared to whatever can be found within the realm of banks, dowries, and stocks. The poem's use of emphases—clearly indicated by underlinings in the manuscript copy reproduced by Franklin in *The Manuscript Books*—and quoted speech may be intended to suggest multiple voices engaged in a bargaining session. The exclamation marks complicate the poem even more, rendering impossible any certainty about the poem's tone, but it seems clear that as with "I took one draught," the language of commerce cannot accurately assess value. As she noted in a later poem, "I am afraid to own a body," to possess a body and a soul is both "profound" and "precarious"; the speaker of "What would I give" doesn't seem to be aware of the value of that possession or perhaps fears to recognize it, preferring instead to negotiate within the capitalist realm. (Franklin dates the manuscript of "What would I give" to 1861 and "I am afraid to own" to around 1865.)

NONCOMMERCIAL MARKETING OF LITERARY GOODS

Melville's first novels were received by his publishers, by reviewers, and by the reading public as essentially autobiographical; their ability to generate symbolic capital was tied to that reception and thus limited to that cultural space—broadly understood as "travel"—about which he was believed to have knowledge. Whatever authority Melville was granted as a critic of his culture both depended on and was limited to his South Sea experiences—he was a man who had "lived among cannibals" (*Correspondence* 193). Thus, he could contribute to discussions of paganism, cannibalism, missionary activity, the beauty of faraway places and peoples, the structure of language, and the superiority of the American or northern European— to some but not all of the interests dominating mid-nineteenth-century American culture.[3] Understanding that his own name as a writer was not sufficiently consecrated, he felt that his productions would fare better with the backing of a "name" like Dana's. He was probably serious when he gestured toward establishing a quite limited field of restricted production, consisting of "sea-brothers," for the exchange of "sea books," but these brothers would almost certainly not be common sailors by birth, education, or social class even though they would have traveled that path for a time. Like South Sea travel, this would be a "natural site" in Bourdieu's terminology: both topics were of interest to American readers, who would assume that the author's experiences made him a credible voice. On the other hand, the travel book and the "sea book" were marginal sites in terms of Melville's developing desire for symbolic capital, a desire that he first began seriously to explore with *Mardi.*

Dickinson presumably read *Typee:* she referred in a letter to "spen-[ding] a few moments profitably with the South Sea rose," and her father's reported reaction to this activity (he "advised wiser employment") supports Johnson's inference that the allusion is to Fayaway (letter of 7 October 1863, Johnson 427–28). She could have known more about Melville's career because of her literary connections and because of reviews she might have read, such as the favorable review of *Pierre* published in the *Springfield Republican* (16 August 1852), although there is no record of her reading *Putnam's* and so encountering his magazine fiction. With the arc of Melville's publishing career nearly at an end around the time Dickinson seems to have dedicated herself to writing, it is tempting, although fanciful, to regard her commitment to publishing by manuscript as her response to his advice—of course not literally so, but by example—that trying to appeal broadly to literary and cultivated readers, let alone the general middle-class audience, was a fool's errand.

That she was so committed is still a matter for debate among scholars, but the idea has been forcefully supported at least since Martha Nell Smith published *Rowing in Eden* in 1992. I am refining this position by arguing, along with Karen Dandurand, that Dickinson actually targeted highly specific markets whose criteria for evaluation she understood and even influenced, and within which she could earn prestige. Dandurand explains that the editors of *Drum Beat* and *A Masque of Poets,* possibly also of the *Round Table*—all of which included Dickinson poems—sent copies to all contributors, meaning that Dickinson's work could have been read by such luminaries as Louisa May Alcott, Oliver Wendell Holmes, William Cullen Bryant, Charles Eliot Norton, Sidney Lanier, and Christina Rossetti (256–57). She well understood that newspapers reprinted material from other papers, and several reviewers of her first published books of poetry remembered individual poems from their appearance decades earlier in the papers and even remembered her as the author (258–59). In short, her strategy seems to have worked.

To read Dickinson as publishing by manuscript is to see her expecting or even demanding to be taken seriously as a producer of literary art and willing to have her productions read by persons outside her intimate circle. A writer publishes to earn capital—economic, symbolic, or cultural. "Publication is the auction" (Fr788) makes it clear that publishing for economic capital is disgraceful, but the poem also invokes the inverse relationship between economic and symbolic capital, implicitly laying claim to the latter by associating it with divinity, the "Creator." She understood that traditional publication includes marketing the writer's very self, as is clear from one of her earliest letters to Higginson, 25 April 1862: "Two Editors of Journals came to my Father's House, this winter—and asked me for my Mind—and when I asked them 'Why,' they said I was penurious—and they, would use it for the world—" (*Letters* 404–5). The editors (probably Samuel Bowles and Josiah Holland, according to Johnson—*Letters* 405) almost certainly asked to be allowed to publish something that she had written. Like "Publication is the auction," this letter shows that Dickinson well understood her culture's inclination to commodify the literary work and to equate it with the writer, an equation that constitutes an erasure of the actual writer: the writer's labor and mind become the literary good and can be owned by the highest bidder (Weinstein 208). Dickinson's use of the word "penurious," as I will explain in chapter 3, also resonates with the copyright issue of whether to privilege the constitutionally protected right of the American public to the fruits of an author's labor ("use it for the world") or an author's perpetual ownership of the right to copy. But Dickinson's point in this letter probably has less to do with that legal context than with her understanding of what audiences do to writers and their works.

Dickinson's experience with publication has often been characterized as negative. As she wrote to Higginson regarding the published version of "A narrow fellow in the grass" that appeared in the *Springfield Republican,* "Lest you meet my Snake and suppose I deceive it was robbed of me—defeated too of the third line by the punctuation. The third and fourth were one—I had told you I did not print—I feared you might think me ostensible" (letter of early 1866, *Letters* 450). This comment historically was taken as yet another sign of her opposition to print publication. Recently, however, scholars have been less willing to make that interpretive leap, noting instead that she was complaining specifically about the change in lineation and was concerned about Higginson's opinion of her—she probably intended "ostensible" to connote "seeming (but not really being) opposed to 'print.'" By this more nuanced reading, she was commenting on the poem within its marketed context. In the view of Habegger, Dickinson's "work was eminently publishable—subject to the usual editorial adjustments, of course"; Samuel Bowles, editor of the *Springfield Republican,* "was always confronting barriers and crossing boundaries and seeking a vital new woman's voice," and Fidelia Hayward Cooke, that paper's literary editor for approximately six years beginning in 1860, would have been especially open to such voices (383–84, 389). Habegger goes on to write that

> [i]t is not the case that Dickinson was denied an outlet, or that her work was deemed too "modern" or "incorrect" or "daring" to be published in her time . . . many conservative nineteenth-century Americans continued to hold the old idea that the best sort of writing circulates in private. This seems to be how Dickinson wanted to be read. Certainly, it was in line with her father's views of feminine decorum, her brother's uneasiness about her "wild" side, and her own profound shrinking from the public gaze. (389–90)

Habegger implies that Dickinson's desire to be read was caused by the expectations set for her within her family. This is a plausible reason, but as a writer in contact with other writers, editors, and other literary tastemakers, Dickinson also understood that the means of production inevitably limit the type and amount of capital the literary good and its author can accrue. Habegger is also correct to point out how the preference for private circulation tended to be held by "conservative Americans"; he could as well have said "economically secure Americans." As I noted in chapter

1, Dickinson's attitudes toward and practice of literary art reflect her position in a family that was privileged in terms of education, social class, and (with some fluctuations) wealth. This was the class within which symbolic capital could be generated by privately circulated writing.

Two other phrases in Habegger's statement deserve special note: "the best sort of writing" and "how Dickinson wanted to be read." Almost all scholars agree that Dickinson wanted her writing to be read—but how, how much, and by whom, aside from her regular correspondents? I argue that like Melville, she desired to reach an audience of "thought-divers" and wished to be understood as writing what was "banned." She obviously wanted to produce "the best sort of writing"—not just socially and aesthetically acceptable to a conservative audience but profound, capable of dealing "heavenly hurt" or "dazzl[ing] gradually" as she put it in "There's a certain slant of light" (Fr320). Thus, the audience's conservatism would have to be limited to the social and perhaps the aesthetic realms and would exclude the intellectual realm. Bowles may have been receptive to such writing: Habegger argues yes, while Sewall cautions that Bowles's "taste in poetry was thoroughly conventional," hence that Dickinson "experienced the frustration of an original mind in an uncomprehending time" ("Emily Dickinson's Perfect Audience" 207). Dickinson had been blessed with receptive audiences even as an adolescent: her friends were all bright and well educated, and she early developed a reputation among them and within her family for the "finesse, the unexpectedly droll turns, and the brilliant resourcefulness of her word spinning" (Habegger 148, 164–65). But if that youthful willingness to perform continued into her mature life, her "profound shrinking" itself needs to be read as a performance of considerable rhetorical sophistication, and her desire to circulate her writing privately must have included the recognition, even the expectation, that it would be shared with people outside her intimate circle.

I suggested in chapter 1 that Dickinson pursued symbolic capital in order to enhance her authority to speak critically, if also cryptically or gnomically, about her culture's dispositions in the realms of organized religion, sexual relations, and transcendent reality—realms that were foregrounded by the subject divisions in the first editions of her poems. Reaching out to Higginson would then be similar to sharing her poems and ideas with Samuel Bowles, her sister-in-law Susan Gilbert Dickinson, or the other tastemakers whose validation she sought in order to become recognized as an author—someone willing to go before a public—by appropriating the writerly context of the personal letter. Agnieszka Salska argues forcefully that Dickinson intended her letters to function this way. The letters "contain the fullest record that we have of the poet's conscious life," demonstrate "the convergence of the principles of poetics for all her writing," often display the oxymoronic quality of "intimate impersonality," and were written within "a culture of intimacy of which the letter was a primary vehicle" (163–65). Dickinson's culture, Salska insists, "persistently encouraged the fusion of literary and personal experience"; "radically and experimentally" she appropriated for "her own use a pervasive cultural habit" (166). Thus, "[t]he essence of her attitude in letting the genre of the private letter color all her writings and pattern her relationship with the reader should be seen as analogous to the innovative use she made in the sphere of prosody of popular ballad and hymn meters" (166–67). Her letters "maintained her connection to the intellectual and literary circles of the New England of her time" and also "prepared and created an audience for her poetry" (167–68).

In other words, Dickinson's letters reveal her as desiring recognition as an author. In the early Higginson letters, "for the first time in her life, Dickinson separates her artistic concerns from her emotional involvements and attempts to test the response to her poetry of a reader who was personally unknown to her but professionally well established. Writing to Higginson seems a 'coming-of-age' gesture of a 'homegrown' artist" (Salska 175). Salska points out that these letters to Higginson followed whatever experience it was that led to the writing of the Master letters; followed within a few days the departure of Samuel Bowles to Europe, and occurred within the "conspicuous two-year gap during 1862–3 in the correspondence with Susan" (175). Her decision to initiate contact with a stranger could thus have been an attempt to fill the gap in her intellectual and writing life that was created by these other conditions—she needed an audience (a fact, as I show in chapter 5, that was ignored by most of those responsible for her twentieth-century career).

The manner of these letters to Higginson is also key. Salska describes the letters as a "coming-of-age *gesture*" (my emphasis): already a master of personae, Dickinson was now trying on yet another mask, this time of the hypothetical "young contributor" to whom Higginson had addressed the *Atlantic Monthly* "letter" that seems to have stimulated her contact.[4] She desired to appear to Higginson as a "homegrown artist" just "coming of age" in the sense of seeking expert evaluation, but it seems unlikely that this is how she imagined herself. After all, she had already written hundreds of poems, and the contact with Higginson did not initiate any significant development or change in her practice, aside from the possibility that it contributed to her ceasing, two years later, the construction of fascicles. She was already thirty-one and had been taking care of her mother for years, had experienced passionate friendships, had known death and other types of personal loss.

These letters to Higginson, like many others, also should be understood as transactions within a sexual economy, intended to "seduce" each correspondent "into an intimate relationship" (Salska 165). Salska describes what she terms Dickinson's "double perspective: subjective—that is, her own as experiencer's—and external, because she had to consider her addressee's response" (172). This double perspective, which Salska says began as an intuitive discovery made by Dickinson through her letter writing, informed her poetry from the beginning, because she crafted and dramatized "the writer–reader bond on the paradigm of the relation between intimate correspondents" (172–73). But it is also possible that Dickinson fully intended to "seduce" that personally unknown but professionally established editor in order to expand her actual or potential symbolic capital. (This is the view of Suzanne Juhasz, one of Salska's sources.) Dickinson certainly understood that she could play the game of sexual flirtation to powerful effect as a way of engaging and holding audiences and that the genre of the personal letter was the ideal field for this game. The end result would then be a conversion of sexual capital into symbolic capital.

It is likely that the letters of many ordinary people would reflect the same development that Salska traces in Dickinson's, the development toward a double perspective or from expressive (writer-centered) toward transactional (reader-centered). The quality of "impersonal intimacy" in Dickinson's more mature letters is unusual, but it is far from unique. This quality, however, would serve to develop symbolic capital while protecting the writer's self from being dragged through the marketplace. Writing at a time when the identity of the author powerfully influenced how a work was received, Dickinson combined manuscript publication with extensive use of personae to signal to a limited and receptive audience that the work was to be the focus and that the writer was not to be possessed through the work, even as she intentionally and playfully offered individualized personae for possession by individual recipients of her work. She could reasonably—and professionally—expect these recipients to recognize the voice as coming from a mask rather than as from the heart, a point I develop in chapter 4. Yet she could also turn to her advantage her audience's predilection to read the author through her work: "Maybe I *can* possess the writer, because the writer really is allowing glimpses of herself to me alone." Furthermore, the writer preserved the right to appear in her own self, if this initial trial proved successful and if she decided that something was to be gained by doing so. Certainly, this strategy was likely to be more productive of symbolic capital than that followed by Melville:

allowing a large audience to identify him so closely with his first fictional protagonist that he could never be wholly free of that label.

Dickinson probably understood that although "nineteenth-century female poets were clearly as engaged as their male counterparts in issues of national importance," they "were denied both recognition and authority for their work" and were able to succeed financially only by relating with editors in ways more resembling marriages than business arrangements (Petrino 10, 23–24). The goods produced by women also risked being devalued if presented to readers as "portfolio poetry" (Petrino 36). Such poetry "offered a culturally defined space for the seriousness of any writer's unpublished and unpolished (and, to that extent, unconventional) work"; the poetry could function this way in part because Emerson had written in support of its value, although Dickinson's reworking and polishing of her poems went contrary to the expected spontaneity of portfolio poetry (Miller, "Whose Dickinson?" 245). However, portfolio poetry was unlikely to be consecrated, especially during the middle third of the nineteenth century: it was deemed valuable because it was closer in spirit to inspired first drafts than was poetry crafted specifically for the common marketplace, but the "culturally defined space" was a marginal one until near the end of the century (Petrino 36–37), similar to the space "Mr Typee" was allowed to occupy. In his preface to the first edition of Dickinson's poems, Higginson, (in)famously, wrote that "she must write thus, or not at all," which within the context of the 1890s was only modest praise. Higginson did not mean that Dickinson had put herself through an apprenticeship, practicing and learning all available forms and committing herself to one; he meant that her form and style chose her. She sang this note well, but it was the only note she could sing. Such an artist, who was simply expressing an inner drive, could be interesting as a spectacle of nature and might even command substantial economic capital, but to be taken seriously as an author of lasting value required overt signs of conscious control (adherence to norms of diction, syntax, and meter, for instance), signs that were lacking in her poetry.

Any "culturally defined space" both empowers and limits, a fact of which Melville and Dickinson were certainly aware. That said, Dickinson's fascicles do not belong within such a space, because as far as we know she never showed them to anyone; they cannot be termed "self-published" as can the poems she distributed in notes and letters. Gabrielle Dean argues that the fascicles reveal Dickinson "imitating the book but refusing print," a tactic by which she "kept her fascicles in print and authorial rights *and* savored the materiality of the text—yet another way of making an unenforceable contract, like that she celebrates in 'Mine!,' beside but outside the reach of the law" (271; emphasis in original). The fascicles thus "present the ideal dream of the book as intimate object, an expression of the author's person outside the law of copyright. The central paradox—and triumph—of the fascicles is that, as much as they invoke self-publication, they are not reproducible because they are not and never were in print" (272). A scholar may read the fascicles as unpublished imitations of published books, but such a reading remains only a *hypothesis* about Dickinson's authorial goals, that is, about "Dickinson as author," and it should carry relatively less weight than what can be understood from her actual practices of self-publication. Domhnall Mitchell's caution must be born in mind when considering what we know to have been disseminated compared to what may have remained private: "Emily Dickinson may not have been fully conscious of the potential her unpublished manuscripts possessed—or would acquire—as published documents. It may be later scholars who invent or reconstruct that potential" ("Revising the Script" 731). As interesting as are the fascicles for what they may show about Dickinson's revising habits and her sense of the groupings into which her poems might naturally fall, they at best support hypotheses, not facts, about her authorial practices.

THE MARKETS FOR SYMBOLIC GOODS AND ART AS INTIMATE CONNECTION

Two types of writing that generated handcrafted goods were especially important for Dickinson's construction of herself as an author—the "poetry of the portfolio" and the personal letter. Both types circulated within markets that had nothing to do with economic capital; Dickinson did not have to imagine herself outside of an economic market, as Melville did until late in his career, but instead explicitly placed her poems in ways that could earn her symbolic capital. These noneconomic, antimimetic markets were also amenable to goods that embodied and reflected household labor of the sort that would have been done or managed by middle- and upper-class women, hence Dickinson's occasional poetic and epistolary depictions of this work. "The Rose did caper on her cheek," for instance, portrays a presumably young woman "fumbl[ing] at her [needle]work" because of the presence of someone else who seems to be a secret lover; it is possible to imagine this scene taking place in a lower-class household, but it is certainly iconic of novels of romance focusing on the gentry (Fr200). A similarly sentimentalized situation is depicted in "Death sets a thing significant," in which the fact of death leads people "To ponder little

Workmanships / In Crayon, or in Wool" that were the final products of the
now-dead hands (Fr640). Much less sanguine, "Severer service of myself"
portrays work as an unsuccessful method to "fill the awful Vacuum" caused
by a loved one's death: "I strove to weary Brain and Bone—/ To harass to
fatigue / The glittering Retinue of Nerves—" (Fr887).

The genres of letter and portfolio poetry continued the eighteenth-
century tradition of genteel amateurism, in which the work of writing
was relatively more prominent than the work of authorship: imagination
and self-expression, as valorized by romanticism, were tangibly visible to
the audience, unlike with published material. These modes also required
money to purchase diaries, albums, scrapbooks, and the like, and they
did involve labor. Dickinson's writing life may have commanded a good
deal of her thought on a daily basis, but as a woman with a household to
manage she probably did not spend much time actually putting pencil to
paper (especially given that because of her eye problems and the relatively
poor artificial lighting of the time, she may have needed to fit in most
of her pencil-to-paper time during daylight hours, when the household
duties would also have been most demanding). Even in a family that had
a servant, running a household was a demanding job: "Simply for Sun-
day dinner, chickens would have to be slaughtered and plucked, the spices
ground for breads and pies, or puddings. The designated family baker,
Dickinson . . . rose before dawn to make the fires and to prepare the family breakfast . . . chores were endless" (Barker 81). In fact she expressed
resentment about the amount of work, and it is likely that she would have
been much less productive during the crucial years 1858–62 were it not
for the presence of a maid (Murray 703, 724).

Does this mean that Dickinson intended her collage-type texts using
domestic household materials to "invoke" the "ideologically valorized"
labor of household management, as Newbury says of middle-class male
authors in the context of other types of labor (693–94)? This interesting
thesis has been advanced by scholars such as Jeanne Holland and Melanie
Hubbard. It is also possible that the genteel-amateur tradition and the cultural significance of letters and other forms of personal, intimate writing
allowed Dickinson to regard her writing as a culturally sanctioned, seam-
less blending of her intellectual work and her household work. That is,
for her this type of labor was not at all "emergent" (Newbury's term) but
long-standing, although she gave it her own distinctive imprint. It could
further be the case that other women whose authorial authority tended to
center on the domestic sphere (the magazine poets discussed by Cheryl
Walker, the prose writers discussed by Susan Coultrap-McQuin and Jane
Tompkins) had ready to hand a realm of labor (the household) within

which they could plausibly situate their themes and characters. But that possibility is beyond my scope here; suffice it to say that Dickinson experienced writing as labor and understood it as such. For her as for Melville, the labor was real, an inescapable component of her authorial authority.

GIVEN THAT portfolio poetry, letters, and other hand-produced forms functioned as fields of restricted production within which symbolic capital could be earned, Bourdieu's theory calls for investigation into the evaluative criteria that were applied to these forms. Bourdieu insists that the criteria would have differed from those of the mass market, would be directed at other producers of symbolic capital, and would overtly suggest an "art for art's sake" orientation. For several reasons, however, this aspect of Bourdieu's work must be modified for the period I'm considering. First of all, mass audiences and highly limited audiences equally expected that they would be able to have an experience of intimacy mediated by the work. The technique perhaps is most tellingly captured in a famous pair of lines from Whitman's "Song of Myself": "This hour I tell things in confidence, / I might not tell everybody, but I will tell you" (conclusion of section 19 of the 1888 version—the lines were present in every edition from 1855 on, differing only in the later addition of the comma after "everybody"). By publishing the poem, Whitman does tell everyone, but he still allows an individual reader to feel individually and even intimately addressed, singled out as worthy of this confidence. Second, both types of audience were ready to grant poetry a higher value than prose, deeming it more likely to convey enduring truth. Third, because egalitarianism and pragmatism loomed so prominently in American ideology, an author would be expected to avoid overt expressions of superiority and of "art for art's sake," but at the same time, the American emphasis on self-reliance would respect an individual offering a high estimation of his or her own value if that estimate was backed up in some way. All of these qualities can be summed up in the phrase "art as intimate connection"—they are the autonomous criteria for evaluation within the extremely limited circles which Dickinson throughout her writing life and Melville from *Clarel* on desired to reach.

Melville appealed equally to intimacy and egalitarianism—for instance with his expressed interest in writing "sea-books" for "sea-brothers," even if these brothers were not imagined as common sailors. His statement to Duyckinck that he believed his "illustrious name" to be "famous throughout the world" need not be taken as pure vanity but fits well with the tone of the rest of that letter, a tone of frustration with a republic of letters that seemed unable to value genius—a common complaint in America at this time, unlikely to be read as elitist (*Correspondence* 180). Allowing his homodiegetic narrators, most famously Ishmael, to establish an intimate and privileged relationship with narratees similarly conveys the sense of an extremely limited field of reception. Parker speculates that until the early 1850s Melville was influenced by the "art for artists" theory propounded in Hawthorne's tale "The Artist of the Beautiful," according to which "what is important is not the created work of art but the artist's feelings" about the work, but that ultimately Melville "had to think beyond" the writer whom he had earlier taken as an ideal model (*Herman Melville* 2:160–61). Certainly the "art for artists" theory was present and not just in a possibly satirical form in the literary culture of Melville's time, but it was not a theory to which he subscribed from the publication of *Pierre* in 1852 until 1866, when *Battle-Pieces and Aspects of the War* appeared. During this period he attempted to achieve both economic and symbolic capital as a writer of imaginative magazine fiction and, later in the period, poetry, and was not overtly pursuing individual, private readers. He almost certainly understood the magazine-fiction and poetry fields fairly well, as I explained in chapter 1. According to Charvat, the magazine world of the 1850s was populated by "the upper middle class," whose taste "was beginning to be interpreted and guided by the editors of national monthly magazines like *Harper's* and the *Atlantic*" (262). This world was "Melville's proper level" in terms of the goals he set for himself as a "thought-diver." The success he did achieve was "as an anonymous magazinist" (the magazine practice being not to print bylines) and was doubtless supported by his skill at embodying his critique of culture in characters and situations, thus preventing readers from easily imputing the critique to the stories' author (279). But this success, such as it was, came too late to be profitable: his income from *Israel Potter* and his magazine pieces from 1853 to 1856 averaged "about $240 a year" compared to $1,600 a year during his first five years (1846–51) as an author (Charvat 193–94), and later he earned even less.

Furthermore, even the success of placing pieces in magazines was qualified, because of the anonymity. Contributors might be listed in tables of contents, as for instance with *Harper's*, but then as now readers tended to "leaf through" magazines rather than scrutinize them. Even if the author's name were initially associated with a magazine piece, the widespread practice of reprinting, which I discuss in chapter 3, meant that authors' names might not follow what they had written, except for those extremely popular authors such as Fanny Fern whose names would help sell copies. The main reason Melville did not continue to pursue magazine publication, however, may have been that he was uncomfortable with the "singular collective identity" and "the amalgamation of art and morality under the rubric *utilitarianism*" that had shaped America's literary magazines during the two decades prior to his magazine career and that were still significant (Bohde 34). Melville would not have embraced the magazines' self-appropriated role "as arbiter of a singular American character" (40), and for that matter neither would Dickinson.

This may partially explain why Melville began to strive around 1856 or 1857 for the status that was traditionally accorded only to poets (Parker, "The Lost *Poems*" 261). By 1860 he had completed a volume, now lost, to be titled *Poems*. He asked Evert Duyckinck to review the volume and to help locate a publisher if he deemed the project worthwhile, and he wrote for his brother Allan "the fullest instructions he had ever given for the publication of one of his works," a memorandum that provides "powerful evidence of how seriously he took his new role as a poet" (Parker, "The Lost *Poems*" 263). Three of Melville's points in the memorandum are especially telling in considering this "new role":

5—For God's sake don't have *By the author of "Typee" "Piddledee" &c* on the title-page.
6—Let the title-page be simply,

Poems
By
Herman Melville.

7—Dont [*sic*] have any clap-trap announcements and "sensation" puffs— nor any extracts published previous to publication of book—Have decent publisher, in short. (*Correspondence* 343–44; emphasis in original)

He understood that his ability to command symbolic capital was still hampered by his early reputation as an author either of travel narratives or of unreadable philosophizing; his hoped-for new identity was to be "Herman Melville, Poet," rather than "the author of 'Typee' 'Piddledee' &c." The proposed title page aptly sketches that identity: brief not prolix, declarative rather than evocative, elegant but not overwrought. Moreover, here is no game with personae or anonymity, no promise (or threat) of metaphysical meanderings.

Parker offers additional evidence that Melville regarded *Poems* as an important step in "reemerg[ing] into the literary scene as a poet" (262), especially the books he read on the round-the-world voyage he began on 30 May 1860 on the *Meteor*, commanded by his brother Thomas. The books were mainly poetry, "most often volumes that contained epic poems or else very long poems," which Melville would have studied to learn how to "write great poetry in his own time" (269, 272). Parker's interpretation fits with everything that is known about how and why Melville read: always in dialogue with voices he hoped one day to match in power and prestige. When he arrived in San Francisco on 12 October, however, he learned that instead of being a published poet, he was "a mere unpublished 'poetaster,'" Duyckinck having been unable to find a house willing to gamble on *Poems* (Parker 273). Regardless of the failure of this endeavor, any complete study of how Melville understood himself as a writer must recognize that *Poems* really existed, was read by George and Evert Duyckinck (the latter responding favorably and agreeing "to help see the poems into print"), and was looked at by two, possibly more, publishers (Parker 263, 261).

Once Melville began working at the New York Custom House in December 1866, his only attempt to accrue either economic or symbolic capital through the medium of commercial publication was *Clarel*, which was published in 1876 with the assistance of a subsidy from his uncle Peter Gansevoort, which fared poorly with both critics and purchasers, and the remaining copies of which were pulped in 1879. From 1866 on Melville was able to adopt at least the practice, if not the leisured posture, of the "gentleman author," who often turned to the handmade book or limited edition in order to distinguish himself from those who wrote for the masses (Reiman 113). Parker emphasizes that the writing of *Clarel* did involve "real work. Melville toiled on *Clarel*, as he had toiled on *Moby-Dick*, in hours when he was exuberantly energized and other hours when he was crushed by fatigue and strain . . . we need to take the composition of *Clarel* out of the realm of the magically appearing artifact and see what writing it must have meant if Melville spent four or five years on it" (*Herman Melville* 2:688). If Melville's handwritten note prior to the first page of the book can be taken as revealing his honest feelings, he had no positive expectation for its reception: "If during the period in which this work has remained unpublished, though not undivulged, any of its properties have by a natural process exhaled; it yet retains, I trust, enough of original life to redeem it at least from vapidity. Be that as it may, I here dismiss the book—content beforehand with whatever future awaits it."

The prefatory note to *Clarel* suggests that Melville was finally, fully embracing the "art as intimate connection" principle as well as moving toward the "art for art's sake" aesthetic of which he had been aware and with which he had at least dallied since working on *Mardi*. During the period of *Timoleon, John Marr,* and what would become *Billy-Budd*, Melville had finally developed a small following of readers who would actually be able to appreciate a presentation copy of one of those last volumes: W. Clark Russell, E. C. Stedman and his son Arthur, for instance. The criteria for evaluation within this extremely limited field were tangibly present in a manuscript or in a self-published work of extremely limited run. The recipient of such a work was automatically privileged; the relationship between author and reader was intimate and sincere (not involving masks); the content of the work was guaranteed to be significant.

Symbolic capital did not remain out of Melville's reach during his lifetime; as I discuss in chapter 5, several of the poems from *Battle-Pieces* frequently appeared in anthologies. There is no record of his response to this modest success. When the name "Herman Melville" did begin to garner symbolic capital in the twentieth century—and to generate significant economic capital as well—it was of course not as a crafter of manuscripts, commercially published poems, or self-published poems. In fact this component of his writing life was almost entirely erased: the twentieth-century Melville was created as a romantic artist whose financial failure was due partly to his own personal and business flaws but more to his contemporaries' inability to appreciate his brilliance. The same is true of Dickinson. In the 1903 *Reader's History of American Literature* he coauthored with Henry Walcott Boynton, Higginson predicted that although her poetry likely "can never attain popularity—the last fate which its author could have wished for it—it is likely, in the end, to obtain the attention of the 'audience fit, tho' few,' which a greater poet once desired of fate" (Higginson and Boynton 131). In praising her poetry's "remoteness of allusion" and "boldness of phrase," Higginson enunciated qualities that at this time would position Dickinson not among the popular poets but in the same category (although of lesser stature) with John Milton.

On the other hand, Dickinson was able to put into long-term practice Melville's wish to send individual manuscripts to individual readers, appealing to them partly because of her "remoteness of allusion" and "boldness of phrase" but more so because she practiced the "art of intimate connection" while presenting herself as a representative voice. Her statement to Higginson that "[w]hen I state myself, as the Representative of the Verse—it does not mean—me—but a supposed person" (*Letters* 412, letter of July 1862) echoes Emerson's assertion that "the poet is representative," standing "among partial men for the complete man, and appris[ing] us not of his wealth, but of the commonwealth" ("The Poet" 198). Dickinson may also have been alluding to Emerson's essay in the lines "For love of Her ["Nature"]—Sweet—countrymen—/ Judge tenderly—of Me," which according to Wolff show her "intend[ing] to speak of the general condition and for all men and women" (142). Higginson is today the best known of Dickinson's literary correspondents, due to his role in publishing her work, but during her lifetime others were also not just well-known but equally well positioned: Samuel Bowles (editor of the *Springfield Republican*, which in spite of its regional character had a national reach), Josiah Holland (affiliated first with the *Springfield Republican* and then editor of *Scribner's Monthly*), and the novelist and poet Helen Hunt Jackson, to name just three. Jackson may have been the most important in Dickinson's later years, perhaps even regarded as a true peer (Sewall, "Emily Dickinson's Perfect Audience" 212). Although not herself recognized as a literary figure, Dickinson's sister-in-law Sue received the greatest number of known letters, was probably viewed by Emily as a writing-workshop partner, and was for several decades a center of Amherst's literary culture because of her salons, in which Emily's poems were almost certainly read. These individuals and others were able to both value and circulate Dickinson's work among a discriminating readership.

SYMBOLIC CAPITAL AND THE INTIMATE HAND

Ownership, labor, identity, authority, and symbolic capital most visibly coalesce in nineteenth-century attitudes toward the writer's "hand," or penmanship style: a manuscript should be legible, but ideally it would also be visually unique. Even though "print was prior . . . in terms of its cultural status" (McGill, "Duplicity" 41), there was still a significant space for handwritten art. Part of an author's individuality is the author's hand, a trait that Poe for one hoped to preserve, but also, by experimenting with printed imitations of others' handwriting, attempted to exploit. The hand-produced work would be strictly the property of whoever owned the artifact itself; it embodies the writer's labor, should be unequivocally identifiable as that person's work (otherwise forgery would not pay), and if received by someone with the power to consecrate can generate symbolic capital. At the time of Melville's education, handwriting instruction in America attended to both the ornamental and the useful; Melville and his family recognized his "hand" as deficient in both ways, neither beautiful nor legible (Renker 18–19). Melville regarded producing a text by hand as the true mark of "authorship" but knew he could not produce legible copy. By the principle of the art of intimate connection, the original, handcrafted manuscript would stand as the true work of art.

Near the end of his life, Melville may have found a way to combine the technology of print production with the intimacy of handwriting. The American Antiquarian Society collection includes a first edition of *Clarel*, inside the front cover of the first volume of which I found a loose title page from *Timoleon* with the following reproduced on the verso side, in Melville's hand:

> New Book by Harper & Brothers.
>
> "Clarel," published by George P. Putnam's Sons, New York—a metrical affair, a pilgrimage, a what not, of several thousand lines, eminently adapted for unpopularity—the notification to you here is ambidexter, as it were: it may intimidate or allure.
>
> Again thanking you for your friendly note, and with best wishes to yourself and your circle, I am
>
> > Very truly yours
> > Herman Melville

The staff of the Society were unable to help me determine how the loose sheet had come to be inside of this volume or where it had originated, although markings on the front of the sheet trace it as far back as "C. A. Stonehill (Lond.)" and identify it as item 90 in catalogue 137, 1938, with a price of £90.00. (See figure 5.) The text itself (excluding "New Book by Harper & Brothers") is from a letter of 10 October 1884 to James Billson; this letter is also listed in Stonehill's catalogue (*Correspondence* 483). Possibly Melville used this sheet to accompany a presentation copy of *Clarel* late in his life, or even of *Timoleon* itself, but why would he have copied the personal letter? Melville's note, I deduced (from embossing) and was assured by the Society staff, was printed not handwritten. This being the case, it is possible—although certainly a stretch—that Melville intended the sheet to embody the personal intimacy of a handwritten note even though it was mechanically reproduced; perhaps he intended to use the sheets to accompany a number of presentation copies. As such, the sheet itself, like *Clarel,* carries the potential both to "allure" and to put off a recipient—to allure the recipient who feels singled out for a special handwritten note, and to put off the recipient who looked closely at the sheet and determined that it was after all not an original signature.

Dickinson's attitude toward handwriting has remained unstudied, although Thomas Johnson, Ralph Franklin, and others have provided a chronology for the changes in her handwriting and have used that to date her poems and letters. Wolff describes her writing as "very difficult to read, so much so that some of the products of her last years seem little more than hieroglyphics to an untutored eye" (4). The phrase "an untutored eye," however, is telling. As Martha Nell Smith notes, in letters to correspondents other than Sue, Dickinson "almost always used more formal,

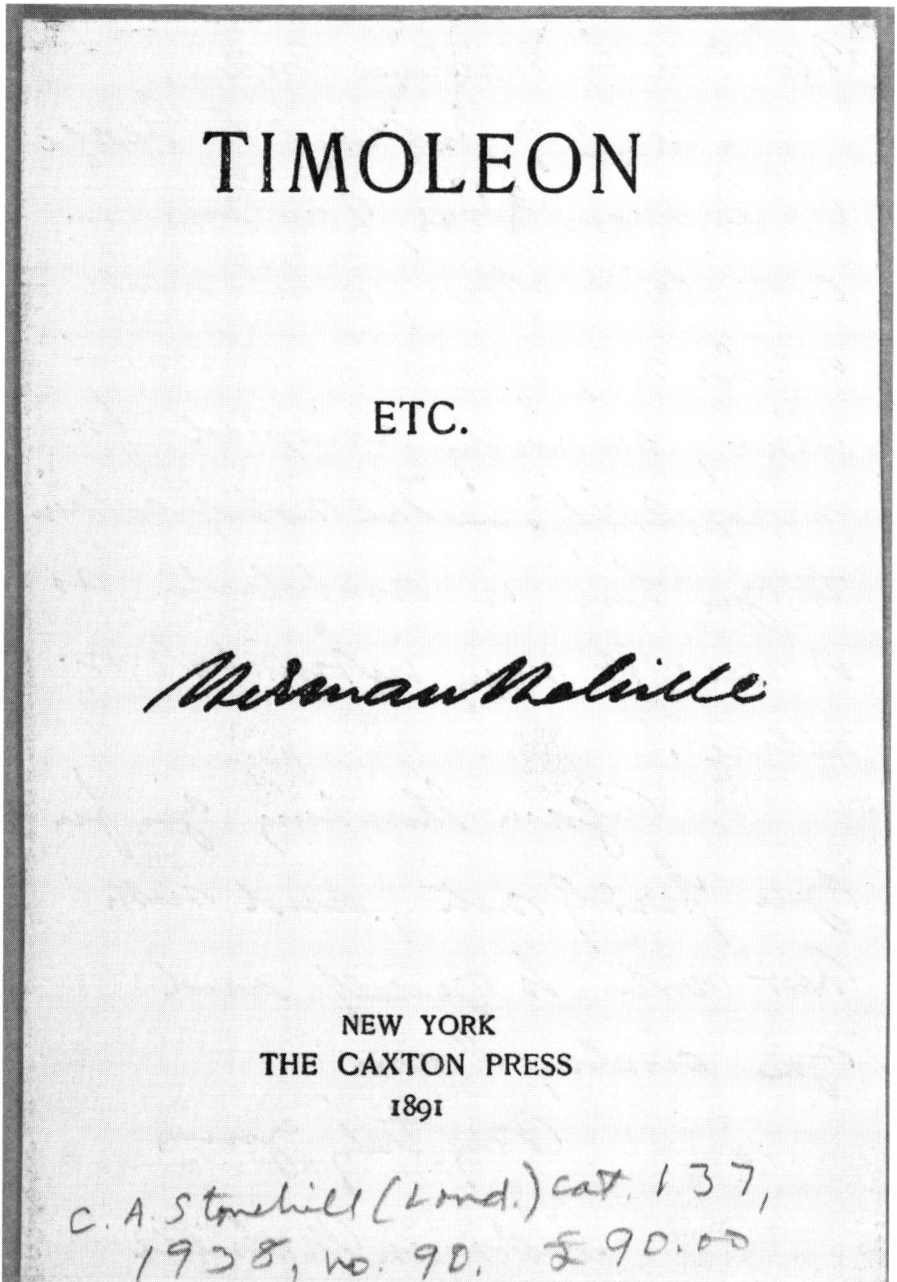

TIMOLEON

ETC.

Herman Melville

NEW YORK
THE CAXTON PRESS
1891

C. A. Stonehill (Lond.) Cat. 137,
1938, no. 90. £90.00

Figure 5. Broadside: title page from *Timoleon* with an inscription on the verso side in Herman Melville's hand. Courtesy of the American Antiquarian Society.

New York by Harper & Brothers.

"Clarel", published by George P. Putnam's Sons, New York. — a metrical affair, a pilgrimage or what not, of several thousand lines, eminently adapted for unpopularity. — The notification to you here is ambidexter, as it were: it may intimidate or allure.

Again thanking you for your friendly note, and with best wishes to yourself and your circle, I am

Very truly yours

Herman Melville

often gilt-trimmed stationery, in effect dressing her texts like a gift edition of poetry or a deluxe edition of biblical scripture" ("Susan and Emily Dickinson" 53–54). The letters, thus, would reach their recipients already making a claim as to their value, regardless of any difficulties created by her "hand." Furthermore, the recipients would not be "untutored"; they would know the writer and after receiving several letters would be familiar with her penmanship. In fact, while Dickinson's very late handwriting does somewhat challenge a reader, the poems she sent to correspondents typically pose no problem. For instance, she enclosed with her first letter to Higginson, dated 15 April 1862, copies of four poems, including "The nearest dream recedes" (Fr304B). As figure 6 shows, this manuscript is quite legible; of course it should be, as she did not yet have any sort of relationship with the famous man of letters and was asking him to determine whether her "Verse" was "alive." She would probably also want her handwritten self to show that she understood the need for truly "fair copy" if one wanted to be taken seriously as a potential author, especially considering how odd were some of her expressions in that cover letter, such as "The Mind is so near itself—it cannot see, distinctly" (*Letters* L260).

Curiously, although Dickinson frequently refers to the hand as engaging in actions, including writing and drawing, she does not figure it metonymically as penmanship style. Equally curiously, in an era when pencils were used for fine drawing but in writing were relegated to drafting (fine copying always being done in pen), she refers in her poems to "pencil" a few times but never to "pen." Or perhaps this is not so curious. She may have regarded the pencil as the technology most conducive to masking, because its marks can so easily be erased and because it does not immediately convey the impression of an actual person who cares enough about the writing to convey it in a relatively permanent form. It could of course also be regarded as suitable for poetry of the portfolio, as such poetry was to convey a sense of immediacy rather than of reflective thought.

In sum, then, within this culture in which "print was prior," a significant space was available for the production of handwritten or otherwise self-produced art. Within this space, symbolic capital could be earned; Melville and Dickinson recognized the opportunity, although he only seized it near the end of his life, while she made use of it throughout her writing life. Melville reveals that even in his ideal situation of sending handwritten manuscripts, the evaluation criteria he imagined were not wholly autonomous: labor after all was widely esteemed. His awareness of the material and economic bases of literary production contrasts with Emerson's portrayal of the relationship between a poet and the poet's nation, according to which the poet, as opposed to a mere maker of verses (a poetaster), would be valued by the nation yet would not be limited by that audience's history, culture, or economic support. Nothing in Emerson's formulation could be taken as advocating art for its own sake, art evaluated solely by autonomous criteria. Emerson's anecdote of the youthful poet makes clear that a discriminating audience is essential, an audience "credulous" not in the sense of casually moved but in the sense of being willing to invest belief in and be spiritually moved by the presence of art.[5] Because, according to Emerson, a poet was to be evaluated in the context of "partial men," an audience was needed. Not surprisingly, Emerson's idealistic theory ignores the labor of production; Melville, on the other hand, grasped that in the literary/cultural/economic system in which he participated, using paid labor to produce a good might aid in or even be necessary to the favorable reception of that good by an audience. Further, as Melville understood, that audience had to be paid for but not "bought" in the derogatory sense. The payment might be in the form of versions of one's self, such as photographic images or verbal stereotypes (the cannibalistic man), a price Melville was not willing to pay. At the other end of the scale, it could be in the form of handcrafted artifacts, a price he idealized. It could also be in the form of a self-published volume of extremely limited distribution, his practice late in life.

Dickinson invested herself solely in the handcrafted forms practiced by the more leisured classes, forms that better tallied with Emerson's description of the ideal poet in terms of being produced without a profit motive and with the expectation of being received by a discriminating audience. But these forms would tend to erase the labor of production and the capitalistic system that made leisure possible for some. She challenged this tendency with her self-conscious use of domestic materials and her frequent incorporation of figures drawn from the language of commerce and finance. She certainly understood, with Melville, that audiences expected a fair exchange: positive evaluation bought with a sense of at least momentarily possessing a bit of the writer's mind. Like Melville, Dickinson met this expectation with lifelike and plausible personae and reinforced it with actual handcrafted works rather than with merely the promise. She learned his lessons well.

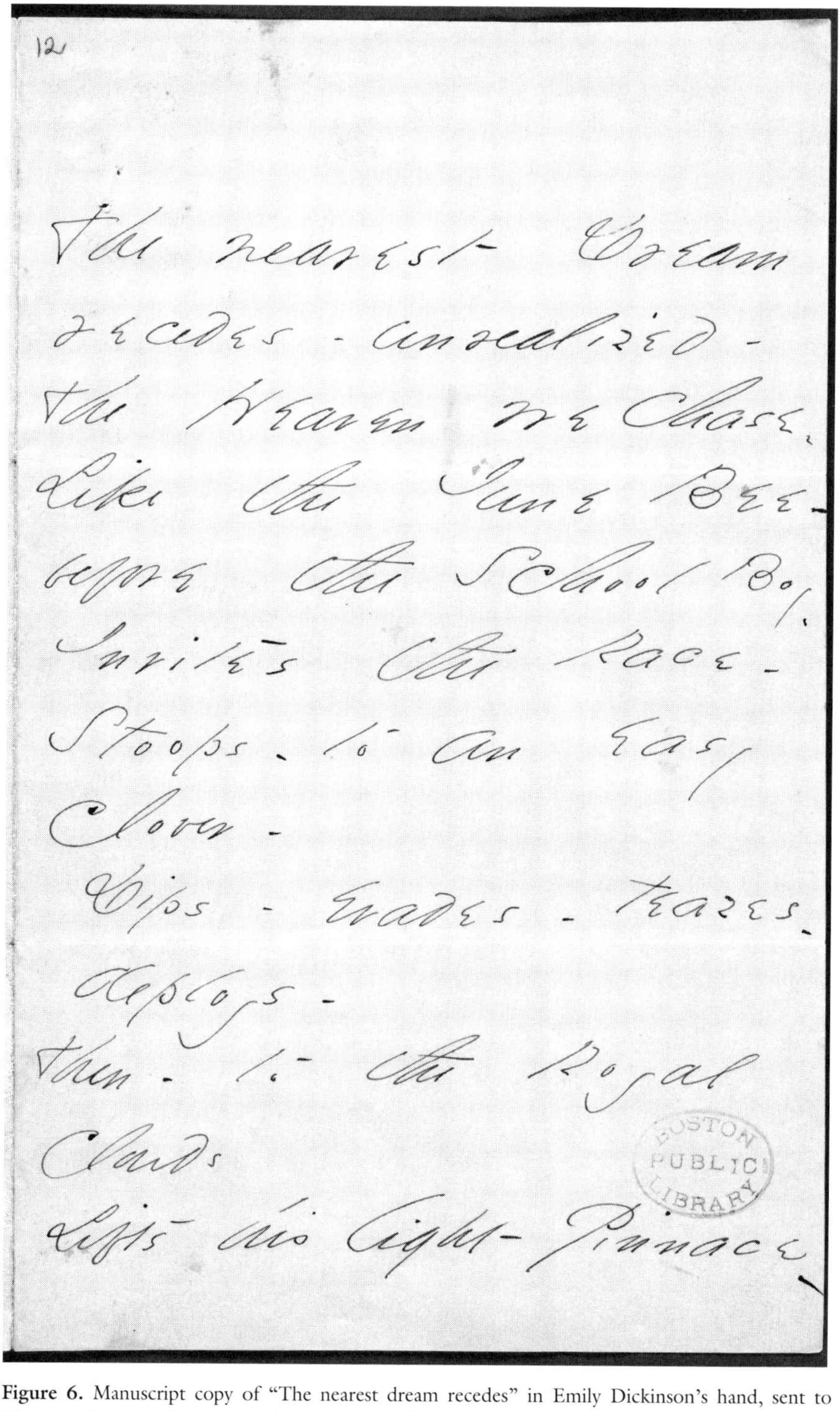
12

The nearest Dream
recedes - unrealized -
The Heaven we Chase,
Like the June Bee -
before the School Boy,
Invites the Race -
Stoops - to an easy
Clover -
Dips - Evades - Teases -
deploys -
Then - to the Royal
Clouds
Lifts his light Pinnace -

Figure 6. Manuscript copy of "The nearest dream recedes" in Emily Dickinson's hand, sent to Thomas Wentworth Higginson. Courtesy of the Trustees of the Boston Public Library/Rare Books.

Heedless of the Boy –
Staring – bewildered –
at the mocking sky, –

Homesick for steadfast
Honey, –
Ah, the Bee
flies not –
that – brews that
rare Variety – !

3

"Firmament" or "Fin"

COPYRIGHT, AUTHORITY, AND OWNERSHIP

Dickinson's famous statement that "I smile when you suggest that I delay 'to publish'—that being foreign to my thought, as Firmament to Fin—" embodies her culture's discourse on creativity and uniqueness (letter to Higginson of 7 June 1862, *Letters* L265). The statement is typically taken at what seems its face value: just as the air-breathing world is fundamentally unattainable to a fish, so Dickinson could not imagine that she might ever want to publish her poetry. Publication, she was telling Higginson, was foreign to her *thought*—incomprehensible or seeming to belong to another realm of being. There is also a suggestion of humility: the fish cannot even dream of something as glorious as the firmament, with its connotations of deity and infinity. But as always with Dickinson, unpacking the analogy reveals some tensions. The opposition between "firmament" and "fin" suggests a realm reachable only in moments of inspiration contrasted with an earthy realm that is soiled by commerce. This figure invites a second turn, however, for the thoughtful reader who reflects on the common trope that published authors constitute a "firmament" and notes that these authors are the source of economic capital for publishers, the brighter stars being more valuable as commodities. Strengthening the turn is Dickinson's strong interest in earthy and earthly depths and her uncertainty (if not skepticism) about things heavenly. By this reading, the humility implied in her association of herself with mere fish becomes pride, and her "smile" is one of superiority: she was playing a verbal game that Higginson would not grasp.

The Firmament/Fin analogy also contains another private joke and the possibility for one complex pun. Dickinson had already been publishing in her own fashion—circulating poems with letters—and by receiving her manuscripts Higginson was unknowingly furthering that end. The sentence's syntactic ambiguity supports such a reading: the second "that" could refer to the phrase "delay 'to publish'" rather than, as is ordinarily understood, simply to the phrase "to publish." She knew well enough what she was doing and why; avoiding commercial publication protected her creativity itself, preserved her independence of thought, and protected the tangible products of her intellectual labor. Her use of the word "fin" may also have been intended to evoke the slang term "finnip," which was used around this time in Great Britain to mean a five-pound note, or its American variant, "finnif," which designated five dollars and which became by the twentieth century our slang word "fin" for a five-dollar bill (*OED*). This pun would twist the meaning yet again, emphasizing the distance between commerce and art.

As a regular reader of the *Atlantic,* Dickinson may have suspected that Higginson would not catch her multiple meanings, but perhaps she intended this letter as a test. Her opposition of firmament to fin could evoke for a superficial reader the romantic tenet that creativity reflected divine inspiration, while by associating herself with the earthly rather than the divine realm, she was overtly indicating that she lacked the heavenly spark of true greatness. However, by creating such a quirky sentence (in terms of both figure and syntax), she offered him the opportunity to demonstrate that he was more of a thought diver than his editorial writings might suggest. Whether in her eyes he passed this test we can't know, but a telling fact is the preface he wrote decades later to accompany the first volume of her poetry, in which he invoked the traditional romantic relationship between originality and unique personality.

Dickinson herself, if she accepted that view, did so only in a qualified way. She was establishing a literary relationship with one of America's most influential literary figures, had drawn in her first letter to him on the romantic metaphor of the work as a living organism, and was here emphasizing her commitment to originality—one of the chief sources of symbolic capital—rather than to the economically attractive accessibility with which Higginson was accustomed to dealing. But her language implies that she understood how the romantic construction of authorial originality limited the artist's claim to both economic and cultural capital. The language also reflects, perhaps intentionally, the debate over moral versus property rights that was central to copyright law at this time: on the one hand, the author's absolute moral right of ownership of her/his productions, and on the other hand the limited right of ownership of the production viewed as a piece of property, especially if anyone else had a hand in its production or distribution.

COPYRIGHT LAW IN NINETEENTH-CENTURY AMERICA

Ownership—of one's name, reputation, visual image, and actual written "hand"—was important to both Dickinson and Melville. Yet in the literary realm, ownership has always been a vexed issue, with ownership depending on the circumstances of the individual case, on local conventions, and on common law. Beginning in the seventeenth century, there developed powerful but conflicting concepts and systems regarding literary property: proprietary authorship, a state's right to the intellectual labor of its citizens and the middle-class appropriation of that type of labor, the value (economic and cultural) of originality, and the mass production and distribution of print as a means to fortune. How Dickinson and Melville constructed both the work of writing and the work of authorship was at least indirectly influenced by copyright law, which most visibly instantiated the polity's stake in intellectual property and established the cash value of the work of writing. That work involves putting words to paper but also research (broadly defined) and simply being still and thinking. The work can be physically demanding, causing or exacerbating eyestrain (hence headaches), back pain, and other problems, as it did for both Melville and Dickinson. The work of authorship requires engaging in publicity, negotiating the best deal, shopping one's goods, reading and marking proof, and other activities that may strike a writer as unpleasantly sordid. Writing can be done in the solitude of the study, although we know from composition scholars that it almost never is and perhaps cannot be conducted without at least a tacit recognition of the cultural context. The work of authorship—which need not be but usually is conducted by the writer—requires engagement with other individuals and institutions. The work of writing is my focus in chapter 4; I mention it here to indicate the limits of the present chapter, which emphasizes the history and function of copyright law in mid-nineteenth-century America in order to enrich our understanding of how Melville and Dickinson constructed their work (both writing and authorship), why both desired to publish but not necessarily by printing, and how both reached toward market types other than the capitalist in order to earn cultural and symbolic capital.

The concept of proprietary authorship originated with John Locke's theory of "possessive individualism" (Rose, "Author as Proprietor" 56–57).

According to this theory, property is a natural right, created by an individual's labor out of "the raw materials of nature" (Rose, *Authors and Owners* 5). Locke described the concept this way in his *Two Treatises of Government,* published in 1690:

> Though the Earth, and all inferior Creatures be common to all Men, yet every Man has a *Property* in his own *Person.* This no Body has any Right to but himself. The *Labour* of his Body, and the *Work* of his Hands, we may say, are properly his. Whatsoever then he removes out of the State that Nature hath provided, and left it in, he hath mixed his *Labour* with, and joined to it something that is his own, and thereby makes it his *Property.* (Quoted by Rose, *Authors and Owners* 5)

Producing a literary work seemed to some legal scholars analogous to getting a crop out of a field, and it also seemed that ownership of one's self necessarily entailed ownership of whatever one produced—ideas no less than crops. Others, however, deemed the products of intellect and imagination significantly different in kind from tangible goods. A poem, after all, did not have to take a tangible material form in order to exist and did not involve removing something "out of the State that Nature hath provided, and left it in." Creativity was understood as an organic expression of divine inspiration rather than as a linking of already existing components, as it had been explained in the eighteenth century with reference to association psychology (Rose, "Author as Proprietor" 61–62); in other words, the "*Work* of the writer's Hands" need not be applied to something tangible taken from its natural state. This discourse led in the nineteenth century to "the romantic elaboration of such notions as originality, organic form, and the work of art as the expression of the unique personality of the artist" ("Author as Proprietor" 75–76). According to Rose, this was when there developed the concept of the literary "work" as separate from both the physical object—the book—and the ideas contained within the book. The work came to be understood as "something else entirely, something consisting of style and sentiment combined" (65).

Copyright law in America emphasized the state's interest in wide distribution of intellectual products. The fundamental legal principle is stated in Article I, Section 8, Clauses 1 and 8 of the U.S. Constitution: "The Congress shall have the Power . . . To promote the Progress of Science and useful Arts, by securing for limited Times to Authors and Inventors the exclusive Right to their respective Writings and Discoveries." As with most of the Constitution, the admirable brevity of the original language has left interpretation and application to subsequent generations. One of the most important copyright cases was *Wheaton v. Peters,* heard by the United States Supreme Court in 1834. The majority ruled as follows: "(1) that an author's common-law property in his text ceased upon publication; (2) that strict compliance with all statutory requirements was necessary for establishing title in a work; and (3) that there could be no common law of the US," meaning that "the common law did not extend beyond state boundaries" (McGill, "Matter" 41). The key point of this ruling was that an author preserved the common-law right by keeping the work in manuscript form even if it was presented to audiences in the form of performances, but once the work was printed and distributed, the author had to share proprietorship with all components of the mechanism of production as well as with the buying public (42–43).

The process by which copyright was secured and announced served to emphasize the right of the state to act on behalf of the public's interest in having access to a work. According to the Copyright Act of 1790 and the addition of 1802, the person desiring copyright was to deposit a copy of the title of the book with the local district court, to have a copy of the record of this deposit printed in at least one newspaper in the United States, to deliver a copy of the book to the office of the Secretary of State, and to place on the title page of the book the copyright information (McGill, "Matter" 44). The copyright notice printed in the book was an outward sign "that *the correspondence between an author and his copyrighted text was fully mediated by the state*" (45; emphasis added). The *Stowe v. Thomas* case of 1853 dramatically illustrates this mediation. The court ruled that Stowe did not have copyright protection against a German translation of *Uncle Tom's Cabin* published in America. According to the court,

> [b]efore publication [the author] has the exclusive possession of his invention. His dominion is perfect. But when he has published his book and given his thoughts, sentiments, knowledge or discoveries to the world, he can have no longer an exclusive possession of them. Such an appropriation becomes impossible, and is inconsistent with the object of publication. The author's conceptions have become the common property of his readers, who cannot be deprived of the use of them, or their right to communicate them to others clothed in their own language, by lecture or by treatise. (Quoted by McGill 50)

These and other copyright cases demonstrate that "the development of a market for literature in America depended on the suspension of private property rights in texts" (51). *Stowe v. Thomas* in particular also represents the literary work as "something consisting of style and sentiment combined." The court recognized the work as consisting of "thoughts, sentiments, knowledge or discoveries" and "conceptions"; when the readers "clothe" these thoughts "in their own language," they change the style, hence style must also be a component of the work. Because style is untranslatable and because a work's uniqueness inheres in its style and concepts together, so the justices reasoned, a translation is always a new work in which the author of the original has no right of property. To try to limit "the world's" use of the author's conceptions would be fruitless; once a conception has entered the mind of a reader and has been "clothed" in the reader's language, it necessarily belongs to the reader.

In the commodity-oriented market of nineteenth-century America, the law gave relatively less weight to the concept of copyright as "an inalienable right vested in the very person of the author of an original work" and instead privileged wider dissemination of, hence greater public access to, a literary work (Saunders, "Approaches" 509–10). However, there was also a tradition in American law to emphasize the relationship between creativity and economic reward rather than strictly to protect publishers' property rights embodied in printed works (Bettig 144). This tradition is seen in the copyright laws passed in twelve of the original thirteen states, for instance that of Connecticut from 1783: "[E]very author should be secured in receiving the profits that may arise from the sale of his works, and such security may encourage men of learning and genius to publish their writings; which may do honor to their country, and service to mankind" (quoted by Bettig 146). Similarly, the Massachusetts law proclaimed that "there is 'no property more peculiarly a man's own than that which is produced by the labour of his mind'" (147). In short, copyright law in America in the middle of the nineteenth century was still developing, with concepts such as intellectual property, publishers' rights, the asymmetry between British and American law, and public and private interest contending.

COPYRIGHT AND CAPITAL

A perfect copyright law, if such can be imagined, would need to regulate not only mercantile exchange but the "aesthetic play" of art, in which the activity of involving oneself with art, being a consumer of art, so to speak, is "a labor (or game) of accumulating symbolic capital that refuses the crude calculations of market rationality. . . . [I]ts very resistance to conversion into such terms must be seen as incorporated into the experience itself, as the sign of its innate complexity" (Guillory, "Bourdieu's Refusal" 385). By way of analogy, Guillory contrasts "the scene of museum going with that of the video game": the latter is "explicitly directed toward the accumulation of profit in the mimetic form of a score," whereas the goal of the former "cannot be reduced to such a quantifiable measure of its profitability," and its resistance to such reduction is "the sign of its innate complexity" (385). To a limited extent, American copyright law did take into account such intangibles as prestige and reputation. The Connecticut and Massachusetts laws quoted earlier, for instance, imply a notion of intellectual property. The former refers to an author's writings "which may do honor to their country, and service to mankind," and this doing of honor and service will redound to the credit of the author in terms of reputation. The Massachusetts law refers to "property," implying commodity, but because this type of property is "produced by the labour of [the author's] mind" it need not be limited to the markets where commercially published works circulate.

Copyright law may even facilitate the transformation of types of capital. Symbolic capital is earned within a very limited field of production and on the basis of autonomous criteria; economic capital is earned within the broadest possible field on the basis of market share. In both fields, the right to copy is legally protected. For example, a poem may be esteemed by the producers of symbolic capital according to autonomous criteria; these criteria themselves are valued because the products of creation are understood to be esteemed under moral law, which otherwise would have no value within a strictly capitalist system. When enough such esteem (symbolic capital) has accrued, the work/author becomes recognized as part of the society's culture, and when this happens—for instance, when the poem enters anthologies or course syllabi—economic capital is generated for the owner of the copyright. The fact that a work can be evaluated on the basis of criteria other than market share, criteria that may be agreed on by only a small number of producers of cultural capital, itself conveys the value of exclusivity.

As far as we know, Dickinson never negotiated for publication; she had no direct experience with the differences between American and British copyright law; by entirely avoiding print publishing (aside from the few poems she allowed and may have allowed to be printed), she retained ownership of her ideas as well as the physical documents that expressed them; her livelihood never relied on marketing her intellectual labor. On the other hand, the copyright issue was broadly interesting to writers and authors, and because Dickinson's father and brother were attorneys, she may even have heard it discussed from their perspective. It is common knowledge that she was opposed to participation in the capitalist market, but to stop there is to miss the sophistication of her opposition and the significance of the choices she made. In chapter 2 I noted that discussions of Dickinson's attitude toward publication always comment on her most explicit statement in this regard, in the poem "Publication—is the Auction / of the Mind of Man" (Fr788). This "auction" was so distasteful to Dickinson (and feels so distasteful to today's readers) because it seems to be violating the moral right of an individual to own herself—"every Man has a *Property* in his own *Person*. This no Body has any Right to but himself" in the words of Locke that I quoted earlier. Dickinson's diction in this poem emphasizes that it is not just a commodity that is being sold, but the identity of the work's creator as embodied in that person's mind.

Sensitivity to copyright may also inform Dickinson's letter to Higginson of 25 April 1862, about the "two Editors" who asked to be allowed to use her "mind" (*Letters* 404–5). Regarding this letter, I made the point in chapter 2 that her reaction, at least as she describes it to Higginson, reflects her abhorrence at the practice of identifying an author's works with the author herself; she did not want to be put to use in some public fashion. The language of this letter gives an impression that what was being discussed that day between her and the editors was a physical product or commodity: the phrase "asked me for my Mind" is sufficiently different from both "asked me for my opinion" and "asked me for a poem" that it evokes the "use" value of her mind, a connotation further strengthened by the capitalization of "Mind." To produce whatever commodity was being discussed required the writer's labor; to disseminate the commodity required her subservience to a system that was grounded in a capitalist market and that at least in this case seems to have expected the author to donate her labor, invoking the notion of the publishing system's obligation to serve "the world" but conveniently glossing over the fact that those editors could benefit financially—even more so if the artist provided the commodity *gratis*. She may have used the word "penurious" ("they said I was penurious") further to evoke that tension between the author's ownership, the public's need for new ideas and inventions that could serve national progress, and the desire of intermediaries to profit from bringing the author to the public.

This letter shows Dickinson on the side of private right; she expressed no interest in serving "the world" with the products of her mind, if that service was mediated through "editors," nor did the social obligation implicit in the word "penurious" carry any weight with her. Part of her negative reaction to those "editors" may also have resulted from her recognition that if indeed they not only transmitted but transformed what

she had written, they would have a claim on it. In other words, the minia-
ture narrative contained within this letter reflects the entire publishing system and the copyright laws that supported it. Other letters and poems as
well suggest that she understood the fundamental tension of the copyright
debate in America and that her strategy of publishing by manuscript was
intended to preserve her ownership while generating symbolic capital.

Dickinson's commitment to private right was supported by the circulation of some of her poems (White 10). For instance, it is possible that
her cousin Fanny Norcross presented Dickinson's poems to the Concord
"Saturday Club" as early as 1878, and Higginson is known to have read
Dickinson's poems to crowded meetings of the New England Women's
Club; significantly, the notes of one such meeting refer to these as "'portfolio poems'—such as could only be privately enjoyed in this way" (White
11, 14–15). This kind of circulation resulted in an "extended audience for
Dickinson's manuscripts," both poems and letters; although the manuscripts might ultimately reach readers who were unknown to Dickinson,
the distribution would be governed by "clear social codes," and attention
would be paid to preserving "the sense of a private, individual context"
(White 12, 14).

These various settings in which Dickinson's physical manuscripts circulated and in which her works were actually performed constitute an
excellent example of an antimimetic market. The market is governed by
conventions and expectations that comprise autonomous criteria, especially the values of "intimacy, uniqueness, domesticity, and antiquarian-
ism" characteristic of manuscript transmission (White 14). The fact that
some of Dickinson's correspondents were also involved in publishing, such
as Bowles, Higginson, and later Helen Hunt Jackson, signals the fluidity
and permeability of these markets in America at this time, as does the common practice of sharing manuscripts with people who might be unknown
to the author.

No existing evidence allows us to ascertain Dickinson's attitude toward
such extended distribution. Surely she knew that her sister-in-law "publicized" some poems in her "salons," for instance. There is no record of
her having opposed such distribution, and it is even reasonable to infer
that she expected and was pleased to know that her "mind" was being
appreciated by the agents of symbolic capital in Amherst. Did she ever fear
that this procedure would lead to the theft of her work? It would seem
unlikely. She could rely on the social structures governing the exchange
of portfolio poetry; the social classes (middle and upper) who practiced
this exchange would respect a writer's implicit desire to remain unpublished. Habegger speculates that her first known publication, a prose Val-

entine in the February 1850 issue of the *Indicator*, Amherst College's literary magazine, "earned a paternal reprimand" and taught her that "all future writing would have to be conducted more discreetly" (236–37). He also attributes to her "the conservative view that feminine self-respect was not compatible with public life" and writes that "she reportedly asked Helen Hunt Jackson how she could bear to 'print a piece of your soul,'" a question that certainly accords with her notion that one's words literally embody one's self (354). Habegger reads Dickinson as "tortured" by "the profound contradictions in [her] history and character" and suggests that as a writer she would experience "a deeper isolation, a more ferocious and even masochistic self-abasement, a terror of coming apart" (392). Perhaps. Certainly she experienced conflicts. Habegger notes two instances when she reacted in a strong and negative way to the revelation of her authorship of a particular poem; interestingly, however, both instances involve her sister-in-law, so perhaps other issues than publication and identity were involved (508, 559).

In the absence of evidence to the contrary, and given the strong circumstantial evidence in favor, it seems reasonable to regard Dickinson as intending to avoid entanglement in the copyright net by limiting her works to manuscript distribution. Copyright law was clear that an author's right to her own manuscript was absolute as long as the manuscript had never been printed. Reading poems aloud in a salon or at the meeting of a literary club did not endanger that right. Once a work entered the public arena by being published, however, the author's rights were severely curtailed, as dramatized by the case of *Stowe v. Thomas*. It has frequently been asserted that Dickinson's class and economic status allowed her not to publish; a more accurate statement would be that her status allowed her to distribute her work while retaining full control.

Melville's case is instructively different—because his work was owned by several different producers of economic capital, he easily could have felt that his mind was being auctioned, a hypothesis supported by his vigorous attacks on the economic system in letters and in *Pierre*. His personal and secondhand experience with the operation of copyright and more generally with the power of publishers could certainly have led him to such a conclusion. An apparently minor detail in the publication of *Typee* is telling in this regard. In the weeks immediately preceding the American publication of *Typee*, when there was some confusion about whether that book would come out in Wiley and Putnam's Library of Choice Reading (the publisher had not informed Melville of the change to the Library of American Books, which was edited by Evert Duyckinck), Melville was "[p]anicked at the possible loss of American copyright for *Typee*, and very likely mindful of the horror story of Dana's loss of copyright to *Two Years before the Mast*" (Parker, *Herman Melville* 1:404–5). Melville was panicked, of course, because American copyright law required first publication in America, but he feared that Murray's London edition would come out first. According to Parker, "everyone in Melville's Boston circle knew the story of how, in 1839 and 1840, the Harpers had haggled with the genteel elder Richard Henry Dana and William Cullen Bryant over the manuscript of young Dana's *Two Years before the Mast* until they got the book outright for $250 and made a fortune from it, fair and square" (Parker, *Herman Melville* 2:76). Parker writes that Lemuel Shaw, Melville's future father-in-law, while advising the young man to take up writing as a way of making a name for himself that could be used to further other job prospects, "probably knew" that the Harper brothers "had all but stolen the copyright" from Dana (1:309). *Two Years before the Mast* had come out in the Harpers' Family Library Series in 1840. It sold quite well, Dana estimating later in life that the publisher had earned $50,000 on the title (Metzdorf 321). The elder Dana wrote to William Cullen Bryant, who had provided advice during the early stages of negotiation, "I can hardly go out on the street without being attacked for disposing of the entire copy-right at all—& especially for such a mere song. The booksellers say it must be a handsome affair to the Harpers, & one house told an acquaintance of mine, that he would have given $1000 for it, & made a good profit on the purchase:—it is looked upon as a stock book" (quoted by Metzdorf 320–21). From the beginning Dana apparently planned to acquire the copyright after it lapsed in 1868, which he did, publishing a revised "author's edition" (322).

Dana's profit between 1840 and 1868, aside from some presentation copies and the small payments from the Harpers and Moxon (the first London publisher), was strictly prestige. However, that symbolic capital was significant, partly because what had happened to him with respect to the copyright was widely known; his case fitted the stereotype of the artist being taken advantage of by greedy, troglodytic merchants, allowing him to be thought of as uninterested in economic capital.[1] There is no record that Melville commented on what had happened to Dana, but the two met on 9 July 1847 and remained friends for decades (Parker, *Herman Melville* 1:541–42). Parker states that Melville actually "decided to take up authorship—perhaps for the nonce only, mindful of the author of *Two Years before the Mast*" (*Herman Melville* 1:355). Melville did read "some or all" of that book soon after it was published, and it may have contributed to his decision to return to sea as a whaler (*Herman Melville* 1:181); he later wrote to Dana that the reading experience created in him "strange, congenial feelings" and "a sort of Siamese link of affectionate sympathy" (letter of 1 May 1850, *Correspondence* 160). This letter suggests, however, contrary to Parker's suggestion about "authorship," that Melville took Dana as a model of the role of writer at least as much as that of author, well before the two met, and that this writerly connection had reinforced the younger man's romantic view of writing.

The correspondence relating to publication of Melville's fourth novel, *Redburn,* reflects his continuing commitment to that view and his failure to grasp the inverse relationship between artistic prestige and economic success. The Harper brothers agreed on 2 July 1849 to publish that book. Meanwhile, on 20 June, the London publisher Richard Bentley wrote and offered Melville 100 pounds—less than what the author sought—his stated reasons being that he had lost money on *Mardi* and that on 5 June 1849, in the British court case *Boosey v. Purday,* it was ruled that foreigners would no longer be able to gain copyright in England (Horth 595—headnote to letter from Bentley of 20 June). Bentley wrote to Melville that "[t]his driveling absurdity [*Boosey v. Purday*] can scarcely be suffered to remain . . . but in the mean time this decision will expose publishers like myself, who am so largely engaged in this department of publishing to the risk of attack from any unprincipled persons who may choose to turn Pirate" (*Correspondence* 596). Bentley went on to refer to the decision as "stupid" and to offer the following suggestion: "Why do not you a people, with the grand literature the United States now has, why not at once with dignity come into the International copyright Act. Surely your literary men have power to accomplish this, and now is the time to do it & shame, our miserable, paltry, shabby lawgivers, & settle the matter beyond question" (*Correspondence* 596–97).

Melville's reply suggests that he missed Bentley's point:

> Notwithstanding that recent decision of your courts of law [*Boosey v. Purday*], I can hardly imagine that it will occasion any serious infringement of any rights you have in any American book. And ere long, doubtless, we shall have something of an international law—so much desired by all American writers—which shall settle this matter upon the basis of justice. The only marvel is, that it does not now exist. (Letter of 20 July 1849; *Correspondence* 134)

Horth points out that Melville and other notable writers of the time, including Cooper, Bryant, and Irving, "signed a petition calling for an international copyright agreement that was belatedly submitted to the Senate in 1852" (133), but nothing came of this petition. This is not surprising; the politics surrounding the Anglo-American copyright issue seem to have had more to do with historical accident and individual personalities than with the principles (Barnes). Did Melville actually believe that an "international law" was on the near horizon? Did he believe that Bentley's "rights" would not be put at risk by *Boosey v. Purday,* and did he understand that Bentley's comments referred less to such rights and more to Bentley's economic situation? As shown by his refusal two years later to have his "mug" advertised, the answers to these questions are perhaps "yes" and certainly "yes" and "no." Although Melville signed the petition, he does not seem to have taken much interest in the international copyright issue. If we take him at his word, he didn't grasp the economic point Bentley was making, that a publisher who "turned Pirate" cared nothing about another publisher's "rights."

Melville, however, was not being willfully obtuse with his adherence to the romantic model, because this model continued to shape commentary on the copyright issue, especially commentary coming from the institutions that granted symbolic capital. For example, a long, favorable *Blackwood's* review of *Redburn* noted that praising an American book was an act of "graceful courtesy," might "encourage Americans to the cultivation of literature" (because the opinions reflected in *Blackwood's* were valued in the United States), and might encourage America to pass an international copyright law. On the third point, the reviewer wrote, "For surely it is little creditable to a great country to see her men of genius and talent, her Irvings and Prescotts, and we will also say her Coopers and Melvilles, publishing their works in a foreign capital, as the sole means of obtaining that fair remuneration which, although it should never be the sole object, is yet the legitimate and honourable reward of the labourer in literature's paths" (quoted in Parker, *Herman Melville* 1:668–69). Like Bentley with his contrast between American "literary men" and the "shabby lawgivers" of Great Britain, the *Blackwood's* reviewer notes that a person of "genius and talent" should never be solely interested in "fair remuneration." Describing such remuneration as "the legitimate and honourable *reward*" for literary labor makes economic capital almost seem an afterthought, consistent with the romantic model.

Nothing Melville wrote or is reported to have said suggests that he was functionally aware of how transatlantic piracy had aided the growth of American publishers (most notably his primary publisher, the house of Harper) or of how attractive it could be to London publishers to be able to avoid paying an author for his or her work. Developing such an awareness, which was basic to the authorial habitus in America at this time, required becoming involved with the gritty details of publication and spending a great deal of time with publishers. (His early ventures into authorship, prior to going to sea, were strictly belletristic—letters to the editor, polemics having to do with societies to which he belonged, and so forth—and probably had little influence on his later conception of both authorship and the writer's work.) Melville did hobnob with the Duyck-incks and other literary figures and was involved in the publication details of *Typee* and *Omoo*. But his patience for such involvement was limited, and he may in a sense have succeeded too quickly with those first books, not spending enough time in a kind of apprenticeship situation.

It may be the case, as John Evelev argues, that Melville's participation in the Young America literary movement in New York City in the later 1840s, with its salon culture, enabled him to write into *Mardi*, especially, a vision of the author as an autonomous professional, and into *Moby-Dick* "an epic about American professional-class cultural politics, a veritable lexicon of the distinctions to be made between other available models of cultural politics and the skills needed to construct one's self as a cultural professional" (67–72, 144). Certainly his membership in the Duyckinck circle allowed him to think of himself as an artist, not as a hired hand. It would seem likely, however, that if Evelev's thesis were correct, Melville would have understood and been able to accept that his early success in the economic marketplace—stereotyped as a popular writer whose reach was limited to travel and autobiography—disqualified him for success in the symbolic marketplace. His famous lament to Hawthorne, "dollars damn me" (*Correspondence* 191, letter of 1 [?] June 1851), encapsulates this dilemma: not only could he not make money writing what he wanted, but having once made money he was tarred by the capitalistic brush. On the other hand, as Evelev emphasizes, the American professional class was still emergent at this time, so Melville's awareness of himself as a "cultural professional" may also have been only germinal.

OWNERSHIP, LABOR, AND PRIVATE PUBLICATION

Melville's enthusiasm for manuscript publishing (the "sea book," the endless letter to Hawthorne) reflects a desire to gain prestige within a market which is not subject to governmental regulation in the form of copyright, is organized around autonomous criteria, and involves primar-ily original creation rather than the drudgery of preparing manuscripts to meet the needs of print publication. All three of these characteristics of the antimimetic market foster freedom of the producer. Given Melville's negative portrayal of assembly-line production in his story "The Tarta-rus of Maids," in which the female laborers are essentially feeding with their lives the paper-producing factory, his use of the language of book production and publication in his letters—essentially writerly rather than authorial creations—suggests that he understood this private market to be structured around the same methods used to produce commodities for the capitalist market. This market was certainly not organized to foster "art for art's sake," but the possibility of preparing a manuscript simply by recording the flow of one's thoughts or by attending only to the expectations of a single reader intrigued Melville because his manuscript would be evaluated only by that one reader even though produced, like mass-market commodities, with paid labor. It would be art for the sake of intimate connection.

The letters to Bentley, Dana, and Hawthorne reflect Melville's conflicted attitude regarding literary economics. On the one hand, he desired to be evaluated on the basis of autonomous criteria (the opinions of single readers) rather than of heteronomous criteria (the fickle tastes of one or more book-buying publics). On the other hand, he imagined this system functioning like a capitalistic market. Even while speculating that he might prepare manuscripts that would never be published as books, he relied on images related to book production (the paper factory, the use of a copyist's labor to prepare a readable manuscript).

These contradictions reflect the transitional state in Melville's time of the concepts of authorship, copyright, the ownership of intellectual property, and labor itself as a basis of value. The stream of an individual's thoughts would seem to have no cultural value and would be wholly owned by that individual, yet if this stream were produced by the same system that produced books, would not the public have some claim to it as well? Would not the same be true of a "sea book" existing only in manuscript that nevertheless had been produced with someone else's labor for the purpose of earning symbolic capital? Yet the public would never pay what the work was worth, and if the audience was limited to a single reader, Melville would realize little symbolic capital. Perhaps he was aware of these contradictions and of what they reflected about his own habitus. Such awareness would help account for the physical violence he directed at his manuscripts as Renker describes it: "The pasteboard mask that can't be struck through, the text that can't be stabbed through, and the copies that he must himself punctuate are dramas of composition in which paper acts as a material site of blockage, frustrating the author's desire to penetrate and so to transcend material conditions" (67). His "'striking through' is a materially loaded gesture for Melville, in terms of his violent frustration with the pages over which he labored and with the laboring women in his household" (68).

Melville's willingness to rely on someone else's labor may also have derived from his sense of class. When finishing the book that became *Moby-Dick*, he wrote to Evert Duyckinck on 13 December 1850:

> Can you send me about fifty fast-writing youths, with an easy style & not averse to polishing their labors? If you can, I wish you would, because since I have been here I have planned about that number of future works & cant [*sic*] find enough time to think about them separately. (*Correspondence* 174)

He would use these youths for what is arguably the most laborious component of the work of writing—actually putting words on paper and then "polishing" those words. If he didn't imagine paying the youths, he would be exploiting them as he did the women of his household. If payment was part of his mental image, then he saw himself as similar to the inventor who patents a new product or process and then sets up a manufacturing facility that relies on the labor of others. In keeping with the American way, Melville would enhance his class status (regaining the position his family had before his father went bankrupt) by becoming a manufacturer. Delbanco offers this thought on Melville's landing in Boston from his sailing travels in October 1844:

> But even if he only glanced up from Boston Harbor toward Beacon Hill, where the Shaws' four-story brick house with its pillared brownstone entrance stood on Mount Vernon Street, he must have felt a twinge of envy, or at least resigned awareness of his own family's fall. As a child he had walked on that street with his eminent grandfather, whom passersby greeted with bows and salutes; now, for lack of alternatives, he was headed west to a rented house in Lansingburgh ruled by his mother. (63)

New York City may indeed have had a democratizing influence on Melville, as Delbanco suggests (119), but it probably never overcame his youthful sense of his own family's fall or made him more tolerant of mass audiences.

In the best of worlds, Melville would have elaborated on what he meant by "an easy style & not averse to polishing their labors." Did he imagine that he would dictate to these youths, or would he sketch out his ideas for them and have them fill in the details, which he would then critique in order for the appropriate level of polish to be maintained? Either possibility would have the effect of literally placing another "hand" (another's script) between him and his readers, and the second in particular would complicate the issue of ownership, because the same legal principle that held in *Stowe v. Thomas* might also be applied to individuals who gave shape to someone else's ideas—the youths might end up with at least partial ownership of whatever they produced, unless this possibility were contractually blocked. Even Duyckinck might have a share, as the provider of the laborers. This letter strongly suggests that Melville is imagining these works being produced for both an antimimetic market and a capitalistic market. The latter requires polish; this has always been one way a writer establishes credibility with the producers of economic capital—a manuscript must be clean and readable in order easily to be converted into print. (In fact, Higginson emphasized this requirement in his "Letter to a Young Contributor.") On the other hand, polish would not be expected if the work was circulating among the same producers of symbolic capital who read and distributed portfolio poetry. For them the relevant criteria would be spontaneity and inspiration, which would be well captured by the fifty fast-writing youths: readers could experience Melville's creative flashes with true immediacy, almost as if they were listening to him talk, because the flow of his ideas would not be slowed by writing (or muddied by his poor handwriting).

Melville's decision, near the end of his life, to print *John Marr* and *Timoleon* but to do so privately can be interpreted as a resolution of these contradictions of class, prestige, and ownership. Howard P. Vincent regards *Timoleon* as "the distillation of the matured thought and poetic art of Melville, who by 1891 had fairly overcome the technical tangles which had troubled him in the writing of much of his previous poetry" (473). Vincent further suggests that while some of the poems in the volume date from the decade when he was working on *Clarel* (roughly 1866–1876), others were written after Melville retired in 1885 from his customs inspector position (473). The fact that the manuscript's corrections are in the hand of Melville's wife, "undoubtedly made at Melville's dictation" (Vincent 500), strongly suggests that as always he was reaching for an audience beyond family members; he had always done this by publishing. Now, at last, by turning to private, limited-run publishing, he achieved the ideal that he had first noted in his letters to Dana and Hawthorne. These privately printed volumes would engage individual readers on an intimate level while also carrying the authority of print.

DICKINSON'S EXPRESSED willingness to be penurious rather than useful, her perhaps irreverent characterization of publication as akin to being placed in the celestial firmament, and her implied preference for swimming among deep and murky thoughts rather than standing in the broad daylight of public view help explain why she was opposed to print publication but not why she adopted the practice of publication by manuscript. Were she simply a reflector of her era's values and practices, she probably would have kept her poetry to herself or shared it only with close friends. Rather, like Melville, she apparently felt called to contribute to her culture's discourse on some of the same topics that engaged him, and she understood that to do so she needed readers whose opinion mattered in the larger cultural enterprise. Her extensive communication with Higginson thus functioned as a type of negotiation conducted with full awareness that tastemakers like him influenced reputation and status.

To place Dickinson in this context complements recent work on the women writers who desired both to make money and to make a social or political difference. Why would women attempt to write marketable verse and prose (both fiction and nonfiction) rather than striving for the more elite status of Poet as described by Emerson? One key reason was the presumption that neither by nature nor by nurture were they well suited for deeper thinking, and the antimimetic market—where the status of Poet would be conferred—was controlled by the same men who ran the rest of the culture industry. Additionally, while the representative antebellum female writer was affluent, some needed to earn a living. Although authors themselves were not supposed to esteem "commercial aims," and although the Gentleman Publisher was supposed to have other aims as well, more money could be made by commercial publishing, and more by publishing prose than verse. Finally, there was always the chance of earning symbolic capital within the mimetic market, as long as they conformed to elements of the dominant culture. Harriet Beecher Stowe was successful in this endeavor with *Uncle Tom's Cabin,* and Helen Hunt Jackson with *Ramona,* for example. The women studied by Coultrap-McQuin were all seriously professional about their literary careers; at least in the middle of the century "enjoyed a considerable degree of autonomy"; and, "like their male counterparts, wanted to say something worthwhile to their culture that would elevate their work above the commercial, material realm" (195–97). But because they participated in the business of print publication, they were judged by heteronomous criteria, and as with Melville, their economic success limited their ability to earn symbolic capital.

Helen Hunt Jackson is of particular interest in this context, because of her long friendship with Dickinson, her literary apprenticeship under Higginson, the fact that her publisher (Roberts Brothers) also published the first volumes of Dickinson's poetry after her death, and Jackson's careful attention to the market value of her writing. Coultrap-McQuin takes Jackson as an example of a writer who worked hard under Higginson's guidance "to perfect the most respected literary techniques of her time" (152). She paid close attention to her market value and told Fields that she wrote "for love" but printed "for money" (quoted by Coultrap-McQuin 155); she wanted her market value to be determined by literary quality and not by popularity (156). Her practice of anonymity and pseudonymity suited her adherence to the ideal of True Womanhood—it kept her from feeling as if she belonged to the public—and also may have increased her market value by piquing public curiosity (159–60). Jackson's career shows that a writer could be somewhat successful in the mimetic market while still achieving commercial success; for example, *Ramona*, her fictional dramatization of Native American life, was well received by both reviewers and the book-buying public. However, she was also at times regarded as a creation of Higginson, lacking sufficient originality and power significantly to challenge either the literary or the cultural status quo; neither in substance nor in style was *Ramona* the sort of book that would send shock waves through the literary or political establishments.

Dickinson's economic and class position allowed her to avoid the type of negotiation between art and success to which Jackson was forced. Had her goal been to write prose fiction, however, she might have experienced a very different curve; the same speculation applies to Melville, had he begun as a poet. At the end of chapter 32 of *Moby-Dick*, in which Ishmael attempts to put forth a system for classifying whales, this unfortunate exclaims, "Oh, Time, Strength, Cash, and Patience!" (145). All four of these qualities can be associated with the actual economics of writing book-length prose works; this is surely one of several points in the novel in which Melville ventriloquizes his own frustrations through his narrator. Poems can be written in stolen moments on scraps of paper, and most people will find it easier to keep a poem draft in memory, working on it that way even while engaged in some other task, than to keep a chapter or scene of a novel. I don't mean to make light of the work of writing poems, but it seems likely that writing novels is more physically demanding, requires more time, and certainly requires more money both for writing materials and to buy the needed time. Given these economic realities, Melville could scarcely have avoided the commercial marketplace and the accompanying necessity to hand over to the government, standing in for the polity, a piece of himself in the form of copyright agreements.

MCGILL DESCRIBES the "discourse of authorship" during much of the nineteenth century as developing "at odds with" mass production ("The

Matter of the Text" 25), but the tension was significant only within the mimetic market because of that market's ability to convert economic into cultural capital and vice versa. Strictly as a mercantile product, a book was like other items within the capitalist market: its value was wholly determined by the amount of available market share it could command. Similarly, any artist only interested in evaluation on the basis of autonomous criteria should in principle feel no tension with the demands of a public marketplace. As Bourdieu emphasizes, however, in practice artists who adopt this position will attempt to legitimate their work in part by deriding that marketplace (think of Dickinson's term "admiring Bog") and the other artists, those perceived as hacks, who allow it to dictate their work. The "cultural weight" of a book (or any other printed piece) was determined within the mimetic market and depended on whether it contributed to the impression of America's cultural maturity and independence from Great Britain or to other elements of American ideology.

The overall literary market, however, exhibited several tensions: between the desire of American writers to earn a living and the desire of American publishers to maximize profits by keeping expenses low (including royalty payments to native authors), between the belief that an individual owned the products of his or her intellectual labor and the legal principle of governmental regulation for the good of the polity, between the notion of the artist as superior and therefore justified in breaking new ground for the public to follow and the public's preference for what it already knows, between the work of writing and the work of authorship, and between the culture's overt valorizing of manual labor and its covert erasing of that labor in favor of intellectual labor. Melville and Dickinson understood that authorial work could be deemed useful by the polity and that American copyright law recognized and protected the polity's interest. On the other hand, they felt that originality had an intrinsic value independent of any use to which it might be put, that effectively to criticize their culture they had to remain independent of demands from a mass market, and that such independence required creative alternatives to the work of authorship as generally practiced.

4

"The brain is just the weight of God"

HAND, MIND, AND MANUSCRIPT

So far I have concentrated on the economic and aesthetic components of the literary culture within which Dickinson and Melville wrote. I have shown that they attempted or at least desired to operate outside of the capitalist and mimetic markets (especially opposing advertising), that they desired to publish in ways that preserved their total control over and ownership of their work, and that they accepted the romantic notion that individual authorial authority was grounded in imagination and inspiration. Another context is also important: how their era recognized the human mind as both material and immaterial but gave more weight to the latter. Dickinson's and Melville's representations of the mind and its relationship to the writing hand and the written text reflect their era's root metaphor of the mind as a physical entity. This metaphor informed their interest in (and Dickinson's commitment to) the hand-produced text and contributed to the impact of their eye problems and other ailments. It also bears on how each writer actually put words on paper. Neither writer's composing habits are well documented, and much critical discussion is based on inference, guesswork, or current attitudes toward textuality and authority. Of Dickinson, Habegger cautions that "we know almost nothing about the daily originating matrix of the writer's work. . . . We have . . . no authorial memoirs telling us how the writing connected with the events of life . . . it often happens that the poems that speak of the most vital of private experiences were preserved in the manuscript books only, giving us virtually no context" (405). The same caution, *mutatis mutandis,* applies to Melville.

Nevertheless, we do have some knowledge about how each writer put words on paper, knowledge that is based on texts they generated (manuscripts, letters, page proofs), on their own statements, and on what was said about them by family members and friends. (These latter two categories of information must always be used with caution.) Melville began his career by following the journalistic model: writing quickly, emphasizing impressions and information, and expecting to connect with his audience in a fairly ephemeral way. He wrote in pencil; this fact, coupled with his poor handwriting, meant that he needed someone else to prepare fair copies for the printer. (When he shipped out on his first voyage, in 1839, his name was mistakenly entered as Norman Melville, "probably as a consequence of his unimproved penmanship"—Delbanco 28.) These copies he punctuated himself. Once he began attempting to make a career out of writing, he treated himself as if he were involved in manual labor. His father-in-law wrote on 1 September 1856 that Herman had been "very ill" and that, according to Elizabeth, "When he is deeply engaged in one of his literary works, he confines him to hard study many hours in the day,—with little or no exercise, & this especially in winter for a great many days together. He probably thus overworks himself & brings on severe nervous affections" (quoted by Parker, *Herman Melville* 2:289). This had been his practice at least since he began *Moby-Dick* six years earlier—to treat writing as a different sort of "trying out," with no rest until the last scrap of blubber was rendered into oil. There was some respite: occasionally, after a day of writing, he might read his work aloud to members of his household, although the reports of this practice do not indicate that he expected or solicited any critical response. Perhaps he hoped for a scene of performance like those he had enjoyed as a young man, regaling his fellow sailors with his "fine yarns" and similarly "enthralling" his bride-to-be (Parker, *Herman Melville* 1:220, 264–65, 311). A final and extremely important practice was relying heavily on other works such as published books and articles, magazine illustrations, and his own journals, something he did throughout his writing career. These were Melville's practices, somewhat modified as his living and financial situations changed, for a writing career lasting more than forty years.

During his twelve years at Arrowhead (from the completion of *Moby-Dick* through *The Confidence-Man* to the lost *Poems* and after), he used a large writing table. The table now in that room may have been the one at which he composed *Moby-Dick,* but has not been proved to be so; however, it is certainly large enough to contain a substantial collection of books and still afford plenty of room to write. (See figure 7.)

Diminutive Emily Dickinson used a tiny writing table in her bedroom

Figure 7. Period table in Herman Melville's study at Arrowhead. Used by permission of the Berkshire Athenaeum, Pittsfield, Massachusetts.

Figure 8. Emily Dickinson's writing table. Dickinson family artifacts collection, Houghton Library, Harvard University. Used by permission.

at the family "homestead"—at least, we assume that this was where she actually put many of her words on paper, and scholars are certain that the table now in the collection at Harvard's Houghton Library was indeed Dickinson's own. (See figure 8.) Another intriguing element of her physical environment was the "Centre Burying Ground" of Amherst (now referred to as the "West Cemetery"), with its imposing new "Town Tomb" that had been constructed in 1850–51. Before the family returned to the Homestead in 1855, they spent fifteen years on North Pleasant Street, directly across from the Centre Burying Ground. Figure 9 gives a sense of what Emily saw out of her second-floor bedroom window—the quite imposing Town Tomb, not more than about eighty yards distant. Figure 10 suggests the scale of this structure, the young woman in the photograph being, at five feet tall, slightly taller than Emily

This tomb was a very different "swelling of the ground" than Mount Greylock, which Melville could see from his study window (see figure 11), but it is equally suggestive. Dickinson quite possibly valued that cemetery view in the same way that Melville was influenced by the whalelike shape of Greylock. (Wolff points out that the touring of cemeteries was a common practice in New England and that in 1846 Dickinson had visited and commented on the Mount Auburn cemetery in Boston.)

Fruitful as it can be to compare the (stereotypical) novelist's large table with the (stereotypical) poet's tiny table, the man's expansive view with the woman's view of ultimate constraint, we actually know even less about how Dickinson put words to paper than we do about how Melville did so. I will discuss her fascicles in a later section of this chapter; it suffices here to note the standard view of her composing process: earlier in her writing career she wrote initial drafts of her poems in pencil and made fair copies in ink on high-quality paper, which she then bound into booklets; she apparently regarded those fair copies as still under revision because they show variants. Later she ceased to make fair copies and tended to compose drafts in pencil on scraps of paper. Like many people of her era who conducted extensive correspondence, she took letter writing seriously, first drafting and then making fair copies. Marta Werner's description of Dickinson's composing and drafting process, as inferred from the textual evidence, exemplifies this view:

> In Dickinson's work two broad scriptural "styles," two hands—one for rough copy drafts, another for fair copy drafts—reflect and translate into space two interior movements of the mind. . . . The style for rough copy drafts, which remained constant even throughout the late years, is also the style of the dictation—a way of *writing in speaking:* the hand jolts into

Figure 9. The Amherst Town Tomb from the approximate location of the Dickinson family's house on North Pleasant Street. Photo by Candace and Craig Fehrman. Used by permission.

Figure 10. Close-up view of the Amherst Town Tomb. Photo by Candace and Craig Fehrman. Used by permission.

Figure 11. Mount Greylock from a north-facing window of Herman Melville's study at Arrowhead. Courtesy of the Berkshire Historical Society.

action. . . . Executed quickly—it is possible to imagine involuntarily—these drafts or inscriptions in which she fixed the nuclei of still unwritten poems reveal the rhapsodic quickenings of thought before their coalescence into a "work." . . . The cometary pace of her thought determines her choice of materials—whatever lies close by—and is registered in the disturbance of the scribal hand: the script is small and angular, text is superimposed over text, fault lines interrupt the narrative, and, all along the margins, words and solitary letters appear sideways and upside down. (*Open Folios* 21; emphasis in original)

Like the assessments of Melville's composing process, those of Dickinson's reflect our contemporary notions of how texts get produced. A novel, we tend to assume, requires long stretches of writing that may feel laborious. Because novels typically are grounded in a quotidian reality, it is not surprising that a writer will rely on sources or even that a writer needs considerable physical space—a large desk or table—for the work. Lyric poems, on the other hand, reflect "quickenings of thought," direct dictations from the imagination to the hand.[1] Both genres begin with the production of written (or typed) text that then must be revised.

These general points about the composing processes of Melville and Dickinson, as well as the assumptions about composing in general, will be contextualized and expanded in the following sections, in which I discuss the cultural basis for the mind/brain metonymy expressed by Dickinson and Melville as well as their conceptions of writing as a craft, in order further to explain their commitment to publishing outside of the commodity-oriented literary marketplace. I will also apply some general points from the field of composition studies to the conventional description of each writer's process. Any reading of the writers' metaphors and of the stereotypes they were challenging must be tempered with an awareness of how writers have always worked, in order to avoid interpreting every element of a writer's process as signifying writerly intent or cultural influence. Certainly, the available writing implements, the type of paper, the lighting, the desks and chairs, all had some influence on how they put words on paper, and certainly these material conditions existed within a discourse and an ideology of materiality. But it would be a mistake immediately to apply current theories of the materialist ideology without fully considering the conditions strictly as material constraints and how the two writers consciously located themselves within their era's ideology as they understood it, according to which a text really was the embodiment of the author's mind.

The "Body-Minded Brain" and the Materiality of Writing

The phrase "body-minded brain," coined by Antonio Damasio, aptly captures the convergence among a number of biological and linguistic avenues of research. "Thought and its representation in language [are shaped] . . . by the innate and universal physical parameters of our bodies and brains, as we attempt to make sense of and successfully negotiate what surrounds us, in nature and culture" (Crane and Richardson 127). From this perspective, the brain is "the material site where culture and biology meet and shape each other" (131). The extreme formulation of this approach is "the mind is what the brain does."

This late-twentieth-century development can be traced to the materialist psychology of the middle of the nineteenth century, a psychology that figured the mind/brain relationship as organic rather than as mechanistic, as had the association psychology of the eighteenth century, and that challenged the other prominent model of the era, the idealist, according to which mind and soul have no material basis. Melville ironized the idealist model, which took as a given the "primary harmony of the soul and the universe" in the words of John D. Morell (quoted in Kearns 40). Melville's writing reflects a psychology that recognizes a "functional and developmental" connection between the mind and the world, rather than the "divine, harmonious, magnetic" connection described by Emerson and others (Kearns 49). Likewise, Dickinson frequently figured mental phenomena as based in a material reality. For both Dickinson and Melville, physiological responses to phenomena were themselves significant phenomena but should not be interpreted in the idealist manner proposed by Emerson, every natural fact symbolizing a spiritual fact, as he expressed the point in the first two propositions of chapter 4 of *Nature* (*Nature* 13; Kearns 49, n. 11). Thus, each writer's descriptions of mental phenomena should be understood both metaphorically and metonymically, revealing the writers' sense of a physical connection among words, thoughts, and sensations.

Certainly, neither writer would have endorsed (although both probably would have been able to appreciate) the theory that the mind is solely a by-product of the brain's physical processes. Equally certainly, however, both understood the brain as the "material site" where a number of forces "meet" (not just "culture and biology" but also the writer's personal history, immediate environment, and inspiration), and both understood writing (the process and the product) as another such site. Scholars generally agree that each writer was aware of and probably influenced by Emerson's theory that words are signs of natural facts, but both seem to have moved beyond that assertion to understand and render words as natural facts no different from "[t]he meal in the firkin; the milk in the pan; the ballad in the street; the news of the boat," as Emerson wrote ("American Scholar" 50). In line with this understanding, both represented the acts, not just the outcomes, of reading and writing, acts that featured the struggle honestly to render surfaces within a print culture that treated those surfaces as transparent to a submerged meaning but represented authors as the print surfaces to which their names were attached, and within a legal system that seemed designed to limit the author's role to producing such surfaces while granting to the public the use of the surfaces' significance.

FAIRLY EARLY in his writing career, Melville was referring to texts as tangible entities whose content could be tasted, hefted, and otherwise perceived in the same way as any other physical item. Writing to Hawthorne on 29 June 1851, he asked, "Shall I send you a fin of the *Whale* by way of a specimen mouthful? The tail is not yet cooked—though the hell-fire in which the whole book is broiled might not unreasonably have cooked it all ere this" (*Correspondence* 196). And responding to a letter from Hawthorne, he wrote on 22 July 1851, "I thank you for your easy-flowing long letter (received yesterday) which flowed through me, and refreshed all my meadows, as the Housatonic—opposite me—does in reality" (199). A logical extension of this metonymic relationship among a book, its writer, and its reader is Melville's assertion that a book's physical appearance should reflect its content. In "A Thought on Book-Binding," he wrote that "books should be appropriately appareled. Their bindings should indicate and distinguish their various characters"; he thus praised Fenimore Cooper's *The Red Rover* for the cover's "felicitous touch of the sea superstitions of pirates" (237).

Melville understood a writer's work as involving (but certainly not limited to) physiology. For instance, comparing Hawthorne to Shakespeare, he wrote that the former was "content with the still, rich utterances of a great intellect in repose, and which sends few thoughts into circulation, except they be arterialized at his large warm lungs, and expanded in his honest heart" ("Hawthorne and His Mosses" 245). The difference between his description of his own process as "hell-fire" and that of Hawthorne as reposed and "easy-flowing" demonstrates as well that the physiological relationship between text and author depends on the temperament of the author. Melville's most extensive presentation of this relationship is in *Pierre*. Settled into his squalid rooms at the Inn of the Apostles, Pierre struggles daily to write but can't bridge the gap between what he feels or knows and what he can say: "Two books are being writ; of which the world shall only see one, and that the bungled one. The larger book . . . it is, whose unfathomable cravings drink his blood; the other only demands his ink. . . . Thus Pierre is fastened on by two leeches" (304). A second extended figure aptly characterizes how Melville himself almost certainly felt the tangible reality of the to-be-written book: "Still [Pierre's] book, like a vast lumbering planet, revolves in his aching head. He can not command the thing out of its orbit; fain would he behead himself, to gain one night's repose" (305).

Similarly, Dickinson often characterized both the production and the reception of writing in terms of physiology. Her best-known comment in this direction is her remark, as reported by Higginson in a letter dated 16 August 1870, that if a book "makes my whole body so cold no fire can ever warm me I know *that* is poetry. If I feel physically as if the top of my head were taken off, I know that is poetry. These are the only way [*sic*] I know it. Is there any other way" (Dickinson, *Letters* 473–74). Her second-known letter to Higginson expresses a similar figure, when she refers to the two editors asking for her "Mind" (Letter of 25 April 1862, *Letters* 404–5). While this comment reflects Dickinson's awareness that the literary culture of her time tended to commodify an author's very self, it also can mean what it literally says—Dickinson felt that the editors wanted to carry away a piece of her mind by carrying away either a thought or something she had written. In relaying this anecdote, Dickinson intended for Higginson to see that she valued her work, and she may have wanted him to see that others did as well: her choice of metonymy to make the point demonstrates a belief that she was indeed what she wrote.

Dickinson was well aware that readers tended to identify a writer not just *with* but *as* the words the writer produced, an identification that was essential for marketing, and participated in the general movement in nineteenth-century America toward commodifying labor, as I have shown in chapter 2. However, her choice of figure should not be read merely as a cultural tic. For the literary marketplace, to equate a writer with her work was a convenience, a shorthand, one we still use: "I have studied Dickinson," "I love Daniel Silva." Like every other great poet, Dickinson dove beneath her culture's casual and intentional figures in order to explore their human truth, in this case a truth about relativism that was slowly becoming accepted or at least known. Immediately following the first letter's question she observes that "[t]he Mind is so near itself—it cannot see, distinctly—and I have none to ask—." If producer and product were separate, "weighing" or "distinctly" seeing should pose no problem. In a nonrelativistic universe, one can easily weigh one's self; whenever we step on a bathroom scale, we imply our faith in that technique of measurement. Dickinson, however, seems to have anticipated Heisenberg's Uncertainty Principle here: from a physical and physiological standpoint, the self can't have objective knowledge about itself because it is implicated in the creation and perception of what it knows. With an entire universe of metaphoric vehicles to draw from, that Dickinson twice in such a short period of time chose vehicles grounded in human physiology suggests that these represented for her a cognitive structure—a way she understood the world—and not just an element of style. This structure is present as late as around 1875: "You cannot take itself / From any Human soul—/ That indestructible estate / Enable him to dwell . . . " (Fr1359). This poem overtly makes the same point as the first letters to Higginson, that the soul cannot be divided (analyzed, measured). Her goal was probably to stimulate a deeper thought—that certain components of a human's psyche are susceptible to tangible mechanical operations. Does the soul truly transcend material reality? If so, how do words have the physiological effect they undeniably do have?

For both Melville and Dickinson, reading and writing were two aspects of the same phenomenon: a piece of literature can have a visceral impact on a reader, and the mind is physically embodied in the words one produces. The root metaphor here, mind as a physical entity, is also present in Dickinson's poems "The brain is wider than the sky" (Fr598) and "The mind lives on the heart" (Fr1384). Melville dramatizes it in Ishmael's depiction of masthead dreaming in chapter 35 ("The Mast-Head") of *Moby-Dick,* a dramatization that also criticizes the idealizing of certain emotions. Ishmael describes a youth on lookout duty who is "lulled into such an opium-like listlessness of vacant, unconscious reverie . . . that at last he loses his identity; takes the mystic ocean at his feet for the visible image of that deep, blue, bottomless soul, pervading mankind and nature," and his spirit "becomes diffused through time and space; like Wickliff's sprinkled pantheistic ashes, forming at last a part of every shore the round globe over" (159). The danger for this youth is that he is suspended over "Descartian vortices"; if he even slightly loosens his hold on his perch he may "drop through that transparent air into the summer sea, no more to rise for ever" (159). (See Kearns for an extended discussion of this and related passages.)

In short, Melville's and Dickinson's body-minded-brain metaphors reflect their sense of how the external world, the writer's mind, the writer's body, and the written text could tangibly interact. Melville's proposal to send Hawthorne "a fin of the *Whale* by way of a specimen mouthful" could be taken simply as a fanciful expression, but it can also be read as reflecting his belief that a text literally embodied its creator's thoughts and could be consumed physically and mentally. His description of Hawthorne's "thoughts" as "arterialized at his large warm lungs, and expanded in his honest heart" can be interpreted in the same way. So too can the following frequently anthologized Dickinson poem, probably written during the summer of 1863, a version of which was sent to Susan Dickinson:

> I send two Sunsets—
> Day and I—in competition—ran—
> I finished Two, and several Stars
> While He—was making One—
> His Own is ampler—but as I
> Was saying to a friend—
> Mine—is the more convenient—
> To carry in the Hand—
> (Fr 557)

In chapter 5, I situate this poem in the context of its first publication, according to which "sunsets" refers to the flowers reportedly sent to Susan Dickinson along with the poem. "Stars" might have a similar significance, suggesting perhaps additional flowers, the whole arranged as a colorful

bouquet—either bouquet or single flowers would certainly be "more convenient—/ To carry in the Hand." Here, I want to consider it strictly
as an individual lyric evoking an idealized relationship between a single,
personalized, ideal speaker and an equally abstract reader. By this reading, "two sunsets" would almost certainly have to refer to the idea of a
sunset conveyed by the poem; as the embodiment of that idea, the poem
is certainly "convenient." The poem thus asserts a metonymic equivalence
among the actual sunset, the verbal representation, and the idea. The two
readings converge in the poem's casual, even offhand tone, as if to create a
sunset (whether out of flowers or out of words) were nothing unusual. By
placing the transmission of the poem in the context of a prior conversation
with "a friend," Dickinson invites not only the specific, intended recipient
of this poem, her sister in-law, but also the "lyric" reader to share the cultural circulation of the concept of metonymy. The convention of climactic
organization implies that the last-mentioned item, the created (floral or
verbal) sunset, is superior. This poem's metonymic basis is identical to that
of "The mind lives on the heart" and "The brain is wider than the sky"—
for Dickinson, as for Melville, the mental, spiritual, and physical realms
substantially interpenetrated.

Given this overlap, it is not surprising that both Dickinson and Melville
(not to mention the latter's family) would be troubled by any illness that
could interfere with writing: not to be able to write is to risk the loss of
one's identity. The eye problems both writers experienced would be most
serious, because the eye reifies the transmission of thought to paper and
guides, quite literally, the addition of new thoughts to those already written. The physical activity of writing requires good light—ideally, daylight,
as anyone will attest who has ever tried to read handwriting by candlelight
or oil lamp. While it is possible to write in the dark, most writers find that
in order to hew to a purpose, they must continually reread what they have
written—this is no less true of writers now canonized than for any first-
year college student. Depending on the writer's rhetorical occasion, the
writer might make (or have someone else make) a fair copy and might be
involved in comparing fair copy with printer's proofs, activities that don't
require the author's eyes but still involve someone's visual concentration.
No less important is the writer's collecting of information—by reading
and by looking. Thus, while eyesight is not intrinsically essential for writing, it may be so for the writer who desires to become an author by going
before an audience, unless that writer leaves the proofing process entirely
to someone else.

As far as we know, at least during his Arrowhead years, Melville used
candles for artificial light, a source that barely sufficed him for reading and

writing. This limitation is clear from a letter he sent to Evert Duyckinck on 13 December 1850: "Before I go further let me say here that I am writing this by candle light—an uncommon thing with me—& therefore my writing wont [*sic*] be very legible, because I am keeping one eye shut & wink at the paper with the other" (*Correspondence* 173). A few sentences later he wrote: "My evenings I spend in a sort of mesmeric state in my room—not being able to read—only now & then skimming over some large-printed book" and then immediately made his request for "fifty fast-writing youths" (174). He obviously felt that not being able to work in the evenings was limiting his productivity. In fact, although his second-floor study was fitted with three windows (two facing east, one north), even his daylight hours would not always have been ideal for writing, unless the day were sunny. Dickinson was somewhat better off: during her most productive writing years, the family used kerosene lanterns, which provide a brighter and more consistent light than candles or oil lamps. Thus she would have more easily been able to read and write in the evenings and when daylight was of poor quality.[2]

The labor of writing also requires a modicum of physical comfort—bearable temperature, a properly configured desk and chair, implements that fit one's fingers. Less obvious aspects such as nutrition and exercise also play a role. If any of these conditions is lacking, the physical act, already tedious, can damage one's health, as Melville's biographers have emphasized and as Dickinson's have noted (but not emphasized—a telling lapse). Andrew Delbanco concisely lists some of Melville's illnesses: pain in his eyes while working on *Israel Potter* in 1854 (209); severe back pain in late 1854 (229); sciatica in June of 1855 that caused him "excruciating, paroxysmal attacks of pain" (261); in 1856 eye strain and a chronic back pain (245); Hawthorne's statement that his friend "has been affected with neuralgic complaints in his head and limbs, and no doubt has suffered from too constant literary occupation" (252, from Hawthorne's journal of 20 November 1856). As I mentioned earlier, Melville's family members frequently worried about the physical demands of his writing, demands that also exacted a psychological toll. His mother, for example, wrote that "[t]he constant in-door confinement with little intermission to which Hermans [*sic*] occupation as author compels him, does not agree with him. This constant working of the brain, & excitement of the imagination, is wearing Herman out" (letter of April 1853, quoted by Parker, *Herman Melville* 2:152). According to Parker, Melville's "account of his writing conditions [at Arrowhead toward the end of 1850] made it sound, for the moment, as near to ideal as he could have hoped" (1:798). The conditions probably were ideal in that Melville had enough time to write, but his account also sounds somewhat like self-imposed servitude: he sequestered himself in his cold room each morning and remained at work until 2:30 in the afternoon, a regimen that limited him in the evenings to skimming over "some large-printed book." Anyone who has suffered with sciatica, as did Melville, knows how painful sitting can be; his self-discipline with this condition has to be admired.

Perhaps Parker is correct; at this time in his writing career, especially with the positive distraction and physical labor provided by the Arrowhead farm, Melville was not only healthy but positively disposed toward his chosen profession, but by the mid-1850s his health was a serious worry to his family, who attributed his physical ailments to his writing and who feared as well for his mental health. Melville's acquaintance Charles Fenno Hoffman had placed himself in an institution in 1849, a fact which troubled Melville's mother among others. The report on Hoffman's condition published by Greeley in 1849 echoes the concerns expressed several years later by her and other family members: "C. F. HOFFMAN, whose health had become impaired by too close confinement and incessant application to literary labors, being threatened with a serious affection of the brain, sometime since very judiciously determined to place himself in a position where, with sufficient seclusion, entire avoidance of literary pursuits, and judicious medical treatment, he was likely most speedily and certainly to be restored to his wonted good health" (quoted by Parker, *Herman Melville* 2:153). Greeley's optimism notwithstanding, Hoffman remained institutionalized until his death in 1884.

Because Melville and Dickinson regarded the written or printed text metonymically as part of themselves, organically and functionally connected in the same way a hand or an eye is connected to the self, then it makes sense that the text could also function as the site of a psychological conflict regarding writing. The body-minded brain figure illuminates what Elizabeth Renker terms Melville's "tortured relation to his writing" (57). That relation, along with "his chronic association of writing with maddening forms of blockage," serves to "illuminate a series of textual effects that associate women with blank pages and textual production" (57). "The pasteboard mask that can't be struck through, the text that can't be stabbed through, and the copies that he must himself punctuate are dramas of composition in which paper acts as a material site of blockage, frustrating the author's desire to penetrate and so to transcend material conditions" (67). According to Renker, Melville's "striking through" is "a materially loaded gesture . . . in terms of his violent frustration with the pages over which he labored and with the laboring women in his household" (68). Renker suggests that he moved from believing that language could accurately capture and transmit thoughts (when he was writing *Typee* and *Omoo*) to despair over the intransigence of language (represented most dramatically in *Pierre*), thence to a thematization and even celebration of language's mute surface on which humans project their wishes and beliefs. A final step in this progression might be that he turned away from a focus on language to embrace poetic form during the three decades of his writing life that followed the publication of his prose works; Renker doesn't argue for this step, but it's plausible. I suggest a complementary view of Melville's relationship to the physicality of his writing—that although he may have come to doubt the viability of language as a medium of exchange, so to speak, he never lost his sense of the physical reality of writing as a manifestation of his thoughts—physical as well as linguistic, tangible sign as well as abstract significance.[3]

How HEALTHY Dickinson was, compared to Melville, it is not possible to determine; we can only say that there are fewer references to her being in ill health, but the reasons for that difference could have a great deal to do with her personality, her role in the family, or her gender. We do know, however, that she was afflicted for a time with a serious problem of vision. Habegger writes that the problem began in September 1863; she was treated in Boston "from late April to November 21 in 1864, and again from April 1 to October in 1865" by Dr. Henry Willard Williams (483–84). The diagnosis was probably "anterior uveitis: what used to be called rheumatic iritis" (485). Symptoms were severe and deep-seated pain and intolerance of light; the outlook was positive if the disease was diagnosed and treated in time (485). By late 1865 she seems to have been well enough to skip a scheduled checkup with Dr. Williams, and since she never again referred to the problem, Habegger writes that "there is little basis for suspecting an ongoing, let alone permanent, impairment" (517). Habegger's tone suggests that although the ailment was serious, it had no permanent effect, and he states that there is no reason to take as an early indication of eye trouble her statement in her second letter to Higginson that she "had a terror" she could not tell anyone about (435), although some biographers have interpreted the letter in that way. Vision problems aside, Dickinson's health was always a concern, although probably no more than would be expected given her family status or her role as the chief caregiver of her mother and father in their last days.

More important than the longevity or clinical severity of any disease, but especially eye trouble, is what such a condition would do to any person for whom writing was a passion. Because the treatment included avoiding bright light and above all reading—this avoidance being the only "woe," she wrote to Joseph Lyman, that ever "made [her] tremble" (quoted by Habegger 484)—it stands to reason that Dickinson was exceedingly troubled by the disease and its consequences: not only could she not read printed matter and letters (one of her primary means of social contact), she could not read her own writing. There is also the possibility that as with Melville some members of her family feared for her sanity or at least that she was aware that some of her behaviors and beliefs invited such a reaction. The poem "Much madness is divinest sense" points in this direction, emphasizing that insanity is defined by "the Majority" and that to "Demur" from the majority view would lead to being termed "dangerous" and "handled with a Chain" (Fr620). These consequences, she writes, are certain; the poem's sentences are all declarative, with no palliating modals.

BEYOND THE ART OF BOOKCRAFT

Melville and Dickinson were influenced more by the era's metaphor of an embodied mind than by the opposing and more widely accepted emphasis on the mind as immaterial. Their figurative language reflects that influence, as do Melville's apparently rough treatment of manuscript and proof copies and Dickinson's practice of linking letters and poems with physical objects. It would be a mistake, however, to emphasize this influence without giving equal attention to the physical realities of the craft of writing during the decades when Melville and Dickinson were practicing that craft as well as to what the field of composition studies tells us about how writers work. This is an important perspective, because although Melville and Dickinson have become "world authors," they began by being writers desiring to reach an audience. I showed in a previous chapter that their culture's idealization of manual labor encouraged authors to figure themselves as engaged in such labor in order to enter the market for symbolic capital. But this physicality was not just a means to justify such participation (and to associate oneself with the production of real, tangible goods as opposed to abstract capital that results from investing); it was also an inescapable fact about the activity. Whether one writes in a temperate, well-lighted library or by candle in an unheated garret, one's entire body is involved. The craft of writing has its own set of hazards, more subtle but no less real, to the writer, than is the machinist's risk to fingers and eyes. The technology of typewriting and recent developments in voice-recognition software have tended to blur this fact, but for millennia writing was a handicraft, the hands producing what the mind generates, and the eyes verifying that production. To understand what Melville and Dickinson were doing when they produced manuscripts thus requires becoming familiar with the physical conditions under which they worked. The fact that these conditions were frequently associated with the stereotype of the poet in a garret starving for his or her art does not detract from the reality of the conditions themselves.

The most important source of information about Dickinson's practice of the craft of writing is her manuscripts, but those material artifacts only answer the question "what" and not "why" or "how." Thus, for instance, the manuscript books are usually taken as fair copies, in pen, of earlier drafts. Franklin infers a process: "The stemma for Dickinson's workshop when fascicles were involved may be generalized," from worksheet to intermediate draft to copies sent or retained to the actual fascicle or set, then to further copies sent or retained, perhaps further revised, and then yet more copies sent or retained (Introduction to *Poems* 19). To postulate a "workshop," even metaphorically, assumes that Dickinson conducted her poetic business in a serious and perhaps even professional fashion, that she was relatively well organized, and that she had at least a metaphorical space within which she crafted her language. Certainly the "stemma" reflects what Franklin terms her "long-distance interest in the fascicles," her return to them "over many years" (18); this return is documented by a study of the fascicles' physical details. But other practices that Franklin presents as fact are much more speculative. For instance, he writes that "[h]er workshop did have rules for destruction, though their purpose was orderly preservation. The primary one was that when working drafts were copied to a later form, such as a fascicle, the drafts were destroyed" (11). Because there are few drafts of fascicle poems that can be dated earlier than the fascicles, it is possible that Dickinson destroyed working drafts after making fair copies. This is a fairly standard practice of writers (although some do keep all drafts).

However, we can't be certain that Dickinson followed this practice, or, if she did, for how long. She may have done a great deal of composing in her head, especially because she had the hymn form to lend structure: relying on a standard structure has been a technique of many oral composers. Scholars continue to debate the unit of Dickinson's composition: Did she structure her poems primarily according to line length, stanza form, or the shape of the piece of paper on which she wrote, and did this unit change during her writing life? Cristanne Miller contends that Dickinson was committed to rhythm ("Whose Dickinson?" 247–48). Domhnall Mitchell puts the point even more strongly: "Emphasizing the rhythm of the eye over the rhythms of the ear in reading Dickinson's poems is . . . equivalent to switching off the music: what's left is silence" (*Measures of Possibility* 264). Mitchell suggests, and I agree, that creating verbal music within a context of oral performance was one of her goals, but most scholars—unintentionally, I believe—follow Franklin in emphasizing the written text as the primary vehicle for Dickinson's composition. Thus, of "If those I loved were lost" (Fr20), Franklin writes that "she had the first line immediately, but the second required adjustment before she could go on; the rest came easily until the final line, which had to be recast," and, later, "[t]he composition of this poem was typically fast" (11).

Franklin seems to be carrying on the assessment of Dickinson's first editors and reviewers, that she generally wrote quickly and revised little, so that her work reflects spontaneous outflow rather than laborious crafting but also that her compositional method was written rather than oral and aural. Her "workshop," according to Franklin, was a site (metaphorically speaking) for the production of new copies, not for laborious crafting of lines and phrases. But given the brevity of most of the poems and their recognizable adherence to stanzaic form, it is also reasonable to imagine Dickinson composing early drafts wholly in her head. Franklin's detailed description of the manuscripts and his careful attention to dating them deserve the gratitude of all scholars, but when he reads intentions into the evidence, some skepticism is appropriate. For instance, he writes that "[a]s of Fascicle 5, Dickinson was working with a large batch of stationery. Whereas she had used five kinds of paper in the first four fascicles, she made the next four from one kind. She had found her model and, confident that poems would come, laid in plenty of stock. The poems did come, and every month or so she would prepare another sheet" (21). Further, "for the last decade she made no fascicle sheets and near the end grew indifferent to making even second copies, with a number of poems surviving in their initial draft, laid down in a large running script" (26–27). He consistently assumes that Dickinson's method of composing was based on the written word, an assumption reflected in his speculation that there may have been "as many as 5,000 manuscripts, instead of 2,500" (29). He arrives at this figure by noting that for instance the twenty-seven poems of Fascicle 1 exist in a total of thirty-nine manuscript versions and then by extrapolating, assuming the preparation of working and intermediate drafts (28).

It is tantalizing to think that several thousand more manuscripts await discovery, or even several hundred (perhaps as not-quite-completely burned scraps in a buried heap of ashes or other household rubbish, if not in a sheaf of papers stored but uncatalogued in an archive). But scholars might better invest their energy in considering Dickinson's composing as informed by oral and aural considerations. After all, as she wrote around 1862,

> A word is dead, when it is said
> Some say—
> I say it just begins to live
> That day. (Fr278)

We should never limit a Dickinson utterance to its literal meaning, but neither should we disallow the literal as one plausible interpretation among many, all of which could have been intended. Thus, she may well have meant that speaking brings words into existence and that the life is then preserved by writing, even while she was also sensitive to the performative character of this utterance (the referenced statements are brought into being by "Some say" and "I say") and to the possible irony thus created. Given the gnomic quality of Dickinson's speech, as noted by many acquaintances, some of her poems may have been drafted and revised aloud, although certainly when working with groups of poems or when returning to a poem months later, she needed manuscript copies.

Dickinson's reliance on handwritten letters and poems to communicate with her actual audiences is consistent with a writing process influenced by an oral and aural aesthetic as well as by an aesthetic of the handwritten word. This aesthetic was supported by the metaphor of the body-minded brain as well as by the practice of portfolio poetry, both of which emphasized an immediate, personal, even visceral and physiological response to a poem. Certainly the manuscript evidence suggests that in preparing rough copies Dickinson wrote quickly, but it is equally certain that we just don't know how much composition preceded these copies. Werner's nuanced analysis assumes that Dickinson composed mainly or wholly in writing rather than aloud or in her head. Werner's phrase "the style of the dictation" implies a process in which writing serves mainly to record speech (either inner or voiced), directed at an audience willing to regard her pen or pencil as an extension of her mind, capturing raw inspiration. McGann's assessment of the fascicles as moving away from the "horizon of [print] publication" in their arrangement on the page also supports this line of thought. He speculates that the change in how Dickinson arranged lines on the page from fascicles 1–8 to the later fascicles represents her decision "to use her text page as a scene for dramatic interplays between a poetics of the eye and a poetics of the ear" ("Composition as Explanation" 120).

That is, the poems in the earlier fascicles "have been imagined under a horizon of publication," whereas those of the later show her "reject[ing] a market model of publishing" (122) and applying "writing conventions permitted and encouraged in the textuality of personal correspondence," of "epistolary intercourse" (123).

Dickinson's method of composing may have been aural/oral or her method of presenting her work may have been intended to imply spontaneity and hence unedited inspiration. Both possibilities are supported by the reports of her conversation, especially from individuals like Higginson who were in a position to confer symbolic capital. About his visit to Dickinson in 1870, he wrote to his wife that the poet seemed at first a child (he uses "child" or "childlike" three times in two sentences) but then "talked soon & thenceforward continuously—& deferentially—sometimes stopping to ask me to talk instead of her—but readily recommencing. Manner between Angie Tilton & Mr. Alcott—but thoroughly ingenuous & simple which they are not & saying many things which you would have thought foolish & I wise—& some things you wd. hv. liked" (*Letters* 473). The impression conveyed by this letter and the one he wrote immediately after is that of a stream of talk coming from the poet, punctuated occasionally by questions from him, an impression strengthened by his reflective comment two decades later: "She was much too enigmatical a being for me to solve in an hour's interview. . . . I could only sit still and watch, as one does in the woods" (quoted by Johnson, *Letters* 476). Comparing this experience to one taking place "in the woods" also explicitly situates Dickinson within the portfolio-poetry context, connoting spontaneous inspiration by nature but not careful revision.

Such reports are usually accepted as reflecting Dickinson's personality or the persona she wanted to create for her addressee. Possibly, she intended her conversations with people like Higginson to enhance her cultural stock by strengthening the impression of thoughts flowing without interruption and with relatively little editing from mind to speech or speechlike writing. Like her poems and letters, these conversations—and indeed her penchant for white dresses and seclusion—can be read as crafted, rhetorically sophisticated performances, carried out for audiences who were in a position to grant the symbolic capital of prestige and consecration. Such an interpretation runs counter to the romantic privileging of inspired, spontaneous lyricism, as expressed in Emerson's description of the poetic youth. Recent scholarship holds that Dickinson was a conscientious and reflective artist. This evaluation transforms the poet earlier generations thought they knew; extant texts, both poems and letters, reveal her careful imposture of breathless spontaneity, an imposture present throughout her writing career. I'm arguing for a second, less dramatic transformation, a poet whose poetics was significantly "of the ear" and for whom the handwritten text was not—or not only—an end in itself but a way of stimulating oral performance and aural reception. In fact, as I show in chapter 5, the posthumous, twentieth-century Dickinson has moved well beyond visual renderings of the verbal (whether Johnson or Franklin, reading edition or variorum, type or manuscript, print or hypertext) to include the spoken, heard, and viewed.

If indeed Dickinson was pursuing symbolic capital within the immediate but also ephemeral context of performance, it makes sense that she would shift later in her career from pen to pencil. Werner refers to her use of pencil and paper as "the greatest economy of means": "For, unlike the pen, which produces a permanent memory trace, the lines drawn by the lead point of the stylus are easily erased and retraced so that each act of copying constitutes a new performance—improvisation or extension of a thought-event" (*Open Folios* 23). Writing that appears transitory and improvisatory is unlikely to invite commodification. Werner generalizes: "The economy in which she worked, Love's deviant economy, is also the economy of the Outlaw. . . . And in this alternative economy, opposed to consistency, productivity, and profit, Dickinson issued her private, successive editions of abandonment" (*Open Folios* 27). Werner's lyrical assessment is compelling but also misleading. The "economy" within which Dickinson worked was a respected alternative to that of print publication and was not "deviant" or necessarily related to "Love." Dickinson indeed desired "profit" (capital), just not of the economic sort. And as I demonstrated in chapter 3, she probably understood that her works had absolute legal protection as long as they remained in manuscript: she did not simply decide not to have her work printed, she decided to present it in handwritten form. Whereas Werner advocates a reading of Dickinson as a writer, I argue that she was seeking the cultural authority of "authorship," albeit outside of the mechanisms of commercial print publication.

The materials on which Dickinson wrote, ranging from fine stationery to household scraps, may or may not have contributed to her quest for authorial authority. It is likely that her use of new, high-quality paper for fair copies of poems in both the fascicles and the letters signals her pride in her work and her hope or expectation that this work would be respectfully received. At the other end of the materials spectrum, it is also possible, as Sally Bushell argues, that Dickinson chose specific scraps of paper in order either to "reclaim" them, "giving them a new life as text," or to "liberate" herself by using something that could be "thrown away if it is no good" (44). Bushell also writes that "[p]ut simply, a mid-nineteenth-century flyer from a pharmacist's shop is worth less than an Emily Dickinson manuscript poem, first draft, existing only in a single state" (48), although it seems a stretch to read that twentieth-century cash value back into Dickinson's intention or hope regarding how either her contemporaries or future readers might receive the work. There is no evidence that a writer of Dickinson's time could have accrued symbolic capital by sending scraps of paper to those correspondents whose esteem she valued, although certainly the juxtaposition of her words and the print or illustration on a scrap could be valued for its wit. Without any evidence that she shared these works, however, the cautious scholar will refrain from asserting intentionality. Like Bushell, Melanie Hubbard offers the "working fiction" that Dickinson "had artistic intentions for her more fugitive creations," her scraps of poems on scraps of paper ("Apartments" 56). Yes, "fiction." It is certainly possible that she imagined herself as engaged in (probably ironic) play or dialog with anything printed on those scraps as well as with their original context, but any such interpretation must remain speculative.

Like Dickinson (as far as we know), Melville composed in isolation; unlike her, writing was his main occupation for a number of years. His letters document periods of what we today term writer's block, some of which were doubtless caused by his sense of not being able to write what as he put it he felt "most moved to write" because it would not "pay" (*Correspondence* 191, letter of 1 [?] June 1851). The manuscript evidence of early drafts is skimpy but consistent: it shows him composing rough drafts in pencil in a nearly indecipherable hand, with frequent insertions and deletions. The Northwestern-Newberry editors' discussion of the surviving manuscript leaf of *Typee* applies to Melville's practices in general. As with most writers, his first drafts contained "false starts" and "transpositions"; copying these drafts, he made a few changes, as shown by phrases being canceled and replaced on the same line, and other changes at a later time, inserted above a line (Hayford et al. 363–64). According to Renker, he tended to write dense sentences and then expand them by unpacking (89). When he began his career, the "scene of writing," to use Renker's phrase, was that of the journalist, emphasizing immediate connection between writer and reader through language that had been spontaneously produced. That scene changed twice in a significant way. First, no later than the composition of *Mardi,* he had put off the journalist's hat and began weighing his work in terms of the praise he hoped to receive from the contemporaries he admired. Second, once he finally secured full-time employment in December of 1866 at the New York Custom House, writing became an after-hours activity rather than his ostensible profession.

In his letters, Melville noted a few times that he felt he was getting better at his craft. One of the early comments is in the letter of 15 July 1846 to John Murray, in which he wrote, regarding what would become *Omoo,* that the manuscript "will be in a rather better state for the press than the M.S.S. handed to him . . . by my brother. A little experience in this art of book-craft has done wonders" (*Correspondence* 58). The process of readying *Typee* for the printer probably affected not only that book but Melville's "later habits of writing" (Howard 280). Murray had actually paid an editor, Henry Milton, fifty pounds for one hundred sixty-eight hours of work on that first manuscript, an amount that was "just over half the amount Melville was paid"; this fact must have contributed significantly to Melville's desire to provide a more printworthy copy of his next book (Howard 282).

Three other important aspects of Melville's composing process differ dramatically from what we know of Dickinson's: he made liberal use of print sources; he relied on copyists (the women of his household) to prepare fair copies; and he came to recognize and thematize the limitations of the handwritten page, the printed page, and language in general. It has often been noted that in a literary culture known for extensive borrowing, Melville was an extreme case. Plausibly, his thematizing of writing and his desire to accrue symbolic capital were also influenced by an internal conflict between using sources without acknowledgment and conceiving of authorship as original composition. The practice has consequences as well for a writer's sense of his potential for earning all types of capital: Is the writer's capital actually his own if he has built it on borrowing? Plagiarism, even by the relatively loose standards of the nineteenth century, may be characterized as the equivalent of taking out a loan at a high interest rate; if the book is unsuccessful in any market, the writer may well feel guilt at having borrowed. One way to relieve this guilt is to believe that economic failure connotes artistic success: the garret life, metaphorically speaking, justifies certain kinds of theft.

Certainly, the values of the literary marketplace within which Melville worked were ambiguous. "The culture of reprinting" was prominent in nineteenth-century America, as McGill has shown, a culture that commodified authors and their works but did not condone outright theft. It was also fairly standard for authors to borrow liberally without attribution. But it was something else entirely for an author to claim, as Melville did, that firsthand experience was the principal basis of a work when the facts were otherwise: for *Typee* and *Omoo* he had "used, misused, and downright abused his sources" (Parker, *Herman Melville* 1:456). Parker summarizes the careful detective work of Harrison Hayford on the composition of *Typee:* "Hayford's detailed account of Melville's depredations on his sources conveys something of the reckless fun Melville must have had during the commission of the purloinings and adaptings" (1:456–57). Parker's diction seems intended to keep at bay what Renker terms the "specter of plagiarism"; these weren't thefts but "purloinings and adaptations," and Melville's purpose was only to have "fun," not to profit from someone else's labor. Perhaps.

Dickinson, of course, famously eschewed literary borrowing, noting in one of her earlier letters to Higginson "I marked a line in One Verse—because I met it after I made it—and never consciously touch a paint, mixed by another person—[new paragraph] I do not let go it, because it is mine" (*Letters* 415, August 1862). Melville, too, when he moved to poetry was pursuing a different market that preferred originality. His recognition that this was a different market is clear from his instructions regarding the preparation of the now lost *Poems* that he had completed by 1860. He apparently believed that he could create a new authorial persona, although he was probably still relying heavily on print sources if those poems were anything like what he included in *Battle-Pieces*. For that volume he claimed in a prefatory note that the poems "originated in an impulse imparted by the fall of Richmond" and "were composed without reference to collective arrangement." He went on to say that from "the events and incidents of the conflict" were taken those that "chanced to imprint themselves upon the mind," and, most strongly invoking the romantic convention of inspiration, that "[y]ielding instinctively, one after another, to feelings not inspired from any one source exclusively, and unmindful, without purposing to be, of consistency, I seem, in most of these verses, to have but placed a harp in a window, and noted the contrasted airs which wayward winds have played upon the strings" (*Battle-Pieces*, first edition). Whether the discrepancy between his actual practice and his claimed method caused him any inner conflict in this particular instance, we will probably never know, but such conflict was clearly present throughout much if not all of his writing life otherwise. One wonders where his writer's allegiance lay—was he evoking the Aeolian harp merely to gain traction with readers? If his imagination had necessitated for almost two decades that he write with verbal or visual sources, why could he not finally come clean, so to speak, with the audience he desired to secure?

In shifting from prose to poetry, Melville preserved some aspects of his composing process, such as the use of pencil and the reliance on sources (including his own journal in the case of *Clarel*), but other aspects changed; most dramatically, he could draw on metrical forms, and he need not feel driven to fill up the blank page but could instead exploit its space.

According to Renker, the manuscripts and language of the published volumes show that "the material presence of writing had become a conceptual problem for Melville that had specific and particular consequences in his engagements with individual, physical pages" (101). He took scissors to the manuscript pages of the *Battle-Pieces* poems, a "compositional practice [that] speaks to Melville's awareness of his poems as both materially discrete and materially variable entities . . . whose physical form he consistently engaged as part of his process of production" (102). These were "pieces" not only on analogy with painting but also as in "the nature of the poems themselves as he conceived it" (102). He became interested in "controlling the white page, a space that is both inherently more present to the poet than to the novelist and also more fundamentally visible within the nominal product itself" (103).

Renker's reading of Melville's relationship to "the art of book-craft" appropriately stresses how he connected the material aspects of writing and book production to the ontological and epistemological status and function of language. One can come away from her *Strike Through the Mask* with the impression that no other writer of the time was as fascinated and troubled by the connections or as well suited, by intellect and temperament, to problematize them. This is where the comparison to Dickinson sheds light: she too practiced that art, but her crafted books more resemble commonplace books, keepsake volumes, scrapbooks, and diaries than anything emanating from the publishing industry. As Alexandra Socarides has recently demonstrated, Dickinson possibly (Socarides argues probably) had these types of artifacts in mind when creating her fascicles. Certainly, if Melville only understood book production to involve the preparation of mass-produced novels and volumes of verse, it would be surprising to find him using white space, copying others' words—in general, concentrating on the material aspects of "the art of book-craft." However, the literary culture of his time included many more markets than those targeted by mass-produced print. Insofar as Melville is to be understood not just as the author of published prose fiction and poetry but also as a writer of manuscripts that preceded publication and that he idealized as the "best" format for his ideas, the context of nonprint publishing must also be considered. No less than Dickinson, Melville emphasized the materiality of text, because of both ontological and epistemological concerns and the literary culture of his time. Both writers practiced a complex "art of book-craft" spanning the complete process from composition to production; both celebrated the fact that this art could yield individualized items whose value was qualitatively different from that of the published book.

The Persona as a Commodity
in a Material Economy

This chapter's first two sections demonstrate that the material text represented for Dickinson and Melville a literal embodiment of what was in the writer's mind. While both attended to the craft of writing, their attention differed in kind: for Melville the material processes of writing constituted a "conceptual problem" whereas for Dickinson the conceptual problem had more to do with the material product. They also differed in the outcome of their crafting: printed books for Melville and handcrafted manuscripts for Dickinson (although Melville wished he could indulge himself in the latter). Key phrases that characterize one author's process are interestingly skewed for the other: the "art of book-craft," writing under a "horizon of publication," the processes of writing as a "conceptual problem," "incarnational poetics." Skewed or straight, these phrases remind us that each writer was intensely engaged with the physical act of writing, the material products resulting from this engagement, and the various economies in which the products and processes participated. Whichever kind of "book-craft" the writer practiced involved an incarnation of self into material text; the "horizon of publication" demarcated two vastly different types of market and capital—economic and symbolic—with participation in one requiring or entailing rejection of or failure in the other.

Each writer's attention to the materiality of his or her media illuminates a desire to participate in a field of restricted production. This participation involves the producers controlling evaluation rather than allowing an external, consuming public to establish value. Asserting the primacy of their own physiological responses was another way for Melville and Dickinson to demonstrate their credibility as producers of symbolic capital. It was widely accepted that the human mind had a material basis, that it was not only "soul" but also "brain." Although the pseudosciences of physiognomy, phrenology, and mesmerism had all been seriously critiqued (and the first wholly discredited) by the middle of the nineteenth century, they survived as plot devices and as metaphors and were understood as necessary precursors to the new discoveries in neural physiology. This conceptual context supported the presence or at least the appearance of "naturalness" in writing—both epistolary and poetic. The culture's recognition that naturalness could be crafted is reflected in Emerson's 1840 essay "New Poetry," Higginson's reference to that essay in his introduction of Dickinson to a reading public (in the essay "An Open Portfolio" and the preface to the first edition of poems, both published in 1890), and Poe's 1845 article "Anastatic Printing" (describing a technology by which writers could create, at home, plates of manuscript pages, which would enable the printing of those pages in facsimile) (Esdale 4–6). Such writing was valuable because it reflected a spontaneous eruption of passionate thought.

Both Melville and Dickinson emphasized the material relationship between mind and brain, represented their culture as based on material values, and understood that to their readers—whether individuals or publics—they were in a tangible sense what they wrote. Dickinson and Melville understood that this transformation negates the power of one of the producers—the writer—by replacing the writer with the book, or with the book and a mass-produced photograph. Obviously, artists defend themselves against commodity fetishization by refusing to participate in the mass production of their work. It is not impossible for a unique work of art to be separated from its maker, but it is unlikely: the labor of the artist is visibly manifest in the individual work of art, or, rather, the individual physical work of art represents the intellectual, esthetic, and emotional labor of the artist. A second defense is to craft personae that can be taken as the author himself or herself yet can be disowned by the author if the personae begin to become commodities. (Once the author is dead, of course, the personae can develop a cash value, as I discuss in chapter 5.) Melville's gift of himself to Dana, in the form of a manuscript, could never have achieved commodity status, nor could Dickinson's letters and the poems she included with letters, unless they were mass-produced.

Implementing these two defenses enabled Melville and Dickinson to compete within a material-based economy for symbolic capital. Their similar responses to the logic of consumption resulted from two main causes. First, they recognized that the print establishment was basically conservative, that reviewers set narrow standards, hence that there was little room for experiments that violated either genre or gender expectations and boundaries. Both Melville and Dickinson voiced awareness of the mass market, and their manuscript practices reflect a recognition of and commitment to the value of the manuscripts themselves as both physical artifact and conceptual work—Dickinson in all of her written output, Melville especially in his handling of white space in his poetry manuscripts.

The second cause combined the widespread practice of circulating work in handcrafted formats (portfolio poetry, scrapbooks, commonplace books) with the almost total lack of a restricted field for print publication in America that valued the pure, the abstract, and the esoteric, at least during the most significant decades of these writers' lives (roughly 1840–1870). The dramatic expansion of the reading public meant that publishers did not need to aim for specific and limited markets but could play freely in the field of large-scale production. No significant circle was advocating the autonomy of art; no publisher needed to make a place for abstract or esoteric literature—"thought-diving" literature. As I've shown in chapter 1, the field of restricted production that did exist accommo- dated the "higher literature," that is, "the select standards of [classic] literature, such works as Milton's, Addison's, Johnson's, Gibbon's, Rus- sell's" ("Readers by the Millions" 839) and the analogous contemporary standards.

Under these conditions, consecration and autonomy—two essential conditions for symbolic capital—could reasonably be pursued by empha- sizing the physicality of the discrete text, the materiality of one's response to it, and the uniqueness of the persona embodied in the text. The mate- rialist psychology of Melville and Dickinson gives value to the physical response generated by the individual work, although this value is not spir- itual or transcendent. The discrete artifact has value not because it can be reproduced and sold but because it has been crafted within and for a field of restricted production, can be evaluated on the basis of the physical response it generates, and can earn symbolic capital for the writer. Mel- ville and Dickinson understood that because their culture was driven by a material economy, they had to generate tangible products. Those prod- ucts shaped their twentieth-century "careers," a topic I take up in my final chapter. The "supposed persons" embodied in those products have to a large extent shaped the popular understanding of each author as well as influenced the scholarly view. Yet each writer actually took considerable pains to separate the written self from the biographical self.

We can look to Fanny Fern's novel *Ruth Hall,* published in 1855, for an example of the type of materiality Melville and Dickinson were trying to avoid. Ruth's husband dies, leaving her with two children and no means of earning a living; both his family and hers refuse to aid her. She suddenly conceives the idea of writing "for the papers," remembering that "while at boarding-school, an editor of a paper in the same town used often to come in and take down her compositions in short-hand as she read them aloud, and transfer them to the columns of his paper" (115). She has to contact many papers before placing even one piece, but that first success gives her hope: "[I]t was at least a *beginning,* a stepping-stone" (125). Fern emphasizes Ruth's labor and has her identify with other laborers involved in print production. Her ability to earn her living requires some economic capital, at least enough to pay her rent and buy bread and lamp oil, and the work is not only physically exhausting but painful on her eyes. Clearly, Ruth is to be praised for earning her crust of bread, and she is to be admired for recognizing the cash value of her work so that she does not allow it essentially to be stolen from her, as was done by that editor who used her school compositions.

Ruth's composing practice allies her with portfolio poetry and other nonprint-publication genres, as she seems to do only a single draft. Her productions are valued because they reflect unalloyed inspiration, but they are also understood not to represent the highest level of crafting. An even more important similarity with that set of practices is that Ruth's identity—or, rather, the question of her identity, as she writes under the pseudonym "Floy"—contributes to her economic value: "And so, while Ruth scribbled away in her garret, the public were busying themselves in conjecturing who 'Floy' might be" (133). The career of Ruth/Floy is similar to that of her creator, Fanny Fern, but those similarities are less important here than is the way Ruth manages her pseudonym in order to project a sense of her actual self and ultimately cashes in the disguise in exchange for the promise of marriage to Mr. Walter. Melville and Dickinson were probably aware of the novel's main events even though neither is known to have read it, and they were also probably aware of its basis in fact. In this sense Ruth Hall might have been a model not to follow. For her, the use of a pseudonym was purely a means to achieve economic capital. To drive home this point, Fern included in the novel not just references to Ruth's new prosperity but, in the penultimate chapter, a reproduction of a bank-stock certificate she now holds, worth ten thousand dollars (209).

WRITING WITH PEN, by the light of an oil lamp, in a garret, for a broad and sympathetic public, and protecting her privacy—all of this in order to support her children—Floy was an exemplary female domestic author of her time. Her goal of financial security of course could only be reached with the assistance of men, and she had to rely on men to compensate her fairly and protect her secret identity. Ultimately, the persona became the author and became, as well, a fetishized commodity within the capitalist market. Employing multiple personae, as Dickinson did, was one way to protect oneself against such an outcome. She almost certainly recognized that the single persona was the essential material component, the fetishized commodity, connecting the producing author to the consuming public. Readers in nineteenth-century America understood themselves to be achieving a personal connection with authors, who in turn traded on this expectation. Creating multiple personae, however, allows for indefinite recycling and reconception, thus providing the writer with a defense against being consumed by a public.

Reading Dickinson in this way, however, should be complemented by recognizing that she also used personae in her poems and letters as means to effect the engagement of her readers, not just as part of a rhetorical strategy of self-defense. Salska writes that "[a]s a vehicle of intimacy, the genre of personal correspondence constituted a perfect form for such a 'creative writing' program" as Dickinson practiced, that is, a form within which the writer could "enlarg[e] . . . [her] emotional experience" while "practicing the craft and skill of its expression" (171). Salska's interpretation requires the additional step of reading Dickinson as slyly challenging the expected association of intimacy with honesty: if the writer is revealing her inmost self, the revelation must be truthful. Personal correspondence constituted a field within which symbolic capital could be amassed; in fact, Salska aptly emphasizes that with her letters Dickinson "prepared and created an audience for her poetry" (168)—placed the poems within a limited field where they could be evaluated. That evaluation would not be wholly autonomous, because the era's readers assessed a work in terms of its author; knowing this, Dickinson may have hoped to create, for the secret pleasure of thought-diving readers, an ironic distance between persona and author. That distance would be signaled to recipients of multiple texts by the variations in personae. The genres within which Dickinson preferred to work—the personal letter, the lyric poem, the diary or scrapbook or commonplace book—presumed a truthful and open relationship between writer and reader, and there were surely many times when she honored this expectation. But her personae loom too large in her work, and her comment to Higginson about "supposed persons" is too explicit, to take such honoring as consistent. As Shira Wolosky explains, Dickinson incarnated her work into "a private manuscript-body while refusing the public exposure of publication. . . . She both would and would not incarnate herself in texts . . . would embody herself in manuscript but not in outward publication" (95)—except that it is really not "herself" even in the manuscripts. Her symbolic capital would thus depend on her most astute readers recognizing and valuing a somewhat shadowy figure known by her ability to create masks and known by those masks *as* masks. Not coincidentally, Dickinson's diligent investing of herself in "supposed persons" also resolves the conflict she felt between the desire to preserve herself for herself and the desire to separate herself from both body and soul in order to shake free of the latter: embodying those components, the personae could easily be "spent" without any spending of her self (Katz 70).

MELVILLE'S CASE reveals the same fundamental desire to market not himself but a "supposed person," albeit complexly framed by the novelistic convention of distance between a homodiegetic narrator and the creating author, by the default reading assumption that a narrative's "I" is the author (an assumption that was just as common in Melville's time as in our own), and by his era's strong preference for factually true narratives. The second and third of these frame components determined the reception of *Typee* and *Omoo:* Melville presented them thus to his publishers and advertised the affidavit written by his shipmate Toby Greene. He seems to have accepted the reading public's "fusion of literary and personal experience." *Mardi,* his third novel, however, he obviously wanted to be evaluated autonomously, because a man known as having "lived among the cannibals" (as he referred to himself in the famous June 1851 letter to Hawthorne—*Correspondence* 193) could contribute little of general value to a civilized society. On 28 January 1849, Melville wrote to John Murray, offering him *Mardi.* The editorial headnote to this letter points out that "Melville requests double Murray's original offer . . . and reiterates his confidence that his reputation has reached the status of 'guinea author,' deserving of publication in a more expensive format" (*Correspondence* 114). But he also desired that *Mardi* not be associated with his earlier work: "Unless you deem it *very* desirable do not put me down on the title page as 'the author of Typee & Omoo.' I wish to separate '*Mardi*' as much as possible from those books" (114–15).

For at least the next half-dozen years Melville continued to believe that he could simultaneously earn symbolic and economic capital simply as Herman Melville, not as the author of *Typee* and *Omoo.* Early in his (significantly pseudonymous) essay "Hawthorne and His Mosses," published in the *Literary World* 17 August 1850, he wrote, "Would that all excellent books were foundlings, without father or mother, that so it might be, we could glorify them, without including their ostensible authors" (*Piazza Tales* 239). But such glorification was impossible; he certainly understood that next to subgenre classification, the author's name was "the chief way of describing a book" (Baym 250). A few pages later he described how reading actually happens: "No man can read a fine author, and relish him to his very bones, while he reads, without subsequently fancying to himself some image of the man and his mind" (*Piazza Tales* 249). As with his suggestion that he send Hawthorne a "fin" of his whale book, this statement figures not only writing but the writer as an object for consumption. He then asserted that the writer probably "has somewhere furnished you with his own picture," although he implies that the self-portrait would not stand out as such but would be blended with "the multitude of likenesses to be sketched" (249). If the author is indeed going to be consumed, it is far better that he be "ostensible" rather than actual, even while the actual author flits among the multitude of characters and can be only inferred from authorial personae within a framework of irony. Unfortunately, Melville's authorial self had been fixed by his first two novels. Evert Duyckinck referred as late as 1857 to Melville as "Typee" (Leyda 563), not as White-Jacket or Ishmael; with even his old friend and mentor continuing to hold the actual author and his later personae hostage, as it were, to the first authorial identity, Melville's comment about foundlings seems sadly prescient.

He raised again the title-page issue early in 1856 when negotiating with the firm of Dix and Edwards for the publication of a volume of stories to include "Benito Cereno" and "Bartleby," but his tone in this correspondence is almost fatalistic. He wrote: "About having the author's name on the title-page, you may do as you deem best; but any appending of titles of former works is hardly worth while" (*Correspondence* 284). And as I have already noted, his directions for the title page of the lost *Poems* of 1860 indicated that he wanted to come before the public as a brand-new author, not even claiming *Moby-Dick*. To sum up, then, in 1849 Melville may have failed to grasp that the limited audience composed of "men who *dive*" into thinking was not of commercial interest to Murray (Letter to Duyckinck, 3 March 1849, *Correspondence* 121). By 1856 he had probably learned that no publisher truly "in business" could share his goal of reaching that audience within the medium of prose. There remained poetry, which was sufficiently different from the novel that he probably thought he could escape the *Typee* albatross. We don't know why he was unable to find a publisher for the 1860 volume, and we also don't know what he requested of Harper and Brothers with respect to *Battle-Pieces*. But Harpers did list the volume as "By the Author of 'Typee' and 'Omoo'" in their list of new books for September 1866 and continued the identification, along with several favorable sentences from the *New York Times*, an advertising ploy they repeated in the October list and again in the summary end-of-year list. (All of these announcements were made in the end papers of *Harper's Monthly*.) Melville certainly did not escape his old identity, but at least he was able to add a new component, being recognized as not only the author of travel romances; this transformation would probably not have been possible for him a decade or two earlier.

From this point on, Melville remained almost exclusively within the field of restricted production, practicing the materialist aesthetic to which he had always been drawn. While his relationship to the act of writing would remain somewhat combative, it was no longer a matter of livelihood. Like the Hawthorne he had described in 1850, he could finally "refrain from all the popularizing noise and show of broad farce," rather than like Shakespeare be "forced to the contrary course by circumstances" (*Piazza Tales* 245). Not surprisingly, his manipulation of personae continued. I have already noted the discrepancy between the facts of the composition of *Battle-Pieces* and Melville's introductory description of that composition, a description clearly intended to convey an impression of an authorial persona who was merely capturing thoughts and ideas. A further discrepancy is between that impression and the voice in many of the poems, a voice characterized by lofty and at times archaic diction, frequent inversions of syntax, heroic apostrophes, a somber tone, and other markers suggesting that the author felt himself to be speaking for and to his country. Milder finds that three personae appear sequentially in *Battle-Pieces:* a "meditative speaker" in the opening poems, a "Laureate, who will celebrate Northern victories and heroes in a tone of righteous jubilation," and finally a "Reconciler (heir to Lincoln)" (175, 179). But within this general progression, more voices appear. Some of the poems are explicitly dialogic, incorporating a second identified speaker (in "Malvern Hill" the final stanza is spoken by "We elms of Malvern Hill") or an alternate perspective signaled by italics (most notably "The Armies of the Wilderness"). Melville's penultimate published volume, *John Marr and Other Sailors* (1888), continues the manipulation. The title poem of 62 lines in the voice of John Marr is prefaced by six pages of third-person prose summarizing the life of the speaker; "Bridegroom Dick" is a fifteen-page monologue; "Tom Deadlight" follows the pattern of "John Marr" but in much briefer compass. As with Dickinson, traits of diction and syntax that are consistent across a large number of poems tempt a reader to identify those traits with the writer himself or herself, especially given our New-Critical heritage that privileges the lyric speaker. But such identification ignores the writers' fascination with masks and masking.

The manipulation of personae by Melville and Dickinson should not be surprising, because the persona was an important coin of the realm within the antimimetic market. Melville's career-long use of personae could simply be termed an element of his style, but the question would still remain, why did he keep returning to that element? Edgar Dryden asks why Melville in the final poem of *Timoleon*, in the words "that close his collection and his publishing career, should choose to speak in the voice of an obscure and ambiguous historical figure" (194). Certainly, as Dryden says, this choice indicates Melville's "deeply ironic" response to the concept of a literary career. But why then print this volume, even privately? Dryden makes the same point with respect to *John Marr,* whose introduction reveals a "deep distrust of public performance and the printed page" (152)—again, if Melville so distrusted "the printed page," why print? The plausible answer is that like Dickinson he was committed to coming before readers, and like Dickinson he had determined that using personae allowed him to present a counterfeit self, one that could continually be reprinted, rewritten, or otherwise reinstantiated without any cost to himself. The conclusion of *The Confidence-Man* is emblematic in this respect: it isn't the shifty Cosmopolitan for whom readers fear an unfortunate outcome, but the open and honest (or at least honest-seeming) old man. If anyone is going to profit from the final transaction, it won't be he. The novel concludes: "[T]he next moment, the waning light expired . . . while in the darkness which ensued, the cosmopolitan kindly led the old man away. Something further may follow of this Masquerade" (251). Typically for Melville (and the same can be said of Dickinson), the syntax at this crucial point creates rich ambiguity: possible referents for "this Masquerade" can range from the immediate situation in the novel to the novel itself. It is impossible to determine what the Cosmopolitan's intentions are and equally impossible to determine whether his creator is endorsing, criticizing, or simply presenting him for observation.

In the same way, Melville and Dickinson understood that their writing accrued its value within a self-contradictory framework. On the one hand, the physical, handcrafted or otherwise self-published artifact signified an intimate and sincere connection to the writer's self, after the fashion of scrapbooks, commonplace books, and portfolio poetry. On the other hand, each writer's commitment to the use of supposed persons signified an invitation to a different kind of transaction, more abstract and esoteric, that would take place in an antimimetic market. This was still not a market that welcomed textual "foundlings," but to enter it with a set of counterfeit selves protected the writer from being consumed down to "his very bones." The writer participates in a material, mimetic economy, but the writer's contributions are counterfeit; the antimimetic economy to which the writer is principally dedicated actually values the counterfeiting skills, not least because the aesthetics of this economy are based on rejecting the values of the mimetic economy.

While Melville and Dickinson used personae to defend themselves against being consumed by their contemporaries, those personae are consumed today as if they are the actual authors. Virginia Jackson emphasizes this outcome with respect to Dickinson: "We can (and inevitably will) keep reading Emily Dickinson as one of the great examples of a subjectivity committed to the page. Yet the very insistence of that commitment urges us to reconsider our placement of the subject on the page, or within the identifying loops of reading through which she predicted her writing would be mastered" ("'Faith in Anatomy'" 107–8). Scholars and readers must become aware of the "fundamental problem of identifying writing too transparently with personhood—indeed, of consuming writing *as* personhood" (87, 102). Awareness of this problem was significantly lacking in the twentieth century, as I will show in the next chapter, when both writers were closely identified with their personae, albeit personae filtered through a twentieth-century critique of what was presented as the nineteenth-century's failure to recognize greatness.

5

Not "Convenient to Carry in the Hand"

COMMERCIALIZING MELVILLE AND DICKINSON IN THE
TWENTIETH CENTURY

When Emily Dickinson wrote about sunsets, "But mine is the more convenient to carry in the hand" (Fr557), she could have been speaking to the future, describing the early editions of her poems (first series 1890 and second series 1891), which were published in a form that was indeed "convenient to carry in the hand"—outdoors as a reinforcement of the reader's experience of nature (Dean 257). In the context of my argument, "convenient to carry in the hand" can serve as a metaphor for "accessible to a variety of nonprofessional audiences": consumers, true, but consumers who value the sense of a personal relationship with the writer, who value books sufficiently to give them as personal gifts, and who might wish to have the writer's words physically ready to hand. The terms typically attached to audience-as-consumer, such as "popular," "low-brow," and "mass readership," connote a class division along social, economic, and aesthetic lines, with the privileged audience being interested in "high culture" or "art."

The twentieth-century commercializing of Melville and Dickinson has been profitable in both venues, and the profit has been both economic and cultural. Elizabeth Horan relates a telling detail. Describing the role of Alfred Leete Hampson in the saga of Emily Dickinson's literary estate, she writes that he was responsible for the inventory that led to the 1935 volume *Unpublished Poems of Emily Dickinson* (published by Little, Brown): "[C]hief among his activities in the 1930s was keeping lists of poems by their first lines, which he appropriately inscribed on the reverse sides of bank deposit slips" ("To Market" 109). Hampson's choice of notepaper for this activity was probably inadvertent but nevertheless emphasizes that Dickinson's poems were to her descendants and heirs, but even more to the publishers who were producing the volumes of her work, a significant source of revenue. The same is true for Melville.

In this chapter I will first sketch some personal issues that make the twentieth-century stories of these two authors somewhat dramatic (for Melville) or extremely dramatic (for Dickinson)—"the stuff of American soap opera" (Erkkila, "The Emily Dickinson Wars" 11). These issues repay study because they contributed to the notoriety attached to each author, especially within the academic community. I will then compare their careers, so to speak, among scholarly and high-brow reading audiences and among popular reading audiences. Finally I will consider significant cultural manifestations of each in the visual and performing arts and even in apparently irreverent genres such as rock music, cartoons, and comic books. These twentieth-century careers bear out Bourdieu's prediction that symbolic capital will always in the long run produce economic capital. Each writer was originally "consecrated" by the mechanisms and agents of cultural capital; that consecration has been modified in response to changing priorities in American life. Each has also benefited enormously from the continued privileging of the notion of author as singular and originary. (See Jaszi and Woodmansee.) This privileging influenced not only the development of copyright law, as I discussed in chapter 3, but the creation of the cultural icons associated with each author: Melville is popularly known by his fictional creations Moby Dick (the whale) and Ahab, whereas Dickinson is known by a self-created persona popularly yet mistakenly believed to be authentic—the cracked recluse in the white dress.

NOTORIETY AND THE PERSONAL SIDE OF PROFIT

The interesting piece of Melville drama is sketched by Ralph Maud and centers around the appropriate use of ideas, information, and access to material. Maud is essentially attempting to rescue Charles Olson, author of *Call Me Ishmael* (published in 1947), from charges of academic impropriety raised in the editorial notes of the Northwestern-Newberry edition of *Moby-Dick*, in which, Maud writes, "complaints about Olson's behavior graduated from colloquial myth into the annals of the discipline" (1). Maud refers to "misdemeanors alleged against" Olson, later asks "[w]hat property right was [Olson] violating by using" the concept of two versions of *Moby-Dick,* and suggests that the Northwestern-Newberry editors termed one of Olson's apparent violations of the code of scholarship an "'unconscious' discrepancy so that they [did] not have to contemplate capital punishment" (1, 3, 5). Maud is obviously having fun here, but his point is serious: even such minor matters as footnotes in a scholarly edition carry significant prestige within the markets in which Melville scholarship circulates, and this prestige is worthy of legal protection because it can yield economic capital.

Having been dead roughly thirty-four years when Maud's article appeared in 2004, Olson was not in a position to cash in on Maud's argument. Maud himself is a different story. Already known as a collector, bibliophile, and leading scholar on Charles Olson before he published this particular piece, Maud extends his reputation into a new area by coming before Melville scholars. He demonstrates by marshaling facts from both accessible and obscure sources (such as unpublished letters) that he belongs in the Melville circle and that Olson too belongs in spite of his "eccentricities"—surely, pursuing Melville's copy of Owen Chase's *Narrative* for thirteen years was a worthy quest, not to mention his work on Melville's annotations in his seven-volume edition of Shakespeare. As Maud writes, "Olson had put in his time" (2). The Northwestern-Newberry footnote refers disparagingly to "a graduate student named Charles Olson" who had a period of exclusive use of some Melville material. The full story according to Maud is that Olson was well past his graduate-student period and had "single-handedly tracked down" the Chase volume and other items from Melville's library: "Harvard thought it proper to accept them with a ten-year period in which Olson would get first crack for his foresight and pains" (4). Indeed, "foresight and pains" should earn a person something.

A final point to be drawn about Olson's story is the power held by institutions once a work or author has been consecrated. The "graduate student" label originated with Leon Howard, whose request to see Harvard's "Melville papers" was initially denied. This denial was quickly reversed on the condition that Howard not publicize what he found, but in fact he loaned his notes to Jay Leyda. Maud comments:

> Anyone who wants to is allowed to take [Howard's report] as the story of a greedy "graduate student" who didn't get away with it. The NN editors talk about "how this restriction [Olson's ten-year privilege] was circumvented," but before we enjoy the glee implicit in that formulation we might ask what a Professor of American Literature [Kenneth Murdock, a member of the Houghton committee] and the Director of Houghton

Library were doing in bending the rule for someone who then gives his
notes to a stranger whose use of them can in no way be controlled. (4)

Maud implies that Leyda, the "stranger," had not earned access to Olson's
labor. Equally significant is the fact that the two institutional representatives in what Howard himself termed a "rump session over the window-
sill" held the power to determine who could access the potential capital of
the Melville items.

I imagine that the rump session occurred in a spirit of collegiality and
with the genuine desire to foster scholarship, although that interpretation
is less interesting than Maud's hint of conspiratorial skullduggery. The
goodwill of the Harvard representatives (if such it was) does not seem to
have extended to the Dickinson manuscripts. Margaret Dickie writes that
"[t]he material evidence of the manuscripts seems now beyond the reach
of everyone but the few scholars whom Harvard University will allow to
view them . . . such access must be arbitrarily assigned since [Susan] Howe
has apparently been denied it" (324). Dickie concludes that the editing of
Dickinson's work "offers a close view of Dickinson at her original scene
of writing, a site that feminists—who have done so much to rescue her
from that scene—must now examine for the wealth and variety of cultural
information it contains about the woman writer. Known as the author of
her poetry, Dickinson must now be studied as its editor and publisher"
(332). In earlier chapters I have questioned the assumption that Dickinson's "original scene of writing" can be known through her manuscripts;
certainly these artifacts offer a window onto that scene, but as with any
window the view is partial. That said, Dickie does well to emphasize the
fluidity of Dickinson's writing (both process and product), the cultural
context of that fluidity, and her tripartite role as author, editor, and publisher.

Similarly, in his aptly titled article "Dickinson Sold Short," William
Matchett considers the "issue of institutional, as opposed to familial, legal,
and economic control of literary property." Matchett terms it a "scandal
that America's foremost nineteenth-century poet has no volume of her
own in the Library of Americas [*sic*], which has come down to some fairly
minor figures but still lacks Dickinson," noting that his own attempt to
prepare a reader's edition of Dickinson's poems was blocked by "a Miss
Metzger, [Houghton Library's] permissions dragon," and that even Ralph
Franklin "turned a cold shoulder" to Matchett's work when preparing his
own "reading edition" (25, 27, 30). (Matchett could also have mentioned
that Dickinson is not represented in the Library of America's *American
Poetry: The Nineteenth Century*.) Matchett's diction—hinting at personal

motives and clashes of strong-willed personalities—suggests that more is at stake here than what general readers deserve. It is not just that Dickinson is being "sold short" in either the casual or the technical sense of that phrase but also that Harvard is engaging in an unethical monopolistic practice and thus has deprived Matchett of the opportunity to profit from the labor he invested in examining manuscripts and preparing versions he deems superior to those in any existing edition of Dickinson's poetry. His denigrating reference to "a Miss Metzger" sounds very similar to Howard's "a graduate student named Charles Olson"; both reflect anger stimulated by loss—not immediately of economic capital but of the prestige that accompanies association with a world-famous author.

Much more dramatic is the decades-long conflict between Mabel Loomis Todd and daughter Millicent Todd Bingham on one side and Martha Dickinson Bianchi on the other over the rights to Emily Dickinson's literary estate. Elizabeth Horan writes that Bingham and Bianchi "took up a Dickinson legacy" for reasons of "pride and consciousness of being the 'last' of old New England family lines. Each woman entered into that legacy much motivated to restore, quite literally, her mother's name," "literally" because Mabel Todd had left Susan Dickinson's name out of the volume of letters she published, while Martha restored Susan as both name and presence by her editing and writing and attempted to elide both Mabel and Millicent from the Dickinson story ("To Market" 89). Bianchi seems to have engaged in what would now be considered plagiarism in preparing her 1924 volume *Life and Letters of Emily Dickinson*, because she drew heavily, without acknowledgment, on Todd's 1894 *Letters of Emily Dickinson* (96–97). Todd and her daughter in contrast and almost certainly with calculation "gained further advantage by appearing to be more generous than Bianchi, such as by showing unpublished manuscripts to writers Genevieve Taggard, Josephine Pollit, and Frederick Pohl, who further publicized Mrs. Todd's expertise" as one of the original editors and a person who still possessed "hundreds of unpublished Emily Dickinson texts" (100–101).

Countering that supposed expertise was the fact that Bianchi not only possessed a store of manuscripts but could claim direct blood lineage and the unique knowledge that could have been passed down through the family. An excellent example is the poem "I send two sunsets" (Fr557), which was first published in the 1914 collection *The Single Hound*, prepared by Bianchi; following the text is the phrase "Sent with brilliant flowers," which does not occur on the manuscript and is thus of uncertain origin. Perhaps Martha knew that flowers had been included with the poem, or perhaps Susan made the note, but in either case the credibility of this editorial "line of descent" is enhanced. This note is one of only two in *The Single Hound;* it stands out as a striking attempt to capture some of the physical characteristics of the manuscripts. The other comment added by Bianchi, "Written after the death of Mrs. Browning in 1861," follows the poem Martha titled "Her 'Last Poems'" (Fr600) and establishes the specific occasion for the writing of that poem. Two other poems in this volume have manuscript-like characteristics that would enhance editorial credibility as well as the sense of personal connection with Dickinson herself: "Who is it seeks my pillow nights" has the final line broken into two parts, and the poem "His cheek is his biographer" (Fr1499—probably sent to Ned Dickinson according to Franklin) appends the word "Thief" printed like a signature (as it was written on the manuscript, according to Franklin). These details fully justify Erkkila's term "soap opera": the people involved were strong-willed and apparently selfish, their conflict dragged on for decades, and the general issues are familiar to any family that has squabbled over a legacy.

Making the story more interesting—and the publication rights more lucrative—were the recognition and advertising of Emily Dickinson as an important American author, the increasing scholarly attention being paid her, and the publication figures collected and published by Charles Green of the Jones Library, an action that "allowed Mrs. Todd, indeed anyone, to figure precisely the immense profits that the Dickinsons had realized from the former editors' work" (Horan, "To Market" 97, 101). Bianchi, on her side, repeatedly insisted that Todd had stolen the manuscripts she held and that any remaining unpublished material held by anyone else was certainly like what she herself held—"not up to Emily's standard" as she wrote in a letter in 1930 (quoted by Horan, "To Market" 103). Horan makes the important point that by "[c]alling for standards" Bianchi was "asserting the value of the Dickinson property as it currently stood" (105). That is, she was attempting to block any new entrants who might dilute the market, especially because the *Centennial Edition of Emily Dickinson* was selling well. Todd, her daughter, and Bianchi all stood to benefit from emphasizing their lineal relationship with the poet and from claiming to know what she would have desired with her work—in short, from fostering the cult of personality that had been initiated by the first editors. Bianchi, more so than Todd and Bingham, apparently failed to see that her aunt was becoming a world author and that as such the Dickinson canon could be greatly expanded; expansion would be the rising water that would lift all boats. Bianchi seems to have understood profit in a very narrow and personal sense, whereas the representatives of "the other house" held a broader vision. Certainly, within the relatively capacious teacup that is Dickinson studies, this "war" kept interest in her higher than it would have been otherwise, a notoriety that in turn enhanced the cash value of "Emily Dickinson" the commodity.

THE POSTHUMOUS CAREERS OF EMILY DICKINSON AND HERMAN MELVILLE
Scholarship, Editions, Monuments, and Consumers

A writer's posthumous career depends on whether the writer or the writer's work has been consecrated by those who produce symbolic and cultural capital. If this happens, then economic capital will sooner or later be available for anyone willing to invest time in preparing an edition, reprint, scholarly study, popularization, etc. The posthumous careers of Dickinson and Melville began as the reverse of their careers while alive, with a strong initial surge of interest in Dickinson and almost no attention to Melville. Both careers illustrate the point that Evelev makes about Melville: his work "has been central to the canonization of American literature because it thematizes issues that have been crucial to modern professionalized understandings of American life, such as resistance to the inscriptive demands of the market, the legitimation of vocational autonomy and nonmanual labor, and the importance of cultural capital" (180). Evelev's remarks regarding canonization are based primarily on a study of Melville's reputation from the 1940s to the present, but the same issues were present early in the twentieth century and were intertwined with the development of American literature as a field of academic study. According to Evelev, "[t]he [contemporary] English professor trades economic capital ('I'll always be poor') for autonomy ('I can learn to read and write and think')" in the same way that Bartleby has been read since the 1960s as "opting for autonomy . . . against the lawyer's vision of the market" (183). This expressed "preference" for poverty and autonomy has yielded a fair amount of cultural and economic capital as those same English professors have written articles and books celebrating the preference and establishing our kinship with Melville and Dickinson, whom we read as championing autonomy and spurning economic profit.

MELVILLE'S PASSING in 1891 was scarcely noted; two of his literary disciples, Arthur Stedman (his literary executor) and Titus Coan, "attempted to rekindle an interest in him," but he was such an insignificant presence in the American literary consciousness that even a decade later Frank Jewett

Mather could not secure funding for a biography; the first book-length biography, by Raymond Weaver, only appeared in 1921 (Barbour 13–14). Because so little material was available, Weaver and others "read [the novels] as autobiographical statements," thus "[a]uthor and character merged together"; later biographers "rescued [Melville] from his own fiction, surrounded him with facts, and placed him within the intellectual climate of his times" (Barbour 14).

The rescue, however, did not and still does not extend to popular culture, for which Melville remains an avatar of both Ishmael and Ahab. This outcome reflects the default identification of author with first-person voice and drives home how relatively insulated is a cultural icon from scholarly understanding of that icon. Another possible cause of this identification is that Melville from early in the twentieth century had a significant popular readership. Hennig Cohen documents the presence of an adaptation of *Moby-Dick* in the anthology *Famous Tales of the Sea* published in 1899, as well as selections from *Typee* and the complete "The Bell Tower" in two other volumes of the "Famous Tales" series (179–80). Cohen notes that the *Sea* volume describes *Moby-Dick* as "based upon the actual experience of the author" and that this book stands as "Melville's chief title to fame" (180). According to Cohen, "[t]hat Melville appears in three volumes of a series and that the series warranted reprinting ["in an handsomely illustrated edition" from the Bodleian Society of New York] suggests a larger readership in this country at the turn of the [twentieth] century than has been generally recognized" (180). Thus, although Charles Anderson's *Melville in the South Seas* (published in 1939) was notable because it "put to bed the prevailing notion of Melville as an autobiographer and enabled scholars to examine him as an artist" (Barbour 19), the operative term here is "scholars"; just as Melville understood that in most of his contemporaries' eyes he was "the author of '*Typee*' '*Piddledee*' &c" (*Correspondence* 343), so his popular identification as "Ishmael" or "Ahab" in the twentieth century was solidified by 1939.

A new biography could significantly revise the cultural icon, for instance if it became the basis of a widely viewed film or widely read fictional treatment. For now, however, Melville's posthumous career must be seen in relation to the cultural icon "Melville/Ishmael/Ahab." That icon has determined how, in what forms, and in what venues a significant portion of economic capital can be earned. For instance, no matter how grandiose a claim might be made for Melville's poetry, or how respected the person making the claim, readers are unlikely ever to be drawn to a Valentine's Day gift book of that poetry the way they will be to a similar item featuring Dickinson. On the other hand, a great deal of economic capital has been generated under the name of Herman Melville, although this outcome was not foreshadowed by the meager profitability of his books through the first decade of the twentieth century: $10,444.53 from 1846 to 1887, on sales totaling 34,577 copies in America and 15,905 in England; $379.06 to Melville's widow by 1898 on new editions of *Typee, Omoo, White-Jacket,* and *Moby-Dick* brought out by the United States Book Company; royalties of $117.85 on another 2,347 copies of these titles prepared by Dana Estes & Company and sold between 1901 and 1906 (Tanselle, "Sales" 199–203). Below I will consider in detail the profitability of Dickinson's work during this same period, but here I want to note that alone the first edition of her poems, prepared by Higginson and Mabel Loomis, sold ten thousand copies very quickly, a striking contrast to the early posthumous publications of Melville's work.

By 1907, in spite of these relatively poor sales, *Moby-Dick* was deemed of sufficient value to be included in Everyman's Library, and in 1920 it was published in the Oxford World's Classics series (Tanselle, *Checklist* 9). This development is a telling sequel to Wiley and Putnam's inclusion of *Typee* in their Library of American Books. James Fenimore Cooper, on the other hand, has fallen dramatically in value since 1917, when Carl van Doren assigned him an eminent position in the *Cambridge History of American Literature* and grouped Melville with "contemporaries of Cooper" (Mathewson 245). The fact that a novel selling approximately 3,200 copies during its author's lifetime has become a world classic directly reflects both the development of American literature as a field of academic study during the early years of the twentieth century and the pertinence of Moby Dick and Ahab to American ideology in the twentieth century.[1]

Moby-Dick's status as a cultural monument was much in evidence during the period 1952–76, which saw the preparation of twenty-eight new editions of which twenty-five "contained introductions, afterwords, or editorial material of some kind," a development that signifies both increased scholarly attention and increased classroom use (Tanselle, *Checklist* 19). The scholarly and classroom attention paid to Melville testifies to his centrality in the canon of American literature: his canonicity is now so well established that anthologies designed for surveys of American literature usually even include a selection of his poems. In sum, Melville has gone from being known in the middle of the nineteenth century as "the author of *Typee* and *Omoo*" to being the author of *Moby-Dick,* from being known as a popular writer of sensationalized travel narratives to being a world author, the study of whom has been the source of lifetime employment for quite a few scholars.

What might not be expected is the extent to which the overlapping disciplines of editing and literary scholarship carry the potential for creating cultural and economic capital. Melville was one of the first authors to be enrolled under the MLA banner of the Centers for Editions of American Authors. The early volumes in the Northwestern University/Newberry Library series were significant enterprises; one early reviewer approvingly quotes the *Times Literary Supplement* description of the project as creating "a monument to Melville" (Allen 441, quoting from the *TLS* of 21 January 1972). A monument is a marker of consecration; like many monuments, the comparatively massive *Moby-Dick* volume has elicited significant criticism as a misuse of public funds. According to Julian Markels, this edition, published in 1988, should have been greeted with rejoicing, but instead it "comes embedded in a commodified artifact of our professional culture that can chill the impulse to cut ribbons" (105). Markels is not quarrelling with editorial apparatus in itself; in fact he praises Tanselle for his portion (the publication history of *Moby-Dick*). Instead, he criticizes Hayford and Parker for using their portions to advance their own hypotheses and in general for not honoring the purpose of a scholarly edition. Markels concludes: "[T]he Northwestern-Newberry editors have discharged an intellectual public trust in an unwittingly self-serving manner. . . . [I]t is hard to see how the public whose taxes helped finance this edition or the community of scholars who are its essential audience and who were made to await it for years can be undistractedly grateful for the package as delivered" (119–20). By using the phrase "intellectual public trust" and suggesting that the high price of the volume ($89.95 in 1994) resulted in part from the "inadvertent" yet "self-serving" pursuit of idiosyncratic scholarly interests, Markels draws attention to the commodity aspect of this text and implicitly to the Northwestern-Newberry edition as a whole. The profit (in terms of both economic and symbolic capital) that will accrue to Parker and Hayford by virtue of the association of their hypotheses with the consecrating stamp of the CEAA has not been earned by the regular process of competing in a marketplace of ideas.[2]

DICKINSON'S posthumous career differs from Melville's in several key ways. First, unlike Melville, Dickinson became a significant literary figure soon after her death. Second, her case was complicated by what has become known as a "war between the houses" over control of publishing rights. (The term was coined by Mary Lee Hall, "friend and neighbor" to Lavinia Dickinson—Sewall, *Life* 157. See Sewall's section on this "war" as well as his substantial appendix that collects all of the pertinent documents available when he was working on his biography of Dickinson.) This war advanced her reputation because the combatants were personally and actively engaged: for them it was explicitly a matter of both reputation and money.

The initial consecration of Dickinson as an artist worthy of attention was carried out by Higginson and Mabel Loomis Todd, her editors during the 1890s. Higginson, as preeminent man of letters, was well placed to promote Dickinson's work; he and Todd also paid a great deal of attention to the volumes as physical objects, bringing their "architecture . . . into conformity with others of the period" by adding "generalizing titles" and dividing the contents into categories (Buckingham xv). Roberts Brothers, the publishing house, did their part, binding the first volume "with an eye toward Christmas and wedding sales" (Buckingham xii). As a result of these efforts, the first edition of Dickinson's poems, in 1890, sold out quickly; a second edition followed in 1891 and a third in 1896, with a two-volume set of letters edited by Todd in 1894.

The acclaim for Dickinson, however, was far from universal. The responses were of three types, distinguished according to the ability of the respondent to consecrate: Dickinson was dismissed by "the elite and largely New York critics" (Roberts Brothers was a Boston house), was regarded by "a middle level" as "troublesome but interesting," and was embraced by some reviewers who wrote for newspapers and for "the family, society, and religious weeklies" (Buckingham xiii–xiv). This division was also in part created by "literary rivalries": Andrew Lang versus Higginson and Howells, the *New York Tribune* versus the *New York Post* and *Nation,* and so forth (xvii). Categorizing Dickinson was also difficult: on the one hand "her work was experienced as fulfilling many of the common reader's religious and sentimental expectations for poetry," but on the other hand her originality and willingness to bend if not break poetic conventions was valued by the nascent "art movement" (xvi).

The reviews collected by Buckingham also reflect how those with the power to consecrate tended to denigrate artists whose work achieves popular acclaim: "[W]hen it became evident that booksellers couldn't keep the new poet on their shelves, Dickinson's popularity was charged against her" (xviii). Dickinson was put forward at the end of the nineteenth century as a reticent, native, and naive genius, not as a careful crafter of linguistically and formally complex poems and certainly not as intending to acquire a role or voice in her culture's deliberations about religion, gender roles, commerce, the Civil War, and so forth. This representation of Dickinson in fact had market value; for instance, in promoting a forthcoming edition of Dickinson's letters, Higginson emphasized her reclusiveness in order to appeal to readers "feeding on the idea of the lonely and misunderstood spinster of Amherst" (Christensen 19). According to Buckingham, "By the end of the century the last hope for edging Dickinson into the canon lay with those . . . who . . . rested their case on the subtlety of her art. She ended the decade as she began, a high-brow poet" (xix). That "high-brow" interest, coupled with the publicity efforts of Todd and her daughter and of Bianchi, ensured that Dickinson became part of the "growth of American literature as a discipline in the 1920s" (Horan, "Technically" 36). Martha Dickinson Bianchi "regarded herself as the sole heir, at once owner, keeper, and gate keeper of a family trust," whereas "the publishers regarded a diversity of opinions and approaches as essential to building the cultural capital associated not just with Emily Dickinson and her relation to modern poets, but for encouraging the study of American literature generally" (38).

This development actually contributed to the decline of Bianchi's influence on Dickinson publishing. She continued to conceive of Dickinson's works mainly in the context of gift-giving between women (the marketing tactic initially taken by Roberts Brothers on the advice of Mabel Loomis Todd), failing to realize that the market for college textbooks was highly valued by publishers, because of its stability, especially after the stock market crash of 1929 (Horan, "Mabel Loomis Todd" 68), and that college professors had become, like reviewers, important shapers of taste (84). As a result of these market forces, by 1929, approaching the centenary of Dickinson's birth, sales of her books were "at an all-time peak" and commemorations were being planned by Yale, Amherst, and Mount Holyoke (82). This interest continued into the 1930s, publishers recognizing that their "prestige within the book trade" would be enhanced by developing their Dickinson materials (86).

Dickinson's economic and symbolic value was also enhanced by one of the "founding assumptions" of literary studies in the early part of the twentieth century, that literature stands as "a reaffirmation of the cultural power of mind and genius against the debased imperatives of both the capital marketplace and the democratic masses" (Erkkila, "Emily Dickinson Wars" 12–13). Erkkila points out that Dickinson became a "cultural icon" for such modernists as Amy Lowell and especially some leading New Critics—Winters, Ransome, and Tate (14). Dickinson's poems became for these critics "both the exempla and the occasion for modernist and New Critical definitions of the literary—grounded in distinctions between poetry and history, aesthetics and politics, high art and mass culture, form and feeling—that came to dominate academic criticism and literary studies in the United States during the Cold War period" (16).

THE GROWTH of American literature in college classrooms and in academic circles means that the cultural and economic capital associated with Melville and Dickinson can be gauged by their representation in anthologies. Amanda Gailey has studied the presence of Dickinson in anthologies of American literature and has concluded that prior to 1955, most anthologies followed the lead of the first anthologist to include her, Frederic Lawrence Knowles in his 1897 *Golden Treasury of American Songs and Lyrics*. Knowles's biographical sketch "would become a refrain in almost every anthology to treat her life. . . . Most would emphasize her 'shy' reclusion and her 'intense imagination,' and attribute to her an unthreatening 'witchcraft': an otherworldliness kept safe within her own head, or at least within the confining walls of her home" (63). She was often referred to as "Emily" (63), and her reclusive nature was always explained in terms of family or a failed love affair, never as a calculated choice (64). She was typically "naturalized" as a "feminized private explorer" and was thus more acceptable to anthologists than other women and minorities (65, 67). This creation of Emily Dickinson by anthologists was made easier because there were almost no photographic images of the actual person. The first published image, based on an oil painting done of Dickinson at age nine, appeared in the first volume of the *Letters;* other than that, there were only various retouched and altered versions of the single daguerreotype, photographs of the daguerreotype, and finally the actual daguerreotype plate which was discovered in 1945. (See Kromer Bernhard for a listing of these images.)

Although the norm, such treatment of Dickinson by anthologists was not universal. Gailey notes that one anthology, Louis Wann's 1933 *The Rise of Realism: American Literature from 1860 to 1888,* not only "resist[s] the confined explorer image of Emily Dickinson" but also includes letters, thus "bolster[ing] Dickinson's reputation as a cross-genre writer and challenges the image of her self-containment" (78). Furthermore, Dickinson was the American poet "most frequently anthologized in American literature and American poetry anthologies . . . and the second most frequently anthologized poet in freshman composition readers, introduction to literature texts, and introduction to poetry texts" from 1890 through 1976 (Chappell 87). This prominence was largely due to the influence of New Criticism, whose methods and assumptions privileged and were best suited for the short, complex lyric. In spite of Dickinson's prominence in anthologies, she was not included among the "eight American authors" elevated by the Modern Language Association in the inaugural volume by that name. This volume, published in 1956, covered Poe, Emerson, Hawthorne, Thoreau, Melville, Whitman, Twain, and James; compared to these men, little scholarly work had yet been done on Dickinson, although in his preface Floyd Stovall notes that Dickinson had been considered for inclusion (Chappell 95–96; see also *Eight American Authors*).

Melville was at first more fully represented in anthologies than was Dickinson, but the advent of New Criticism resulted in a warping of his representation. His work appeared in nineteen anthologies while he was still living (Richard Johnson 7). Five of these contained selections from *Battle-Pieces and Aspects of the War* (8), showing that he actually had begun to achieve the recognition he desired as an American poet. Once the canon of American literature began to be developed in the twentieth century, *Moby-Dick* became much more important, but the New Critical emphasis on complete works that could be studied for their "organic unity" led to the curious situation of Melville being known as the author of *Moby-Dick* but studied as the author of shorter prose pieces (Mathewson 243, 252). If chapters from the novel were included in an anthology, they were intended either to whet a student's appetite for the complete work or to demonstrate Melville's "emphasis on style and experimentation with form" and were selected because they could stand alone as unified works (248–49). Similarly, the few poems that were included were meant to show Melville's creative range but not to place him among the then important poets such as Bryant and Longfellow.

An anthology both reflects and furthers a reading strategy. "[T]he *intimacy* we attribute to Dickinson and extend to ourselves in the experience of reading her poetry—a personal quality, a child-like quality, a secrecy, a nun-like quarantine that exalts friendship and places in the interlocutor the sacred trust of friendship—is an effect in part constructed by Dickinson's first editors, her first 'public' readers" (Dean 243). This effect began with Higginson's preface to the first volume of Dickinson's poetry; Higginson drew from Emerson's 1840 essay "New Poetry" (published in the *Dial*) the term "verses of the portfolio" to describe her poetry, explaining that she had produced it "absolutely without the thought of publication, and solely by way of expression of the writer's own mind" (243). Dean suggests that the *Dial* began to train generations of readers, including Higginson, to read by "browsing," thus initiating a type of reading that would be widely enough practiced by 1890 to receive Dickinson's poems as Higginson presented them (245). In preparing this first edition, Higginson was certainly guided by the precepts he had presented many years earlier in his "Letter to a Young Contributor"—that great care should be paid both to the physical manuscript (so that "it shall allure instead of repelling") and to the content, so that "it shall not need the slightest literary revision before printing" (Dean 256 quoting Higginson). The size of the

1890 edition is similar to that of books of poetry published in Dickinson's time: a small book (between seven and eight inches long, between 4½ and 5½ inches wide) was convenient for carrying in the outdoors to reinforce experiences of the natural world and was also convenient as a fetishized object, to be loved and held close (257).[3]

The physical characteristics of this and the other editions of the poems and letters produced during the 1890s significantly contributed to the "private, confidential and mysterious authorial presence" who became the Dickinson known through most of the twentieth century (Dean 263). Thus, for instance, the Dover Thrift Edition of 1990 "demonstrates how, one hundred years later [after the first publication of Dickinson's poems], the Dickinsonian mythology has become so firmly embedded that it can be reflexively invoked at the subtlest invitation—and that each invocation can also serve the purpose of updating the myth to suit later generations of readers" (266). The introductory note, titling of poems, and other details of the Dover edition "do for the twentieth-century reader what Higginson and Todd did one hundred years before . . . ensur[e] that the reading of Dickinson's work will be integrally related to the reading of her life" (268–69). Thus, like Melville, Dickinson was shaped to fit the alienated-artist, garret-dwelling, antimaterialistic narrative of early twentieth-century American literature.

While throughout much of the twentieth century the interests of publishers and scholars converged, that may no longer be the case as electronic resources proliferate and as the copyright-based tension between profit and public interest plays out in this new realm (Horan, "Technically" 49). The question of which Melville and which Dickinson readers will encounter carries significant economic weight. Will "writers and scholars" indeed serve as "mediators" between corporate interests and public interests, as Horan suggests with respect to Dickinson (49)? This seems unlikely, given that "[t]he material and economic conditions of symbolic production in many spheres, especially the Internet and the World Wide Web, are simply becoming less and less compatible with those under which the literary author produces for the market of printed books" and thus that author-centered legitimacy may become a thing of the past (Paulson 405–6). The Internet promises for the first time in human history essentially free and universal access to cultural material. It also promises something even more radical: readers can become editors—instantaneously publishing their own versions of Dickinson poems and letters, of Melville stories and poems and novels. On the other hand, given that access to the Dickinson Electronic Archive is not yet free and universal, one might argue that even this admirable initiative preserves what Paulson terms "traditional intellectual legitimacy" (413). After all, putting up an image of a manuscript on the Web—or, in the case of Melville, not only manuscripts but corrected typescripts, pages of first American and first British editions, and so forth—still requires access to that manuscript as well as access to technology. Legitimacy is a precondition for such access—only those who have established their legitimacy within the scholarly field are allowed to be involved. Thus, while the author-centered view of the literary marketplace may be losing some of its power, there is no doubt that having access to the author's textual body still counts for a great deal.

Once Melville and Dickinson were consecrated, their works existed within a specific and clear set of expectations having to do with what imaginative literature will actually do and reinforced by editorial decisions (Tanselle, "Emily Dickinson" 79). Because these decisions are of their time, they—and the attendant consecration—are continually being reviewed and either renewed or modified. Thus, for example, while Dickinson's first editors presented her as uninterested in a wide readership, current thinking asks whether she intended to be read (and assumes that she did) and goes on to wonder by whom (Horne 737–38). She may have asked her servant, Margaret Maher, to destroy her manuscripts, because they had been stored in a trunk belonging to Maher, but the evidence is regarded as equivocal (Murray 726–27). She apparently did direct that her letters be destroyed. On the other hand, her practice of sending letters and including poems with them constitutes unequivocal evidence that she intended these items at least to be received and expected these receptions to be idiosyncratic and individual.[4]

Setting aside the question of Dickinson's expectations, the question of how she is to be received today remains a site of ideological (and economic) conflict. Should readers have the experience of easily accessing the poems in something approaching the order of their composition or the order of their appearance in a fair copy? The experience of perusing the fascicles? The experience of perusing all versions of a single poem? Should the experience be located in print or in manuscript facsimile, and in hard copy or electronic copy? Should readers be expected to choose among these options? For many decades in America, because Dickinson has long been recognized as a source of cultural capital, it has been taken for granted that the experience in whatever form is valuable, and the market has long been sufficiently healthy to support many different venues. One certainty is that regardless of the actual writer's intentions, "Emily Dickinson" will continue to remain a source of all types of capital and will continue to be marketed to the wider public as a familiarly mysterious oddity.

THE SAME holds for Melville. On the one hand his case is more straight-forward because the best-known texts of his work are in a real sense "pub-lic property," thanks to the efforts of the Centers for Editions of American Authors (CEAA), unlike the Johnson and Franklin editions of Dickinson's poems and letters. Melville was one of the first authors to be selected for publication by the CEAA project, which originated in 1963 under the Modern Language Association with funding from the National Endow-ment for the Humanities. At this time there were only "two completed editions of American authors that aspired to textual reliability," the John-son edition of Dickinson's poems and letters being one (Bruccoli 237). A crucial element of the CEAA program was the seal that was given to an "approved text." This seal indicated that the text had been prepared using the best practices for determining the author's "final intention"; perhaps even more important was that "the published text—without front or back matter—would be made available for reprinting on a non-exclusive basis for a reasonable fee" (240). Bruccoli notes that there was some complaint about the sealing process and about the expectation on the part of the NEH that work be done, progress be made, and so forth; that "textbook publishers did not line up to obtain reprint rights"; and that the publish-ers who did reprint the approved texts were not as careful as they should have been in ensuring textual reliability (240–42). These problems not-withstanding, the Northwestern-Newberry edition of Melville has been in part funded by public money and, as an approved edition, is available for reprinting "for a reasonable fee"; it functions as a public resource. Har-vard University Press, in contrast, has achieved no little notoriety for how much it charges for the reprinting of Dickinson material, a practice con-sistent with the restrictive policy followed by Houghton Library regarding who is allowed to view Dickinson manuscripts.

The fact that both Dickinson and Melville are embodied in editions regarded as complete and scholarly solidifies their canonical status and reinforces their presence within the cult of the author, but these editions and their attendant status, not to mention their economic power, put the actual writers at even greater distance. As John Bryant has been arguing for over a decade and most dramatically in the context of *Typee,* the public-property artifacts fail to allow actual readers to explore or even easily to be aware of the complex interactions among writer, publishers, reviewers, and cultural taboos and preferences, so the "Melville" whom we might think we know as the author of *Typee* (for instance) is far from the dynamic, developing writer and reviser who can be at least glimpsed by means of "fluid texts." Bryant emphasizes that authorship itself is "fluid," that it "unfold[s] historically through the now irretrievable processes of revision and reprinting"; the problem for the editor is how to "give readers access to the unwitnessable" (29–30).

The concept of an edition itself, especially one that purports to be complete, has long been linked with "our modern sense of authorship" (Nash 1). From editions of Chaucer at the end of the sixteenth and beginning of the seventeenth centuries to the nineteenth-century editions of Wordsworth and others, these projects strongly influenced how authors were to be understood because they typically included a narrative of the life and were regarded by authors as "the ultimate embodiment of their artistic endeavors" (2, 4). Nash concludes that "the gathering force of our digital environment makes the re-editing and re-collecting of our 'archive of cultural works' an inevitable necessity" (13). The recent debates over electronic editions of Dickinson and Melville participate in and are framed by this larger context, because these editions can challenge, invoke, or even replace the existing "collected editions" and thus are powerfully implicated in cultural iconicity and the potential for economic capital. These editions, however, should not be privileged as providing closer access to the actual person who did the writing, as Werner and Bryant tend to suggest they can do. Thus, Bryant: "When we read a literary work as the fluid text it invariably is, we have access to concrete evidence of the writer's acts of acceptance and resistance; we can see rhetorical strategies in the shape of revision strategies; we can witness more directly the interpenetration of writing and cultural processes, actual struggle, not allegories of struggle" (34). Certainly, reading in this way brings more information to bear, but part of that information consists of interpretations—for instance, whether a revision constitutes an "act of acceptance and resistance" to a culture, signals a writer's preference of one word over another for its rhythm, or even, as those of us know who regularly teach English 101, marks a moment when the writer couldn't remember how to spell the initially selected word and so replaced it with one she or he knew.

THE CAPITAL OF POPULAR CULTURE

Popular culture is usually thought of as making people rich, in contrast to high culture's function of enriching (Weiner 85). This dichotomy, however, is simplistic; as Weiner shows, popular culture can take an icon such as *Moby-Dick* that serves "as a password for culture and a touchstone for complexity" (86) and make it accessible to a wide audience. Thus, what has been an "object of desire" controlled by the cultural elite becomes a commodity that the public can embrace and own, a "popular icon" (85–

87). Not only is this process applicable to a specific text like *Moby-Dick* and its well-known characters, it also applies to artists themselves. Dickinson has become the "complex artifact." She is the mystery, the iconic figure in the white dress who is most significantly known for being inscrutable and for concentrating on weighty topics such as death and God, and for rendering impressions of nature that sound as if they came from a very wise child. Like the novel *Moby-Dick,* she is grounded in nature and extends beyond nature to the metaphysical realm. Saying "Emily Dickinson," like saying "Moby Dick," is to imply "mystery and power"; to say or recognize either is to invoke an "intellectual status symbol" (87).

A work becomes an "artifact of high culture" when it is "consecrated" by an institution of cultural production (a salon, a taste-shaping magazine's editors). Consecration normally requires that the work not already have been sullied by involvement in a mass market. Such a work may be produced by an artist who accepts the paradigm of the starving poet in the garret, creating literature for posterity and not for her or his own age. On the other hand, the artifact may be produced by any one or a combination of other interested parties such as an editor, publisher, family member, or literary executor. This artifact will still be presented to the public, however, not as a physical object created to earn capital but as the embodiment of an abstract work, an idea given artistic shape by a creative individual whose main purpose *was* such creation.

This process provides the backdrop against which Melville and Dickinson as cultural icons have come to be "objects of desire" within popular culture. Dickinson was available early in the twentieth century as an intimate yet mysterious authorial figure; this identity has only been strengthened by subsequent textual recreations of her works and is easily captured in a few memorable images and verbal clichés: the white dress, the recluse, the somewhat severe albeit youthful face of the only known photographic portrait. The identity is deepened by the apparent simplicity of the most anthologized poems such as "Because I could not stop for death," "I'm nobody," and "There is no frigate like a book." These poems have fairly straightforward metrical and rhyme structures and don't overtly challenge a reader in terms of diction and syntax, yet they convey an impression of thoughtful depth with their aphoristic treatment of serious themes and their reflections of and on ideology. While the "authorial presence" is mysterious, the poems are presented as accessible, individual communications between a writer and a single reader: "Then there's a pair of us? / Don't tell! They'd advertise—you know!" The popular-culture artist or adapter need only reference a couple of these cues to invoke both the authorial presence and the cultural significance of that presence. This "authorial presence" of course has always been a creation of editors; the private Dickinson presumably was committed to preserving privacy and confidentiality.

This dynamic requires a modest revision of Weiner's assertion that *Moby-Dick* or any similar artifact "serves as an object of desire controlled by intellectual elites who market its complexity to affirm their own identity while calling everyone else's into doubt" (87). A superb example of how "intellectual elites" function is Harvard University Press's control over the scholarly editions of Dickinson's poems and letters. These editions by definition "call into doubt" such popular editions as the Dover Thrift. But the proliferation of popular editions also demonstrates that Dickinson is at best imperfectly controlled by the elites: most people who consume Dickinson in the form of a book are consuming the "supposed person" created by a collaboration, so to speak, among (a) the dead Dickinson who adopted memorably strange habits; (b) her first editors, Higginson and Todd, who modified and reified that supposed person in the 1890 *Poems by Emily Dickinson* and subsequent editions; (c) Martha Dickinson Bianchi and her heirs, who also contributed to the reification of the garret-dwelling (metaphorically speaking) Dickinson; and (d) later publishers like Dover who reprint the public-domain editions with new introductions.

Given this context, the discovery of a significant body of work by one of America's world-renowned authors would be major news. Betsy Erkkila notes of William Shurr's *New Poems of Emily Dickinson* that his "discovery" of "new poems" became a "media event," but of course the "new poems" were only "discovered" in the sense that Shurr rearranged, as verse, passages from Dickinson's letters. According to Erkkila, the central issue becomes "the necessity of maintaining the integrity and purity of Dickinson's intentions as individual author and origin of the poetry"; Susan Howe and others are trying to ground Dickinson's intention in the holograph, this intention being based in traditional concepts of creativity and genius, but there is no compelling proof that she did or did not accept those concepts (Erkkila, "Emily Dickinson Wars" 20, 24).

Melville, too, although he has been consumed in a much greater variety of forms and genres than Dickinson, remains fundamentally a creation of the early decades of the twentieth century, when *Moby-Dick* was canonized as both a world classic and a quintessentially American work. M. Thomas Inge in 1986 offered a superb overview of Melville's presence in popular culture, a presence that is rivaled, if at all, only by Edgar Allan Poe and Mark Twain (695). The details of this presence have changed over the past two decades (see Elizabeth Schultz's 2006 essay), but Inge's central points remain valid. He notes that while Melville began his career as "the man who lived among the cannibals," in the twentieth century "[h]e came to represent the danger and tragedy of being an artist in a democratic, capitalist society, where pleasing the tastes of the mob and making money counted for more than producing a classic work of literature" (695). This representation is embodied in his creations, chiefly Ahab, Ishmael, and Moby Dick, with Bartleby and Billy Budd occupying a second tier. Inge aptly notes that there are many complex reasons why *Moby-Dick* in particular has been so influential, including that novel's effort to "push humanity to the outer limits of the universe" and the portrayal of Ahab as a kind of alienated superhero, "a solitary, irredeemable egomaniac . . . determined to fling a challenge in the face of God" (696)—themes with much broader resonance in the twentieth century than in 1850.

Inge locates the source of the popular awareness of Melville and specifically of *Moby-Dick* in John Barrymore's 1926 silent film *The Sea Beast* and his 1930 sound film *Moby Dick* (696). Both versions were huge successes, the latter being "the most successful of five pictures made by Barrymore under a million-dollar contract with Warner Brothers, perhaps because the public wanted to hear the great profile's seductive voice" (701). *The Sea Beast* "was the first popular success that Herman Melville had enjoyed since *Typee* made his name a by-word in this country" (Stone 179). John Huston's 1956 version starring Gregory Peck as Ahab was also a commercial success although denigrated by academic critics (Inge 705).

More recent films continue to solidify Melville's cultural status, for instance three that appropriate *Moby-Dick:* Woody Allen's 1983 *Zelig,* Michael Lehmann's 1988 *Heathers,* and Jon Avnet's 1992 *Fried Green Tomatoes.* Weiner notes that all three directors seem to share Melville's ambivalence about success: they "take their uneasy place in an artistic world where acceptance produces anxiety and rejection becomes subject matter" (86). The directors' statements suggest their belief that popular and artistic/cultural successes are usually incompatible at least within the artist's lifetime. In *Zelig,* Allen references *Moby-Dick* as an "intellectual status symbol" that "presuppose[s] audience recognition" of the novel, allows the public to embrace and own the icon, and so enables a mass-market realization of the "high culture text" (87). Lehmann's film, likewise, presumes that its audience of teenagers will recognize the icon, a recognition that will reinforce the film's critique of the "commodification of culture" (88). This example leads Weiner to conclude that "[d]espite the current fears that our culture is eroding, it seems clear that new cultural constructs evolve through reference to their predecessors" (88). The status of film as a medium is enhanced "by adapting the classics," these adaptations invariably reflecting a culture's immediate concerns: "During more vigorous periods of our century the movies presented *Moby-Dick* to the public as the story of a great quest for a great goal. But in this equivocal age, as our international role is undergoing redefinition and our national identity is in crisis, movies too have become self-reflective and their appropriation of *Moby-Dick* is more mediated" (Weiner 89–90). Randy Last deepens the thematic relationships between *Moby-Dick* and *Heathers* by reading Veronica as an Ishmael character, suggesting that the film "rewrites *Moby-Dick* as a rock video" at the same time that "something of Melville's profound moral vision trickles into *Heathers,* complicating its conventional Hollywood ending" (72).

Like film, the comic book as a medium both reflects and rewrites a culture's notable texts. *Moby-Dick* was the third most popular *Classics Comics* title (Inge 711). (The series was *Classics Illustrated* after 1947.) The 1942 version "familiarizes the novel for its readership by refracting it through the familiar prisms of boy's adventure fiction and the comic book genre itself" (Berthold 1). The readership was assumed to be young boys, and the stated hope of Meyer Kaplan, an employee of and apologist for the Classics series, was that the young reader would become hooked by the stories, would have in his "mind's eye a picture of what the author was trying to portray in words," and thus would later turn to the original (2). In support of this goal, the original Classics version concluded by urging readers to explore the full novel and by "laud[ing] *Moby-Dick* as 'possibly' the 'greatest' of American novels. The comic is merely a single stop in a series of institutional stations that house and eternize such greatness" (3). The more recent Classics version, published in 1990, "employs some of the rhetoric of humanism that informed Kanter's enterprise" but also in its presentation invokes "methodological post-modernism" and "begins to suggest the symbolic, ontological and epistemological complexities of Melville" (4). Berthold notes that the creator of this version, Bill Sienkiewicz, "benefits . . . from the general growth of the Melville industry" which has made both Melville and *Moby-Dick* "recognizable without necessarily being known" (5). This recognizability no doubt has contributed to the freedom Sienkiewicz has felt to dispense with some of the comic book conventions such as speech balloons, verisimilar representations of characters and actions, and multiple panels on a page (5–7). The form— better thought of as graphic novel than comic book—captures the novel's metaphysical and epistemological themes, such as the unknowability of the whale (8).

The novel has been similarly popular as a reference point for thousands of cartoons (Inge 717). Of the latter, Inge writes that "[i]f scholars have taken Melville too seriously, then America's comic artists have compensated by finding inexhaustible uses for him in their humor and satire. It largely is a comedy of appreciation, however, rather than ridicule" (717). Inge goes on to state that in these cartoons "[t]he joke is often on the reader unable to come to terms with the magnitude of the writer and his ideas" (717). I would refine this generalization: the joke requires a reader who recognizes the icons, and the joke may also play in an elitist way on the fact that average Americans who recognize the icons probably have never read *Moby-Dick*, not even extracts. But elitism is not essential; many of Gary Larson's *Far Side* treatments of Ahab, Ishmael, and the whale function perfectly without the reader assuming that others don't get the joke. For instance, a sailor on lookout sings out: "The White Whale! . . . No, no. My mistake! . . . A black whale!" Standing in the bow of the ship and looking somewhat perturbed is Ahab. Obviously, we miss the joke if we don't recognize that the cartoon is referencing *Moby-Dick*, but we need not have read the novel or feel superior to people who don't get it, any more than with any other cartoon that requires some sort of knowledge. The same is true of the single panel simply showing a sperm whale with a harpoon sticking in his forehead and the line curling into his mouth; the best part of the cartoon is the whale's eye, conveying at once irritation and satisfaction—again, no special knowledge is needed.[5]

The most telling bit of evidence for how significantly *Moby-Dick* in particular has permeated culture may be the children's riddle "What's purple and lives at the bottom of the sea? . . . Moby Grape" (725), something that I remember quite well from fourth or fifth grade, that is, 1957 to 1959. Although as a child I read quite a bit, I am almost certain that I had no idea of the literary context for this riddle; the humor, if I remember the workings of my juvenile mind, resulted from incongruity—an animate grape with a name, and a grape that lives in the sea. But the formula "Moby X" lodged in my memory, as it surely did in the memories of my peers, along with the association between that formula and the ocean, establishing a rudimentary cognitive field that would be filled with other popular culture references and ultimately with my first reading of the novel at age sixteen (thanks to a dynamic first-year high-school teacher who decided to challenge her students to read outside of class *Moby-Dick*, *War and Peace*, and *The Brothers Karamazov*, among others, our only reward being her esteem).

Similarly, Dickinson's many personae in poems and letters invite readers with complex, intimate gestures. Another important commonality is less apparent: the icon will typically be appropriated as if it is strictly monologic, although certainly the works and most of the texts of Melville and Dickinson are intrinsically both dialogic in the sense described by Bakhtin (incorporating the speech of others in their own voices—324) and polyvocal (incorporating many explicit voices). Robert Wallace usefully calls attention to the "dialogic voice" used by Rinde Eckert in his opera *Great Whales* in contrast to "narrative voices" used by other adapters of *Moby-Dick* (323). Wallace is referring specifically to Eckert's use of two singers on stage, but his point has a much larger reach. The now-iconic status of the sentence "Call me Ishmael" and the memorable quality of the events involving Ahab, Queequeg, Starbuck, and the white whale tend to dominate adaptations and thus obscure the dialogic quality of the novel that is created by Melville's extensive appropriations from the literature of cetology, by his occasional use of a dramatic mode (as in the Quarter-Deck scene), and by Ishmael's explicit addresses to readers. Popular-culture appropriations of any writer will tend to limit that writer to a single-voiced self, yet such appropriations can also be understood as a conversation between a present-day culture and these voices from the past. These appropriations develop over time and modify the authorial icon. Thus, while a culture may "hear" a single voice from the Melville or the Dickinson it is appropriating, there are probably also echoes of the voices heard by earlier eras.

Scholarly studies of Melville within culture, especially within popular culture, unfortunately often substitute the product for the producer, almost always *Moby-Dick,* and this substitution seems to happen without the scholar even noticing it. Similar studies of Dickinson preserve an emphasis on the person, a difference from Melville that is not at all curious, given the early creation of "Emily Dickinson" as fascinatingly idiosyncratic and mysterious, and for both authors, the icon always looms. Jonnie Guerra, in her superb overview "Dickinson Adaptations in the Arts and the Theater," acknowledges this emphasis when she notes that "[a]daptations of Emily Dickinson's *life* and poetry . . . have been widespread" and that a great variety of "creative projects" have been inspired by "*Dickinson* and her poems" (385; emphases added). Guerra comments that "adaptations . . . signal a collaborative effort . . . between the dead poem and the living artist as well as between their 'texts,'" that the adapting artists express a "strong personal identification with Dickinson," and that adaptations "have continued to reflect the views of her early biographers, editors, and critics" and thus to perpetuate both the "powerful romantic legends" about her and the "thematic categories" into which the first editions were divided (387).

Two other aspects of Dickinson's twentieth-century career are similar to those of Melville's. First, the "collaborative effort" identified by Guerra can be understood as dialogic in that at least two voices typically are heard, that of the adaptor and that of Dickinson. Some very recent adaptations go even farther, for instance Meisha Bosma's dance production *Violet in my Winter,* which features an offstage voice reading selections from Dickinson's poems and letters while dancers move onstage. The presence of multiple dancers adds to the dialogic aspect because it is not possible to say that any one dancer "is" Dickinson; the effect is rather of multiple and shifting personae on stage echoing and occasionally contrasting the voiced words. (See Fraser and Heginbotham for a review of this performance.) Reports of performances of Martha Graham's 1940 *Letter to the World* as well as the overall design of the ballet (two dancers in the role of Emily and other dancers performing as abstractions relevant to Dickinson's time and art such as the Lover and the Ancestress) suggest that *Violet in my Winter* is following in the Graham tradition. (See Guerra 392–94.) These adaptations are far removed from the still best-known *The Belle of Amherst,* written by William Luce, which premiered in 1976; this "monodrama offers a circumscribed view of the poet's life, narrowing the spectator's attention to focus on a 'Dickinson' defined exclusively within domestic space" (Guerra 390). On the other hand, *The Belle of Amherst* can be understood as reflecting cultural, social, and political concerns of its era as the film versions of *Moby-Dick* have done, although it is unlikely that the Broadway run (117 performances) and the public television redaction of the play gave as significant an impetus to Dickinson's presence in mass culture as did those films. That said, as with Melville, Dickinson's presence in popular culture definitely differs from her presence in higher culture, where audiences are less likely to regard Luce's "distorted presentation as a fact of literary history" (Guerra 391).[6]

Second, one of the most interesting markers of the continuing salience of both Melville and Dickinson in popular culture is their use by rock musicians. In 1992, Carlton Lowenberg was able to list over 1,600 musical settings of Dickinson's poems and letters by 276 composers (Guerra 386). Most of those settings are what is usually referred to as "art song," but rock musicians have also been turning to her words. Boston-based Sebastian Lockwood and Nanette Perrotte, for instance, have produced an eight-song compact disc titled *Emily Dickinson: Zero at the Bone* (Fehrman). The best-known use of a Dickinson poem is probably in The Lemonheads' 1988 album, *Creator;* the lead track, "Burying Ground," concludes with the final stanza of "After great pain." Melville has been more prominent in this scene. In August 2007 The New Pornographers evoked *Moby-Dick* in the cover art for *Challengers:* the torso of a man in a boxing pose bears a tattoo of a breaching sperm whale and a small human figure attached to the whale by a harpoon line. An ad for this album, with the same artwork, fills the back cover of the Summer 2007 issue of *Magnet,* an interesting example of the expectation by the band's label, Matador, that the album will be worth this investment. According to Eric Miller, a staff member at *Magnet,* the standard charge for a back-page ad at that time was $3,000, if the label is an independent, a substantial amount for such a label even when the band is as successful as The New Pornographers. The artwork may seem somewhat strange, given that the band's main members are Canadian; on the other hand, because the Pornographers' music is categorized as "indie rock," which is typically considered less mainstream and more artistic, their use of this highbrow allusion surprises less than it otherwise might.

A better known and perhaps more notorious example of how contemporary music has appropriated Melville is the heavy-metal group Mastodon's 2004 album, *Leviathan.* This appropriation was successful, according to Craig Bernardini, because it assimilated not the "generic prestige of high culture" but "the prestige of the sublime masterpiece . . . by invoking the masculine ideologies of size, power, risk, and ambition" (28). Studying online postings as well as professional reviewers, Bernardini concludes that while the novel may not have been read or studied by the teens who comprise the bulk of heavy-metal's audience, they tend to value it precisely because, like their music, it is deemed "unpalatable" by the mass-market consumers, their high-school classmates (35). Both the novel and the music thus accrue "deviance prestige," with additional mutual reinforcement coming from the similarity between the novel's bombastic language and large themes on the one hand and heavy-metal's sonic traits (high volume and distortion) and dark lyrics on the other (35, 37).

MANY MORE popular-culture manifestations could be listed; the tabulations of anthologies, editions, and adaptations could be brought up to the minute; college and university catalogs could be surveyed to document the prominence of Melville and Dickinson in course descriptions. Such an exercise would only underline with a bolder stroke one point to be drawn from the posthumous careers of these two writers: garret work that later becomes successful in the street will always constitute a blue-chip stock in terms of cultural, symbolic, and economic capital. This exercise would also dramatize the continuing debates over who owns the authors (their visual identities, textual identities, canonical and anticanonical identities) and how their identities should be transmitted and received.

A second point to be drawn is that these identities are always and only constructed by the mechanisms of transmission and reception, because the authorial personae are precisely that—personae—surely connected to the flesh-and-blood writers but in ways that can at best be coarsely sketched and must always remain tentative. The personae have truly become commodities; when we refer to Melville and Dickinson as icons of American culture, we are acknowledging their presence in the same category as Kokopelli refrigerator magnets, dashboard Marias, framed prints of George Washington, and indeed coffee-mug caricatures of famous writers. I note that as of today (3 December 2009) I can buy on eBay for $59.95 a coffee mug featuring Steven Cragg's 1992 caricature of Dickinson (a large and large-headed figure inside a transparent box). The capitalist in me mourns my loss of that very mug a year ago after giving a paper, fittingly, on Dickinson as cultural capital. The text on the opposite side of the mug, to the best of my recollection, compares her favorably to "your Aunt Lurleen" who also wrote poems, suggesting that this artifact may appeal both in terms of high culture and in terms of the street—if you don't yourself have an Aunt Lurleen, you can easily imagine someone who does.

The final words spoken in *Pierre*, Isabel's deathbed "All's o'er, and ye know him not!" (362), can serve well as an epitaph for both writers. Like the speaker of T. S. Eliot's "Ash Wednesday," we might say "Consequently [we] rejoice, having to construct something / Upon which to rejoice" (61). We can never "know" any historically distant individual: it is even more hopeless to try to know a writer on the basis of what that writer has produced, especially when the writer has so resolutely practiced and thematized the use of personae in order to create an authorial self or multiple selves. Consequently we know and celebrate exactly and only what we construct, each era constructing its own Dickinson and Melville.

Notes

CHAPTER I

1. Whether quoting from Dickinson's letters or from her poems, I will tend to concentrate on what Jerome McGann has termed the "linguistic" codes rather than the "bibliographic." Recognizing that much recent work on the poems (but, interestingly, not on the letters) has focused on the latter as well as on details that can only be seen by the few scholars with access to the original manuscripts, and recognizing as well that any statement I attribute to the biographical person on the basis of words that person wrote represents my conjecture as to meaning, nevertheless a fairly coherent picture of Dickinson's reasons for pursuing nonprint publication does emerge from these linguistic codes. See McGann, *Textual Condition* 13–15, 66–67.

2. In insisting on the functional difference between cultural and symbolic capital, I find myself at odds with John Guillory, who is probably Bourdieu's most thoughtful commentator and student, at least in the United States. Guillory describes the three main forms of capital thus:

In [Bourdieu's] *Outline of a Theory of Practice* symbolic capital is given the specific concept of "prestige" or "honor," while cultural capital seems best exemplified elsewhere in Bourdieu's work on the educational institution (*Reproduction, Homo Academicus*), where it refers as much to knowledge, skills, or competence as to the honor or prestige that the possession of this capital can command. Cultural capital is certainly a species of symbolic capital generally, but it is a form of symbolic capital certifiable by objective mechanisms . . . most importantly by the credentializing function of the school. In *The Wizard of Oz*, for example, we know that the Scarecrow has more than proven his intelligence and that he has acquired considerable symbolic capital based on that personal embodied quality. He only lacks, as the Wizard says, a diploma. It is the curious property of the diploma to certify his intelligence to those who may not be familiar with the Scarecrow's accomplishments. ("Bourdieu's Refusal" 381)

To term cultural capital a "species of symbolic capital generally" is to downplay the dichotomy insisted on by Bourdieu between symbolic and economic capital. The Scarecrow demonstrates his intelligence; he does not, however, demonstrate "knowledge, skills, or competence" that are located within a highly specific cultural context. The diploma may "certify his intelligence," but it does not certify that he has read the Great Books, can apply Newton's three laws of motion, or can identify chiaroscuro or the Oedipal Complex. Guillory acknowledges that "symbolic and cultural capital are not precisely equivalent concepts"; more dramatically, he says that the "*differentia specifica* of cultural capital would seem to be its convertibility into material capital, and vice versa" (382), a "convertibility" that is essential to the fundamental dichotomy theorized by Bourdieu *and* documented by him in his exhaustive research. In fact, to emphasize this dichotomy is consistent with Guillory's point that Bourdieu conceives of the capitalist market as driven by pure self-interest in contrast to the market of symbolic goods, which is structured by "the most complex social practices" (386). The key point in Guillory's discussion is that cultural capital serves as a common currency, so to speak, between economic and symbolic capital, a currency allowing for their mutual conversion albeit at a real cost—the involvement and payment of the individuals and institutions who bestow one or the other.

3. It is also possible to locate Dickinson's opposition within what Lori Merish refers to as "feminine domestic aestheticism." Merish notes that "[d]uring the early nineteenth century, Protestant and liberal-capitalist traditions were forged into a novel synthesis of 'pious materialism,' in which luxury goods were seen as a primary means to civilize and spiritualize the self while animating economic and moral progress, and which legitimized a rise in living standards, especially among the middle classes" (91). A particular manifestation of this synthesis was "the consumerist ideal of feminine domestic aestheticism," which located "consumer refinement and gracious materiality as a specifically feminine province" (93). Domesticity was understood and constructed as a realm that was relatively separate from the market and safe from its contamination (134)—but Dickinson's prominent use of metaphors from economics and finance indicates that for her this realm was not safely separate. According to Merish, "domestic writers like Sedgwick seem to counsel that it's fine to shop and buy things; but once at home, be sure to take the price-tag off" (134)—perhaps Dickinson understood that the price tag could never really be removed. By the 1860s, Stowe's *House and Home Papers* for instance revealed a "naturaliz[ation of] middle-class patterns of private ownership and helped establish consumerist domesticity as an instrument

of cultural hegemony" (138). That is, the relations between family and property were being constructed as essentially human and natural rather than created by an economic or social system.

4. In the 1851 Crystal Palace Exposition, Americans swept the awards for daguerreotypes. Rudisill notes that Brady's gold prize entry consisted of forty-eight portraits of leading Americans, a choice suggesting that "Americans placed first importance on the truth of the individual sitter and wished to reveal his character before any other consideration" as well as a "belief that American character could best stand contest in the form of national personalities" (208–9).

CHAPTER 2

1. Kristie Hamilton asserts that Fern "relocates women in the public sphere" and "foregrounds the conditions of women's labor" (96). Fern could count on "the predisposed outrage of a bourgeois audience at the prospect of women being forced into public spaces," but even while this publicity was probably experienced by Fern and other women as a violation, it also constituted a means to secure "women's subjectivity (not subjection), insight, and self-protection" (98). Insofar as their authorship was public (and it must be remembered that many authors labored under anonymity), it offered protection against exploitation. Fern emphasizes "the issue of money" when specifying how much Ruth earns for her labors even while preserving Ruth's heroic stature by means of her "character and gentility"; this is true both of Ruth's stitching and of her literary labor, as Fern reveals "the conditions of labor" to be the "bottom line" whether the labor is mental or manual (101). That is, Fern "collapses a central figuration, the manual/mental binary, of class difference accepted in the dominant culture"; we see a variety of laborers, from the typesetters to the author Horace Gates, living "the garret existence of an exploited worker" (102). Hamilton does not note, however, that the "garret existence" itself was strongly identified with the romantic ideology of authorship, was constructed within the culture as an admirable, even noble marker of a life devoted to the pursuit of artistic truth, and thus significantly contributed to an author's potential for symbolic capital. Certainly, this novel can be read "as a record, critique, and partial analysis of the mechanisms by which bourgeois domestic ideology effected . . . the continued identification of womanhood with certain narrowly defined activities and with a particular socioeconomic status" (103). But it must also be read as a validation of that ideology, because Ruth's success in earning symbolic capital very quickly translated into a great deal of money.

2. Many scholars who have studied this topic have failed to account for the difference between writing and authorship. Newbury, for instance, argues that Hawthorne's and Thoreau's writing "attempted to reclaim for authorship the virtues and physical health persistently associated with manual labor and production" and that they did this "by mediating their representations of authorship through

modes of idealized and residual manual work" (683). Newbury generalizes: "Self-declaring middle-class exercise, residual forms of more or less recreational labor, and spiritualized housework and domestic production became the means through which white-collar men and middle-class women could distinguish themselves from working-class people even as they paradoxically claimed the moral, corporal, and spiritual benefits of increasingly transformed modes of physical 'work'" (693). Newbury argues that the "professionalization of authorial work" differed from "the professionalization of the middle class," because while the latter was "characterized by an increasing distance from residually valorized modes of physical work," the former was "a history of evolution from one form of genteel and aristocratic headwork to another form of professionalized headwork. . . . This fact of literary history, however, did not prevent antebellum authors from imagining authorship as outside the market precisely by imagining authorial work through modes of manual labor" (694). Newbury takes this phenomenon as indicating "how powerful the cultural invocation of craft and artisanal production had become as a response to the professionalized sense of self" (694).

Some of the writers Newbury uses as examples were representing neither the work of authorship nor the actual physical and intellectual activity of writing. True, "Hawthorne . . . went to Brook Farm not only to support himself and his wife but also to situate himself in an economy that would re-establish a non-commercial basis for authorship by grounding it in support provided by labors of the hand" (697). But *The Blithedale Romance*'s ironizing of Miles Coverdale shows that Hawthorne was well aware of how difficult it was to unite manual and intellectual labor. In fact, Newbury ignores that Coverdale tried to write and failed, a gap in the novel that Hawthorne surely intended and that obviously does not signify his inability to describe or thematize the labor of writing. Regarding Thoreau, Newbury writes that "[b]ean farming, in the end, represents a model for authorial labor not because it emphasizes the benefits of actual subsistence farming but because it is performed wholly outside the contingencies of material necessity or exchange of any kind" (705). This reading of Thoreau's experiment with bean farming ignores his fundamental principle of economics, that as he put it in the first chapter of *Walden* (Economy), "the cost of a thing is the amount of what I will call life which is required to be exchanged for it, immediately or in the long run" (20). To characterize bean farming as "a model for authorial labor" that is located "outside the contingencies of material necessity or exchange" is to fail to recognize the possibility of markets other than the capitalist one. Thoreau's point was precisely that where noneconomic capital (cultural and symbolic) was concerned, the market of interest was precapitalist or antimimetic, certainly not capitalist.

3. John Murray, the London publisher of *Typee*, wanted to include the book in his "Colonial and Home Library," which "specialized in the experiences of foreigners in strange places," but he was initially skeptical that the book was factual (Howard 279). Wiley and Putnam, the American publishers, were troubled more by some of the book's perceived raciness, an issue that would have less of an

impact on the book's reception because it was not situated within genre. Turning to *Omoo*, Melville relied much more on print sources to refresh his memory about life in the South Seas but wrote with the same lively, personal style he had used in *Typee*, a fact that caused some reviewers to continue to doubt "the authenticity of the narrator as a person" (Roper 325). Murray published this volume in London, while in America Melville offered the book first to Wiley and Putnam but ended up signing a contract with Harper & Brothers (Roper 328–29). Had Melville's first publishers situated *Typee* differently, had he included more elements that could be taken as romance rather than journalism (as did Cooper, for example, with the Leatherstocking series), he might have better positioned himself to accrue symbolic capital either with these books or with those that came later. It is also possible that Melville's lengthy relationship with the house of Harper limited him, as they were interested in seeing him continue to produce profitable material like what they had already published.

4. R. Jackson Wilson offers a detailed analysis of Higginson's "Letter to a Young Contributor," demonstrating that "he had managed to fuse two ethics that his contemporaries worried might be contradictory, the ethic of 'noble' art and the ethic of large profits. He had also managed to celebrate an esthetic of industry and trade, and to justify the artist's pursuit of 'gain.' He had sketched a world where literary 'jobbing' was not tawdry but a rich source of new linguistic 'coinage' and 'exchange.' And in such a world, writing for publication, for the literary marketplace, was not only an acceptable thing to do; it was the only acceptable thing for a writer to do, the only thing that put the artist truly in touch with the 'average judgment of intelligent minds'" (246). Wilson takes Dickinson's third letter as "a cryptic soliloquy on herself, her work, and—most urgently—her relationship to the literary marketplace" (253). Dickinson used the same "strategy that had been deployed by Irving, Garrison, and Emerson" and most other "serious professional writers in the first half of the nineteenth century [to] justif[y] their struggles in the literary marketplace"—that is, they assumed a "modest posture, a barefoot rank, a relinquishment of fame" in order to be able to claim "the moral and esthetic high ground" (255). For every writer at this time "the marketplace was the most important existential reality. Its enticing possibilities, its demands, and its potential for humiliation set the boundaries within which [Dickinson], no less than any other writer of the nineteenth century, defined her work" (259). Dickinson's response to these possibilities, demands, etc. was to construct herself as an apprentice, an archaic position in this "market economy with little place for masters and apprentices in any industry (and no place at all for them in the industry of literature)" (260). Wilson also points out that "[d]ecades earlier, the notion that an author probably will 'starve in some garret' was already conventional, so conventional that a woman like Frances Maria Lloyd Garrison could use it to mock her own son's literary ambitions. Dickinson's use of the cliché [in "Publication is the auction"] gives point to her observation that this poet—whose 'We' may be editorial, but might also be comically regal—is straining after a purity so perfect that it will not allow her to 'invest' her poems" (273).

5. Stephen Railton has noted that while authors have always depended on audiences, during this period in American history they were "peculiarly dependent" and experienced considerable "performance anxiety" as a result (5).

Chapter 3

1. We have not only his father's mention of the word "on the street" but also Poe's 1841 remark in a review of the author's second book, *The Seaman's Friend:* "His '*Two Years Before the Mast*' was, very deservedly, one of the most popular books ever published, and proved immensely profitable—at least to his booksellers" (quoted by Metzdorf 322).

Chapter 4

1. More recently, Werner has reflected, in a fascinating way, on the editorial process of producing electronic facsimiles. However, there is still a tendency to attribute to the markings on paper a particular mental state or process: "On the surfaces of Dickinson's manuscripts, the turbulence of the mind expresses itself in a series of legible signs and illegible marks—in letters, dashes, pointings, strikeouts, pen-tests, blurs, and blank spaces," although Werner oddly also recognizes the difficulty of determining a timeline for many of the marks on a given fragment ("'Woe of Ecstasy'" 33, 41). In fact, one of the goals of the Dickinson Electronic Archive is to enable users to gain a sense of Dickinson the writer as reflected in her manuscripts, the poem variants, the epistolary contexts, and so forth, a goal that seems committed to regarding her work under the horizon of the holograph rather than allowing for oral production. See Christensen, chapter three, for a recent consideration of this commitment.

2. Domhnall Mitchell, in *Monarch of Perception,* documented that the Dickinson household did not have gas at least in 1863—311, n. 19. As shown by the account books of George Cutler & Company, Dry Goods, of Amherst, with whom the Dickinson family primarily traded, kerosene, along with wicks and glass chimneys, were frequently purchased into the 1870s, while no purchases of candles or whale oil are shown. These books are in the collection of the Jones Library in Amherst. According to George Whicher, in Dickinson's girlhood "[a]stral lamps burning whale-oil, or tallow dips, supplied illumination" (3). Murray says that lighting was provided by whale-oil lamps or tallow candles, but this seems not to have been the case when Dickinson was doing the majority of her writing (716).

3. In fact one of the major drudgeries of authorship in the precomputer age—copying—probably weighed at times as much on Augusta as did the labor of writing on her brother. According to Parker, in the winter of 1853–54, for instance, she "had been in charge of servants while being Herman's sole copyist. . . . What

with using daytime for copying and perhaps for necessary sewing, Augusta had no time for reading and for her essential correspondence unless she stayed up far into the night with her candle" (*Herman Melville* 2:207). Some of her copying "was done under great pressure of time, unlike three years before, when she had had the luxury of copying the whale book at her own pace, well behind Herman because he was writing slowly, by his standards" (2:208). Delbanco puts the point even more strongly: "[B]y now [1855], everyone had accepted Herman's defective handwriting as incorrigible, not a personal tic but, because of its consequences, a family problem, although it was becoming clear that Augusta could not be enslaved forever as she had been in much of 1854" (244).

CHAPTER 5

1. This was also the fate of Thoreau's *Walden*. There is probably a point of major significance to be made here about American cultural imperialism, but to pursue that point would be beyond my scope. See, however, Sanford E. Marovitz's discussion of the Melville revival, in which he notes that for some scholars the revival itself was less about Melville or his works than about the cultural and especially ideological uses to which the icons could be put

2. A different perspective is offered by G. Thomas Tanselle, one of this generation's most respected textual scholars. Tanselle states that the Northwestern-Newberry Edition "separates intention from expectation: it attempts to approach Melville's artistic intention, held in the privacy of his own study, before that intention got entangled with the intentions of other persons involved in the publication process (however much Melville may have expected those persons to alter his texts)" ("Text" 333). Tanselle emphasizes that "the intention" of Melville is difficult to specify because it seems to have shifted from work to work and from version to version of a work; the editors of this edition attempt to identify the "intention that emerged from a full engagement with the original conception of a work" (335). Thus, for instance, revisions that seem to have been hurriedly made on a proof copy would not be given precedence over an early manuscript version, but revisions would be selected that seemed to involve "full engagement" with the work as determined by textual or biographical evidence. Tanselle notes that recent editorial theory and practice has generally been driven on the one hand by a recognition that "literature is a collaborative art" involving many individuals and institutions in addition to the artist (336) and on the other by "an increased concentration on earlier intentions—or, more precisely, on textual genesis and development as reflected in successive drafts and revisions" (340).

3. Dean asserts that Higginson and Todd were responding "to the material dilemma posed by [Dickinson's] fascicles" (243). However, there is no indication in the extant material regarding the first editions that these editors regarded the fascicles and sets as posing a "dilemma" in terms of the form the editions should take. Millicent Todd Bingham, for instance, in tracing the discovery of the poems,

quotes from her mother's journal that she did see the "over sixty little 'volumes,'" but her concern was strictly with how "hopeless" the manuscripts would look "from a printer's point of view," because of Dickinson's handwriting and the presence of alternative word choices (17). "Portfolio poetry" itself posed no dilemma; if it was written as sketches, then editors were free to organize the sketches however they chose. Higginson and Todd determined that subject groupings would be most effective, in the same way that watercolor sketches could be organized by subject; although Todd saw the actual sewn fascicles, their form obviously was not compelling enough to cause her to replicate it.

4. The decline of the author-centered view has been motivated in part by the recognition, as Tanselle puts it, that a writer may expect to be published without approving of the publication: "expectation and intention are very different things" ("Emily Dickinson" 68). Referring to Dickinson's well-known complaint to Higginson regarding the publication of "A narrow fellow in the grass" (Fr1096) in the *Springfield Republican,* Tanselle insists that Dickinson's "disapproval here cannot be used either to claim that she approved of everything else or to suggest that she wished to have unconventional punctuation in print—for the inserted question mark does not make the punctuation more conventional but substantially changes the meaning" (68). In fact Tanselle goes on to say that Dickinson "is easier to edit" than many other authors because most of her works do not exist in the multiple versions created during the process of moving from manuscript to print—that is, do not exist in versions over which she had control (69). The same cautions hold for the approach I've been advocating in this book—taking poems sent in letters as published. Tanselle reminds us that "documents (manuscript or printed) are social instruments, enabling texts to be transmitted between people," but also that not every element of these documents necessarily signifies an intention (71).

5. The weight of Inge's article reflects the relative power of the media that have been used to bring Melville to a popular audience: of approximately thirty-one pages of text, he devotes roughly fourteen to a discussion of film, with the remainder of the article treating Melville's presence in comics, radio and television, popular literature (from children's to adult), and "general culture" (advertisements, menus, names of establishments, etc.).

6. Dickinson's presence in music and the visual arts is significant, but as Guerra points out she is also represented in "what traditionally are regarded as women's crafts—china painting and textile art such as sewing, embroidery, and quilting" (398).

Works Cited

Allen, Robert R. "The First Six Volumes of the Northwestern-Newberry Melville: A Review Article." *Proof* 3 (1973): 441–53.

Bakhtin, Mikhail Mikhailovich. *The Dialogic Imagination: Four Essays*. Ed. Michael Holquist. Trans. Caryl Emerson and Michael Holquist. Austin: University of Texas Press, 1981.

Barbour, James. "Melville Biography: A Life and the Lives." *A Companion to Melville Studies*. Ed. John Bryant. New York: Greenwood Press, 1986. 3–34.

Barker, Wendy. "Emily Dickinson and Poetic Strategy." *The Cambridge Companion to Emily Dickinson*. Ed. Wendy Martin. Cambridge: Cambridge University Press, 2002. 77–90.

Barnes, James J. *Authors, Publishers, and Politicians: The Quest for an Anglo-American Copyright Agreement 1815–1854*. Columbus: The Ohio State University Press, 1974.

Baym, Nina. *Novels, Readers, and Reviewers: Responses to Fiction in Antebellum America*. Ithaca, NY and London: Cornell University Press, 1984.

Bernardini, Craig. "Heavy Metal: Mastodon's *Leviathan* and the Popular Image of *Moby-Dick*." *Leviathan* 11 (2009): 27–44.

Berthold, Michael C. "Color Me Ishmael: Classics Illustrated Versions of *Moby-Dick*." *Word & Image* 9 (1993): 1–8.

Bettig, Ronald V. "Critical Perspectives on the History and Philosophy of Copyright." *Critical Studies in Mass Communication* 9 (1992): 131–55.

Bingham, Millicent Todd. *Ancestors' Brocades: The Literary Discovery of Emily Dickinson, the Editing and Publication of Her Letters and Poems*. 1945; New York: Dover, 1967.

Bohde, Cheryl D. "'Magazines as a Powerful Element of Civilization': An Exploration of the Ideology of Literary Magazines, 1830–1850." *American Periodicals: A Journal of History, Criticism, and Bibliography* 1 (1991): 34–45.

Bourdieu, Pierre. *Distinction: A Social Critique of the Judgment of Taste.* Trans. Richard Nice. Cambridge, MA: Harvard University Press, 1984. Published in French in 1979.

———. *The Field of Cultural Production: Essays on Art and Literature.* Ed. Randal Johnson. New York: Columbia University Press, 1993.

———. *The Rules of Art. Genesis and Structure of the Literary Field.* Trans. Susan Emanuel. Stanford, CA: Stanford University Press, 1996.

Brodhead, Richard. *Cultures of Letters: Scenes of Reading and Writing in Nineteenth-Century America.* Chicago: University of Chicago Press, 1993.

Bromell, Nicholas. *By the Sweat of the Brow: Literature and Labor in Antebellum America.* Chicago: University of Chicago Press, 1993.

Bruccoli, Matthew J. "What Bowers Wrought: An Assessment of the Center for Editions of American Authors." *The Culture of Collected Editions.* Ed. Andrew Nash. Hampshire and New York: Palgrave Macmillan, 2003. 237–44.

Bryant, John. "Witness and Access: The Uses of the Fluid Text." *Textual Cultures* 2 (2007): 16–42.

Buckingham, Willis J., ed. *Emily Dickinson's Reception in the 1890s: A Documentary History.* Pittsburgh: University of Pittsburgh Press, 1989.

Buell, Lawrence. "American Civil War Poetry and the Meaning of Literary Commodification: Whitman, Melville, and Others." *Reciprocal Influences: Literary Production, Distribution, and Consumption in America.* Ed. Steven Fink and Susan S. Williams. Columbus: The Ohio State University Press, 1999. 123–38.

Bushell, Sally. "Meaning in Dickinson's Manuscripts: Intending the Unintentional." *Emily Dickinson Journal* 14 (2005): 24–61.

Chappell, Diane Landry. "The Selection of Emily Dickinson's Poems in College Textbook Anthologies, 1890–1976." PhD diss., University of Tennessee, 1980.

Charvat, William. *The Profession of Authorship in America, 1800–1870.* Ed. Matthew J. Bruccoli. Columbus: The Ohio State University Press, 1968; New York: Columbia University Press, 1992.

Christensen, Lena. *Editing Emily Dickinson: The Production of an Author.* New York and London: Routledge, 2008.

Cohen, Hennig. "The 'Famous Tales' Anthologies." *Papers of the Bibliographical Society of America* 68 (1974): 179–80.

Coultrap-McQuin, Susan. *Doing Literary Business: American Women Writers in the Nineteenth Century.* Chapel Hill and London: University of North Carolina Press, 1990.

Crane, Mary Thomas, and Alan Richardson. "Literary Studies and Cognitive Science: Toward a New Interdisciplinarity." *Mosaic* 32 (1999): 123–40.

Dandurand, Karen. "Dickinson and the Public." *Dickinson and Audience.* Ed. Martin Orzeck and Robert Weisbuch. Ann Arbor: University of Michigan Press, 1996. 255–77.

Davidson, Cathy. Introduction. *Reading in America: Literature and Social History*. Ed. Cathy Davidson. Baltimore and London: Johns Hopkins University Press, 1989. 1–26.

Dean, Gabrielle. "Emily Dickinson's 'Poetry of the Portfolio.'" *Text: Transactions of the Society for Textual Scholarship* 14 (2002): 241–76.

Delbanco, Andrew. *Melville: His World and Work*. New York: Knopf, 2005.

Dickie, Margaret. "Dickinson in Context." *American Literary History* 7 (1995): 320–33.

Dickinson, Emily. *The Letters of Emily Dickinson*. Ed. Thomas H. Johnson and Theodora Ward. Cambridge, MA and London: Belknap Press of Harvard University Press, 1958.

———. *The Poems of Emily Dickinson*. Variorum Edition. Ed. Ralph Franklin. Cambridge, MA and London: Harvard University Press, 1998.

———. *The Single Hound: Poems of a Lifetime*. Ed. Martha Dickinson Bianchi. Boston: Little, Brown, 1914.

Dryden, Edgar A. *Monumental Melville: The Formation of a Literary Career*. Stanford, CA: Stanford University Press, 2004.

Eight American Authors: A Review of Research and Criticism. Ed. Floyd Stovall. New York: Modern Language Association, 1956.

Eliot, Thomas Stearns. *The Complete Poems and Plays 1909–1950*. New York: Harcourt, Brace & World, 1962.

Emerson, Ralph Waldo. "The American Scholar." *Ralph Waldo Emerson*. Oxford and New York: Oxford University Press, 1990. 37–52. First published 1844.

———. "The Poet." *Ralph Waldo Emerson*. Oxford and New York: Oxford University Press, 1990. 197–215. First published 1844.

Emily Dickinson Lexicon. Brigham Young University. http://edl.byu.edu/index.php (accessed 27 October 2007).

Erkkila, Betsy. "The Emily Dickinson Wars." *The Cambridge Companion to Emily Dickinson*. Ed. Wendy Martin. Cambridge: Cambridge University Press, 2002. 11–29.

———. *The Wicked Sisters: Women Poets, Literary History, and Discord*. New York and Oxford: Oxford University Press, 1992.

Esdale, Logan. "Dickinson's Epistolary 'Naturalness.'" *Emily Dickinson Journal* 14 (2005): 1–23.

Evelev, John. *Tolerable Entertainment: Herman Melville and Professionalism in Antebellum New York*. Amherst and Boston: University of Massachusetts Press, 2006.

Fehrman, Craig. "Amherst House Rock: *Emily Dickinson—Zero at the Bone* and Pedagogy." *Emily Dickinson International Society Bulletin* 19:2 (November/December 2007): 24–26.

Fern, Fanny. [Sara Payson Willis] *Ruth Hall and Other Writings*. Ed. Joyce W. Warren. New Brunswick, NJ and London: Rutgers University Press, 1986.

Franklin, Ralph. Introduction. *The Poems of Emily Dickinson*. Variorum Edition. Ed. Ralph Franklin. Cambridge, MA and London: Harvard University Press, 1998.

———, ed. *The Manuscript Books of Emily Dickinson*. Cambridge, MA and London: Belknap Press of Harvard University Press, 1981.

Fraser, James, and Eleanor Heginbotham. "'They Can Dance Upon Their Feet': A Blend of Poetry and Dance for Emily's Birthday at the Folger." *Emily Dickinson International Society Bulletin* 18:1 (May/June 2006): 1–2.

Gailey, Amanda. "How Anthologists Made Dickinson a Tolerable Woman Writer." *Emily Dickinson Journal* 14 (2005): 62–83.

Guerra, Jonnie. "Dickinson Adaptations in the Arts and the Theater." *The Emily Dickinson Handbook*. Ed. Gudrun Grabher, Roland Hagenbüchle, and Cristanne Miller. Amherst: University of Massachusetts Press, 1998. 385–407.

Guillory, John. "Bourdieu's Refusal." *Modern Language Quarterly* 58 (1997): 367–98.

Habegger, Alfred. *My Wars Are Laid Away in Books: The Life of Emily Dickinson*. New York: Random House, 2001.

Hamilton, Kristie. "The Politics of Survival: Sara Parton's *Ruth Hall* and the Literature of Labor." *Redefining the Political Novel: American Women Writers, 1797–1901*. Ed. Sharon M. Harris. Knoxville: University of Tennessee Press, 1995. 86–108.

Hayes, Kevin J. "Poe, the Daguerreotype, and the Autobiographical Act." *Biography* 25 (2002): 477–92.

Hayford, Harrison, Hershel Parker, and G. Thomas Tanselle. Editorial apparatus. *Typee: A Peep at Polynesian Life*. Evanston and Chicago: Northwestern University Press and the Newberry Library, 1968.

Hayford, Harrison, and Alma A. MacDougall. "Related Documents." *The Confidence-Man: His Masquerade*. Ed. Harrison Hayford, Hershel Parker, and G. Thomas Tanselle. Evanston and Chicago: Northwestern University Press and the Newberry Library, 1984. 401–518.

Higginson, Thomas Wentworth, and Henry Walcott Boynton. *A Reader's History of American Literature*. Boston, New York, and Chicago: Houghton, Mifflin & Co., 1903.

Horan, Elizabeth. "Mabel Loomis Todd, Martha Dickinson Bianchi, and the Spoils of the Dickinson Legacy." *A Living of Words: American Women in Print Culture*. Ed. Susan Albertine. Knoxville: University of Tennessee Press, 1995. 65–93.

———. "To Market: The Dickinson Copyright Wars." *Emily Dickinson Journal* 5 (1996): 88–120.

Horan, Elizabeth Rosa. "Technically Outside the Law: Who Permits, Who Profits, and Why." *Emily Dickinson Journal* 10 (2001): 34–54.

Horne, Philip. "The Poetry of Possibilities: Dickinson's Texts." *Women's Studies* 31 (2002): 725–40.

Horth, Lynn. Editorial Notes. *Correspondence: The Writings of Herman Melville*. Ed. Lynn Horth. Evanston and Chicago: Northwestern University Press and the Newberry Library, 1993.

Howard, Leon. "Historical Note." *Typee: A Peep at Polynesian Life*. Ed. Harrison

Hayford, Hershel Parker, and G. Thomas Tanselle. Evanston and Chicago: Northwestern University Press and the Newberry Library, 1968. 277–302.

Hubbard, Melanie. "As there are Apartments: Emily Dickinson's Manuscripts and Critical Desire at the Scene of Reading." *Emily Dickinson Journal* 12 (2003): 53–79.

———. "'Turn it, a little': The Influence of the Daguerreotype and the Stereograph on Emily Dickinson's Use of Manuscript Variants." *Mosaic: A Journal for the Interdisciplinary Study of Literature* 38 (2005): 115–32.

Inge, M. Thomas. "Melville in Popular Culture." *A Companion to Melville Studies.* Ed. John Bryant. New York: Greenwood Press, 1986. 695–739.

Jackson, Virginia. "'Faith in Anatomy': Reading Emily Dickinson." *Dwelling in Possibility: Women Poets and Critics on Poetry.* Ed. Yopie Prins and Maeera Shreiber. Ithaca, NY: Cornell University Press, 1997. 85–108.

Jaszi, Peter, and Martha Woodmansee. Introduction. *The Construction of Authorship: Textual Appropriation in Law and Literature.* Ed. Woodmansee and Jaszi. Durham, NC and London: Duke University Press, 1994.

Johnson, Randal. "Editor's Introduction: Pierre Bourdieu on Art, Literature and Culture." *The Field of Cultural Production: Essays on Art and Literature.* Ed. Randal Johnson. New York: Columbia University Press, 1993. 1–25.

Johnson, Richard C. "Melville in Anthologies." *American Book Collector* 21 (1971): 7–8.

Juhasz, Suzanne. "Reading Emily Dickinson's Letters." *ESQ: A Journal of the American Renaissance* 30 (1984): 170–92.

Kaenel, André. *"Words Are Things": Herman Melville and the Invention of Authorship in Nineteenth-Century America.* Bern: Peter Lang, 1992.

Katz, Daniel. "Satin Cash: Dickinson's Reserves." Ed. Jean-Jacques Lecercle. *L'Argent comme échange symbolique.* Nanterre, France: Université Paris X, 1999. 49–71.

Kearns, Michael. "Phantoms of the Mind: Melville's Criticism of Idealistic Psychology." *ESQ: A Journal of the American Renaissance* 30 (1984): 40–50.

Kelly, Wyn. "'Lying in Various Attitudes': Staging Melville's Pip in Digital Media." *"Ungraspable Phantom": Essays on Moby-Dick.* Ed. John Bryant, Mary K. Bercaw Edwards, and Timothy Marr. Kent, OH: Kent State University Press, 2006. 337–53.

Kromer Bernhard, Mary Elizabeth. "Lost and Found: Emily Dickinson's Unknown Daguerreotypist." *New England Quarterly* 72 (1999): 594–601.

Last, Randy. "Profiles in Ontological Rebellion: The Presence of *Moby-Dick* in *Heathers.*" *Leviathan* 11 (2009): 72–78.

Leyda, Jay. *The Melville Log: A Documentary Life of Herman Melville, 1819–1891.* New York, Harcourt, 1951.

Loeffelholz, Mary. "'Question of Monuments': Emerson, Dickinson, and American Renaissance Portraiture." *Modern Language Quarterly* 59 (1998): 445–69.

Markels, Julian. "The *Moby-Dick* White Elephant." *American Literature* 66 (1994): 106–22.

Marovitz, Sanford E. "The Melville Revival." *A Companion to Herman Melville.* Ed. Wyn Kelley. Malden, MA and Oxford: Blackwell, 2006. 515–31.

Matchett, William H. "Dickinson Sold Short." *Literary Imagination: The Review of the Association of Literary Scholars and Critics* 6 (2004): 25–38.

Mathewson, Stephen. "Cutting In, Cutting Out: Herman Melville, *Moby-Dick,* and Anthologies of American Literature." *Essays in Literature* 18 (1991): 243–53.

Maud, Ralph. "Charles Olson and the Northwestern-Newberry *Moby-Dick.*" *Melville Society Extracts,* no. 127 (July 2004): 1–5.

McGann, Jerome. "Composition as Explanation." Ed. Katherine O'Brien O'Keefe. *Cultural Artifacts and the Production of Meaning: The Page, the Image, and the Body.* Ann Arbor: University of Michigan Press, 1994. 101–38.

———. *The Textual Condition.* Princeton, NJ: Princeton University Press, 1991.

McGill, Meredith L. "The Duplicity of the Pen." *Language Machines: Technologies of Literary and Cultural Production.* Ed. Jeffrey Masten, Peter Stallybrass, and Nancy Vickers. New York and London: Routledge, 1997. 39–71.

———. "The Matter of the Text: Commerce, Print Culture, and the Authority of the State in American Copyright Law." *American Literary History* 9 (1997): 21–59.

Melville, Herman. *Collected Poems of Herman Melville.* Ed. Howard P. Vincent. Chicago: Hendricks House, 1947.

———. *The Confidence-Man: His Masquerade.* Ed. Harrison Hayford, Hershel Parker, and G. Thomas Tanselle. Evanston and Chicago: Northwestern University Press and the Newberry Library, 1984.

———. *Correspondence: The Writings of Herman Melville.* Ed. Lynn Horth. Evanston and Chicago: Northwestern University Press and the Newberry Library, 1993.

———. "Hawthorne and His Mosses." *The Piazza Tales and Other Prose Pieces.* Ed. Harrison Hayford, Alma A. MacDougall, and G. Thomas Tanselle. Evanston and Chicago: Northwestern University Press and the Newberry Library, 1987. 239–53.

———. *Moby Dick; or, The Whale.* Ed. Harrison Hayford, Hershel Parker, and G. Thomas Tanselle. Evanston and Chicago: Northwestern University Press and the Newberry Library, 1988.

———. *Pierre; or, The Ambiguities.* Ed. Harrison Hayford, Hershel Parker, and G. Thomas Tanselle. Evanston and Chicago: Northwestern University Press and the Newberry Library, 1988.

———. *The Piazza Tales and Other Prose Pieces 1839–1860.* Ed. Harrison Hayford, Alma A. MacDougall, and G. Thomas Tanselle. Evanston and Chicago: Northwestern University Press and the Newberry Library, 1987.

———. "A Thought on Book-Binding." *The Piazza Tales and Other Prose Pieces.* Ed. Harrison Hayford, Alma A. MacDougall, and G. Thomas Tanselle. Evanston and Chicago: Northwestern University Press and the Newberry Library, 1987. 237–38.

Merish, Lori. *Sentimental Materialism: Gender, Commodity Culture, and Nine-*

teenth-Century American Literature. Durham, NC: Duke University Press, 2000.

Metzdorf, Robert F. "The Publishing History of *Two Years Before the Mast.*" *Harvard Library Bulletin* 7 (1953): 312–32.

Michaels, Walter Benn. *The Gold Standard and the Logic of Naturalism.* Berkeley and Los Angeles: University of California Press, 1987.

Milder, Robert. *Exiled Royalties: Melville and the Life We Imagine.* Oxford and New York: Oxford University Press, 2006.

Miller, Cristanne. "Whose Dickinson?" *American Literary History* 12 (2000): 230–53.

Miller, Eric. Personal e-mail communication. 5 October 2007.

Mitchell, Domhnall. *Emily Dickinson: Monarch of Perception.* Amherst: University of Massachusetts Press, 2000.

———. *Measures of Possibility: Emily Dickinson's Manuscripts.* Amherst: University of Massachusetts Press, 2005.

———. "Revising the Script: Emily Dickinson's Manuscripts." *American Literature* 70 (1998): 705–37.

Murray, Aife. "Miss Margaret's Emily Dickinson." *Signs* 24 (1999): 697–732.

Nash, Andrew. "The Culture of Collected Editions: Authorship, Reputation, and the Canon." *The Culture of Collected Editions.* Ed. Andrew Nash. Hampshire and New York: Palgrave Macmillan, 2003. 1–15.

Newbury, Michael. "Healthful Employment: Hawthorne, Thoreau, and Middle-Class Fitness." *American Quarterly* 47 (1995): 681–714.

Oxford English Dictionary. 2nd ed. Oxford and New York: Oxford University Press, 1989.

Parker, Hershel. *Herman Melville: A Biography.* Volumes 1 and 2. Baltimore: Johns Hopkins University Press, 1996.

———. "The Lost *Poems* (1860) and Melville's First Urge to Write an Epic Poem." *Melville's Evermoving Dawn: Centennial Essays.* Ed. John Bryant and Robert Milder. Kent, OH and London: Kent State University Press, 1997. 260–75.

Paulson, William. "The Market of Printed Goods: On Bourdieu's Rules." *Modern Language Quarterly* 58 (1997): 399–415.

Pease, Donald. *Visionary Compacts: American Renaissance Writings in Cultural Context.* Madison: University of Wisconsin Press, 1987.

Petrino, Elizabeth A. *Emily Dickinson and Her Contemporaries: Women's Verse in America, 1820–1855.* Hanover and London: University Press of New England, 1998.

Phegley, Jennifer. "Literary Piracy, Nationalism, and Women Readers in *Harper's New Monthly Magazine,* 1850–1855." *American Periodicals* 14 (2004): 63–90.

Post-Lauria, Sheila. *Correspondent Colorings: Melville in the Marketplace.* Amherst: University of Massachusetts Press, 1996.

———. "Magazine Practices and Melville's *Israel Potter.*" Ed. Kenneth M. Price and Susan Belasco Smith. *Periodical Literature in Nineteenth-Century America*. Charlottesville and London: University Press of Virginia, 1995. 115–32.

Railton, Stephen. *Authorship and Audience: Literary Performance in the American Renaissance*. Princeton, NJ: Princeton University Press, 1991.

"Readers by the Millions." *Harper's New Monthly Magazine* 19 (November 1859): 838–40.

Reiman, David H. "Gentleman Authors and Professional Writers: Notes on the History of Editing Texts of the 18th and 19th Centuries." *Editing and Editors: A Retrospect*. Ed. Richard Landon. New York: AMS Press, 1985. 99–136.

Renker, Elizabeth. *Strike Through the Mask: Herman Melville and the Scene of Writing*. Baltimore and London: Johns Hopkins University Press, 1996.

Roper, Gordon. "Historical Note." *Omoo: A Narrative of Adventures in the South Seas*. Ed. Harrison Hayford, Hershel Parker, and G. Thomas Tanselle. Evanston and Chicago: Northwestern University Press and the Newberry Library, 1968. 319–44.

Rose, Mark. "The Author as Proprietor: *Donaldson v. Becket* and the Genealogy of Modern Authorship." *Representations* 23 (1988): 51–85.

———. *Authors and Owners: The Invention of Copyright*. Cambridge, MA: Harvard University Press, 1993.

Rudisill, Richard. *Mirror Image: The Influence of the Daguerreotype on American Society*. Albuquerque: University of New Mexico Press, 1971.

Salska, Agnieszka. "Dickinson's Letters." *The Emily Dickinson Handbook*. Ed. Gudrun Grabher. Amherst: University of Massachusetts Press, 1998. 163–80.

Saunders, David. "Approaches to the Historical Relations of the Legal and the Aesthetic." *New Literary History* 23 (1992): 505–21.

———. *Authorship and Copyright*. New York: Routledge, 1992.

Scholnick, Robert J. "'Don't Tell! They'd Advertise': Emily Dickinson in the *Round Table*." Ed. Kenneth M. Price and Susan Belasco Smith. *Periodical Literature in Nineteenth-Century America*. Charlottesville and London: University Press of Virginia, 1995. 166–82.

Schultz, Elizabeth. "Creating Icons: Melville in Visual Media and Popular Culture." *A Companion to Herman Melville*. Ed. Wyn Kelley. Malden, MA and Oxford: Blackwell, 2006. 532–52.

Sewall, Richard B. "Emily Dickinson's Perfect Audience: Helen Hunt Jackson." *Dickinson and Audience*. Ed. Martin Orzeck and Robert Weisbuch. Ann Arbor: University of Michigan Press, 1996. 201–13.

———. *The Life of Emily Dickinson*. Cambridge, MA: Harvard University Press, 1974.

Shurr, William H. "Melville's Poems: The Late Agenda." *A Companion to Melville Studies*. Ed. John Bryant. New York: Greenwood Press, 1986. 351–74.

Smith, Martha Nell. *Rowing in Eden: Rereading Emily Dickinson*. Austin: University of Texas Press, 1992.

———. "Susan and Emily Dickinson: Their Lives, in Letters." *The Cambridge Companion to Emily Dickinson*. Ed. Wendy Martin. Cambridge: Cambridge University Press, 2002. 51–73.

Socarides, Alexandra. "Rethinking the Fascicles: Dickinson's Writing, Copying, and Binding Practices." *Emily Dickinson Journal* 15 (2006): 69–94.

Stone, Edward. "Ahab Gets Girl, or Herman Melville Goes to the Movies." *Literature/Film Quarterly* 3 (1975): 172–81.

Stoneley, Peter. "'I—Pay—in Satin Cash—': Commerce, Gender, and Display in Emily Dickinson's Poetry." *American Literature* 72 (2000): 575–94.

Taft, Robert. *Photography and the American Scene; A Social History, 1839–1889.* Macmillan, 1938; New York: Dover, 1964.

Tanselle, G. Thomas. *A Checklist of Editions of Moby-Dick, 1851–1976.* Evanston and Chicago: Northwestern University Press and the Newberry Library, 1976.

———. "Emily Dickinson as an Editorial Problem." *Raritan: A Quarterly Review* 19 (2000): 64–79.

———. "The Sales of Melville's Books." *Harvard Library Bulletin* 18 (1969): 195–214.

———. "The Text of Melville in the Twenty-First Century." *Melville's Evermoving Dawn: Centennial Essays.* Ed. John Bryant and Robert Milder. Kent, OH and London: Kent State University Press, 1997. 332–45.

Thoreau, Henry David. *Walden and Civil Disobedience.* New York: Norton, 1966.

Trachtenberg, Alan. "Mirror in the Marketplace: American Responses to the Daguerreotype, 1839–1851." *The Daguerreotype: A Sesquicentennial Celebration.* Ed. John Wood. Iowa City: University of Iowa Press, 1989. 60–73.

———. *Reading American Photographs: Images as History, Mathew Brady to Walker Evans.* N.p.: Hill and Wang, 1989.

———. "Seeing and Believing: Hawthorne's Reflections on the Daguerreotype in *The House of the Seven Gables.*" *American Literary History* 9 (1997): 460–81.

U. S. Constitution. The National Archives Experience. http://www.archives.gov/national-archives-experience/charters/constitution_transcript.html (accessed 27 November 2007).

Vincent, Howard P. Introduction and Notes. *Collected Poems of Herman Melville.* Ed. Howard P. Vincent. Chicago: Hendricks House, 1947.

Wallace, Robert K. "Fusing with the Muse: Eckert's Great Whales as Homage and Prophecy." *"Ungraspable Phantom": Essays on Moby-Dick.* Ed. John Bryant, Mary K. Bercaw Edwards, and Timothy Marr. Kent, OH: Kent State University Press, 2006. 321–36.

Weiner, Susan. "Melville at the Movies: New Images of *Moby-Dick.*" *Journal of American Culture* 16 (1993): 85–90.

Weinstein, Cindy. "Melville, Labor, and the Discourses of Reception." *The Cambridge Companion to Herman Melville.* Ed. Robert S. Levine. Cambridge: Cambridge University Press, 1998. 202–23.

Werner, Marta L. *Emily Dickinson's Open Folios: Scenes of Reading, Surfaces of Writing.* Ann Arbor: University of Michigan Press, 1995.

———. "'A Woe of Ecstasy': On the Electronic Editing of Dickinson's Late Fragments." *Emily Dickinson Journal* 16 (2007): 25–52.

Whicher, George F. *This Was a Poet: A Critical Biography of Emily Dickinson.* New York: Charles Scribner's Sons, 1938.

White, Melissa. "Letter to the Light: Discoveries in Dickinson's Correspondence." *Emily Dickinson Journal* 16 (2007): 1–26.

Wilson, R. Jackson. *Figures of Speech: American Writers and the Literary Marketplace, from Benjamin Franklin to Emily Dickinson.* New York: Knopf, 1989.

Winship, Michael. *American Literary Publishing in the Mid-Nineteenth Century.* Cambridge: Cambridge University Press, 1995.

———. "The Transatlantic Book Trade and Anglo-American Literary Culture in the Nineteenth Century." *Reciprocal Influences: Literary Production, Distribution, and Consumption in America.* Ed. Steven Fink and Susan S. Williams. Columbus: The Ohio State University Press, 1999. 98–122.

Wolff, Cynthia Griffin. *Emily Dickinson.* Reading, MA: Addison-Wesley, 1998.

Wolosky, Shira. "Emily Dickinson's Manuscript Body: History/Textuality/Gender." *Emily Dickinson Journal* 8 (1999): 87–99.

Yannella, Donald. "Writing the '*Other* Way': Melville, the Duyckinck Crowd, and Literature for the Masses." *A Companion to Melville Studies.* Ed. John Bryant. New York: Greenwood Press, 1986. 63–81.

Zboray, Ronald J. "Antebellum Reading and the Ironies of Technological Innovation." *Reading in America: Literature and Social History.* Ed. Cathy Davidson. Baltimore and London: Johns Hopkins University Press, 1989. 180–99.

Index

American Antiquarian Society, 56–57

antimimetic market, 27–28, 49, 72, 77–78, 117–18, 150n2; and status, 39, 80–81

art as intimate connection, 15, 22, 46–52, 54–56, 78, 80, 118, 142

"art for art's sake," 20–21, 51, 54, 78. *See also* autonomous evaluation

Atlantic Monthly, 4, 46, 52, 65, 130

authorship, 82, 136–37, 149n1; contrasted with writing, 32–33; and Dickinson, 105–6; labor of, 32–33, 50, 66, 83, 152–53n3; and Melville, 73–78, 107; romantic view of, 56

autonomous evaluation, x, 9–10, 19, 21, 51, 60–61, 70–72, 77–78, 112, 114–15. *See also* "art for art's sake"

autonomy, and manuscript publication, 28–29, 60–61, 72, 77–78. *See also* capital, symbolic

Bakhtin, Mikhail Mikhailovich, 142

Belle of Amherst, The (Luce), 144

Bentley, Richard, 75–76, 78

Bianchi, Margaret Dickinson, 124–25, 131, 139; *The Single Hound,* 124–25

Billson, James, 11, 57

Bingham, Millicent Todd, 3, 124–25, 153–54n3

Blackwood's Magazine, 76

Boosey v. Purday, 75–76

Bosma, Meisha, *Violet in my Winter,* 144

Bourdieu, Pierre, x–xi, 147–48n2; applied to American culture, 18–20, 29, 42, 51, 83, 121; and capital, types of, 8–12; and copyright in America, 70; *Distinction,* 29; *Field of Cultural Production, The,* xi, 8–12, 18; *Rules of Art, The,* xi

Bowles, Samuel, 43–46, 56, 72

Bryant, John, 136–37

Bryant, William Cullen, 20, 26, 43, 74–75, 133

Cambridge History of American Literature, 128

capital, cultural, 147–48n2, 150n2; and Dickinson, 104, 120–21, 126, 131–32, 135, 139, 142–44; and Melville, 126–29, 137–42, 144–45

capital, economic, and author as commodity, 25–27, 43, 110–13; and capital, symbolic, 10–13, 28, 30, 49, 115, 147–48n2; and copyright, 70, 73–74, 80; and photography, 4–6, 8; and posthumous profitability, 126–32

capital, symbolic, x–xi, 4, 9, 13, 20, 74, 107; and capital, economic, 10–13, 28, 30, 49, 115, 147–48n2; and consecration, 10, 12, 56, 76, 104, 112, 126; and copyright, 69–70; and labor, 78, 100; and portfolio poetry, 80; and private publication, 28–31, 35, 45, 47, 60, 105–6, 114

Centers for Editions of American Authors (CEAA), 129, 136

Charvat, William, x–xi, 13, 18–19, 52

Classics Comics (and Classics Illustrated), 141

commodity, 10, 17–18, 27, 69–71, 113, 126, 129, 137; persona as, 110–19; photograph as, 4–5, 16, 18, 25

commonplace books, x, 20–21, 31, 109, 111, 114, 118

composition studies, 91, 100

Concord "Saturday Club," 72

consecration, 42, 48, 135, 138; agents of, 9–10, 31, 56; and economic capital, 121–22, 126, 129, 130; and symbolic value, 8–11, 104, 112. *See also* capital, symbolic

Cooper, James Fenimore, 75–76, 93, 128

copyright, x, 19, 23, 49, 65, 134; and capital, symbolic, 69–70; and creativity, 38, 69, 76–77, 83; history of, 66–69, 121; international, 75–76; and labor of writing, 43, 71, 78–80; and publication, 68–69, 72–74, 82

daguerreotype, and American character, 5–6, 15–16, 27, 149n4; and capital, cultural 8–9, 13, 16–17, 27; of Dickinson, 3, 18, 132; history of, in America, 4–6, 16–17, 27; and Melville, 1–2, 7–8, 13, 17, 27

Dana, William Henry, Jr., 29–31, 35, 38, 42, 74, 75, 78, 80; *Two Years before the Mast*, 74–75

Dean, Gabrielle, 48–49, 120, 133–34, 153–54n3

Delbanco, Andrew, 34, 79, 85, 97, 153n3

Dial, 133

Dickens, Charles, *Bleak House*, 24

Dickinson, Edward, 18, 70, 99

Dickinson, Emily: in anthologies and collections, 43, 132–33, 138; and antimimetic market, 49, 72; and art as intimate connection, 51, 55–56; attitude toward photography, 4–5, 18, 27; and capital, symbolic, 31–32, 43–45, 47–49, 65–66, 72, 104–6, 110–11, 114, 120–21, 151n4; *Centennial Edition of Emily Dickinson*, 125; and commercial publication, 26–27; compared to Melville, ix–xii, 26–27, 28, 31, 51, 61, 73, 81, 83, 84, 87, 91–92, 96–98, 106–7, 109–11, 118–21, 126, 128, 129, 134,